THE ILLUSTRATED GUIDE TO
SNOWBOARDING

written & illustrated by

Kevin Ryan

MASTERS PRESS

NTC/Contemporary Publishing Group

Library of Congress Cataloging-in-Publication Data

Ryan, Kevin.
    The illustrated guide to snowboarding / Kevin Ryan.
       p.   cm.
    Includes bibliographical references.
    ISBN 1-57028-144-0
    1. Snowboarding.   2. Snowboarding—Psychological aspects.
    I. Title.
GV857.S57R925   1997   97-31314
                                            CIP

Published by Masters Press
A division of The McGraw-Hill Companies
4255 West Touhy Avenue, Lincolnwood (Chicago), Illinois 60712-1975 U.S.A.
Printed in the United States of America
International Standard Book Number: 1-57028-144-0
01 02 03 04 05 06 RCP 21 20 19 18 17 16 15 14 13 12 11 10 9 8 7 6 5 4

contents

SECTION THREE: AFTER THE SNOW INFORMATION

I dedicate this book to my family — Alyson, Bill, Jenny and Kerry Ryan — for without their love and support my life would be hollow. You have given me education, purpose and the ability to give back and teach others. I would be nothing without you.

a c k n o w l e d g m e n t s

I would like to thank the following people for their contributions to The Illustrated Guide to Snowboarding *and for their devotion to the growth of this great sport:*

The instructors who have taught me to ride better than I ever thought I could. Especially the five men who have had the biggest influence on my ability as a rider and an instructor: Will Garrow, Alex Birch, Brian Dunfey, Dave Lewis and J. Randy Price.

The resorts that have hired me as an instructor giving me the opportunity to teach and learn. Dan Raliegh in particular, the ski school director who originally gave me the idea to start this project. His advice was to fill this book with humor, to "keep it light and interesting" — for this I dedicate every bad joke to Dan and his family.

The snowboarding professionals who dedicated the time, effort and patience to make this project a stronger reference for learning.

Tim Byers and Aggression snowboards for permitting photo access to their factory for the "Birth of a Snowboard" section.

John Stouffer and partners in crime at Transworld Snowboarding Business for helping to supply logistical information regarding the various snowboard organizations worldwide.

Jonathan B. Smith, a close friend whose help with the "Caring For Your Ride" chapter transformed a mess of information into a succinct recipe for board maintenance...and pampering.

Monique Cole, Ann Mitchell and Lisa Wertz, three talented women who's writing skills and intelligence helped to make the "ideas" into understandable concepts.

Arn Menconi and the Snowboard Outreach Society for helping to make this world a better place through the sport of snowboarding.

Tom Bast and the people at Masters Press. A special thanks to Holly Kondras who believed in my proposal for such a book and gave me the chance to pass this knowledge on to a wider audience. And to Chad Woolums, my editor, for his support and suggestions along the way.

And finally I would like to thank my students, the people who continue to teach me more about snowboard instruction than anyone else.

Credits:
Cover Photos ©Mark Gallup
Illustrations ©Kevin Ryan
Cover Design by Suzanne Lincoln
Edited by Chad Woolums

This book is a must read for anyone involved with or thinking about being involved with snowboarding. Never in my thirty-three years of pioneering, shaping and defining this sport was there ever any access to such material, and never was there a definitive resource explaining all of the technical aspects of riding in such an easy to understand manner. Whether you are a beginner (at any age) or a "seasoned lifer," these tips, lessons, descriptions and illustrations will change the way you think and ride.

Kevin Ryan zero's in with a zen-like approach to setting goals and achieving those goals. He breaks down every aspect of a move and incorporates the interaction between the mental, physical and spiritual components of riding like never before. It's that simple.

If you truly want to improve the quality of your time on the snow, then this is the guide you've been waiting for. This is an "encyclopedia" of how-to snowboarding instruction that should be on the shelf of every ski area, snowboard park and bookstore in the snowbelt. Learn from the straightforward Question & Answer sections, try out suggestions on tuning boards, follow helpful tips from some of the sports most reknown riders and coaches. There is truly something in this book for everyone — and if its not here, then we haven't tried it...yet.

So, if your thinking about giving snowboarding a shot, here's a great place to start. And if you are sitting there dreaming about last year's big hits and drops in endless powder, do yourself a favor — immerse yourself in this book and see if you can't teach an old dog some new tricks! It worked for me!

May you ride forever,

Paul Graves

WELCOME TO SNOWBOARDING

Hello, and welcome to "The Illustrated Guide to Snowboarding." Snowboarding is one of the fastest growing sports in the world. It is one of those activities that will make people spend large amounts of hard earned money and countless hours of time either riding or trying to get to someplace where they can ride. It can cause normally quiet and shy people to dream, smile madly with wide eyes, and speak with passion whenever the subject of snowboarding surfaces. People have been known to leave secure, high-paying jobs and travel hundreds even thousands of miles away from loved ones just to ride. Some have given up skiing altogether. Why? Simple, SNOWBOARDING IS FUN. It is so much fun that it's addictive. And once you are hooked, it's almost guaranteed to change your life forever.

This book is designed with fun in mind. The information is presented in a manner suitable for both sides of your brain. The left (logical/verbal) side of the brain will learn from reading the text while the right (visual/intuitive) side draws from the images that fill the book. If what you read does not make complete sense...the corresponding images should help to clarify those ideas that you may be unsure about and vice versa. This guide is meant to serve as a means to assist in your learning process and help you achieve more for yourself in snowboarding. The images contained in this book represent both regular and goofy riders. If you see an image or sequence of images that are opposite the way in which you ride, flip the image around in your mind or look at it in a mirror. Some portions of text are extremely technical. If you are having difficulty at any point understanding what is being explained, the glossary definitions found in the back of the book should prove helpful. If you prefer, pass over the more technical sections. You can always refer back when the context of the information is more suitable to specific skill level.

The techniques described in this book are geared to take you from your first day through to your thousandth and even further on. However, this book is not meant to serve as a replacement for trained instruction or "on the hill" experience. Take lessons, especially when you are first starting out. Supervised instruction by trained snowboard instructors is the most effective means to learn how to ride. This book is a reference (for your own endeavors). You can read this book all you want, but until you experience, until you feel what is being discussed in this book, your riding will not improve. So go out and experience snowboarding for yourself.

One of the best things about snowboarding is that it is an individual sport that has many different interpretations and avenues of expression. There is no "right or wrong" way to ride a snowboard. There are many different ways to ride. I have tried to present to you a variety of approaches and the best "options" (to quote a friend of mine) to work with. Some of these ideas will be easier to follow than others. Some of the approaches discussed will at times conflict one another largely because of differences in equipment and riding styles. The book has been written with this in mind, and the illustration sequences show both soft and hard boot systems. Use your own judgment in regard to what information will relate to your own personal riding preferences. As I said before, the only real requirement is that you go out and ride.

MESSAGE TO THE CROSSOVER SKIER

As a skier, you will find snowboarding easy to learn. Just look at the bottom of a snowboard. It has a P-tex base and metal edges on the sides — really, it looks a lot like a chubby little ski. On the snow, a snowboard and a ski act quite similar. As a skier you already possess a working knowledge of edge control, direction control and the sensation of flying down the hill at high speeds. What makes snowboarding so much different than skiing is what you'll find on top of the board. The bindings are aligned sideways and do not release. Both feet are bound to a single board. But, never fear, you are already a natural candidate for becoming a snowboarder. All you really need to do is get equipment, sign up for a lesson, and begin.

If you are concerned about your knees, take heart. Snowboard systems are much less stressful on the knee joint than ski systems. Ski systems pose a greater danger to the knee joint for a few reasons in particular.

Snowboarders place both legs on one board. Non-releasing bindings keep the individual legs in safe positions attached to the board. Since the board/binding system is not designed (unless you have special bindings) to release, all the weight is kept on both legs at all times. Equipment — soft boots allow for a great deal of ankle flexion which distributes the forces placed upon the knee more evenly throughout the entire leg. This translates to less stress on each individual leg. I've got to be honest, my knees have stopped aching since I started to snowboard.

When you ski, almost (if not) all of your weight is placed upon one leg and then the other. Because our ankles are held tight in a frozen plastic boot, we do not have the benefit of movement at that joint. This means that all the forces from the ski are transmitted directly to the knee joint first and then to the rest of the body. In reference to that idea, the professional life expectancy of a snowboard racer is many years longer (5-7) than a professional ski racer. It is true that you do spend more time kneeling on your knees, and it is easier to fall on them, too. But with both feet anchored upon a single board, the chances of ACL (anterior cruciate ligament of the knee joint) injuries are significantly reduced.

When a skier falls their legs move about in individual directions. If the skis do not release, serious damage to the leg and particularly the knee can occur. If the skis do release, they can travel a ways down the hill or possibly even hit someone.

When a snowboarder takes a spinning fall, their whole body spins. The risk of being hit by flying equipment is eliminated. When the snowboarder is ready to move again, the rider just stands up and rides away.

As a snowboarder, you will find a much more diverse range of movement down the mountain. You can go backward, fast. You can spin around like a top. You can get away with spinning multiples of 180 instead of 360. A hill that has 500 feet of vertical can be cruised down in less than a minute on skis. Riding a snowboard opens up many possibilities for riding creativity, improvisational use of the environment, and whatever else you can think of. I believe that this is why so many skiers try snowboarding and never go back.

Finally, if you try snowboarding just to say you tried it, you're missing the point. Don't try it for a couple of runs and then write it off. That's like saying you tried candy once, but decided better not — it might rot your teeth out. If you try snowboarding a half dozen times and still don't have the desire to ride, you gave it an honest chance. Maybe snowboarding just isn't for you. But if you want to ski sideways and all other sorts of ways, give it a real chance. I hope that this book can make your familiar alpine environment as fresh and interesting as it was when you first strapped on skis and fell in love with the winter.

INHERENT RISKS OF THE SPORT

Do remain mindful that snowboarding can be a dangerous sport. Riding down the side of a mountain on a rocket sled over frozen water at high speeds can be dangerous. As a snowboarder you must take into account your own abilities and the dangers of the environment you inhabit. You must also realize and accept your own responsibility as a member of the entire snowboarding community. You are in control of the way you ride, where you ride, and the choices you make in between. Be responsible, be safety conscious, and enjoy this wonderful sport.

LEARNING TO LEARN
HOW TO SNOWBOARD

The sum and substance of snowboarding is the process of learning and growing as a snowboarder. No one is created absolutely equal and no one learns at the same rate. Some people pick up snowboarding very quickly — it is natural for them. Some people have the advantage of already knowing how to surf or skateboard. For others it takes more time. I hear people say "I want to ride just like him" or "She's the best, I want to look that cool on a board." Well, no matter how hard you try you will never be able to ride exactly like someone else. Your mind and body are your own, and the same goes for each individual. I'm not saying don't check out other riders — drawing inspiration from outside sources is great. Just don't let yourself become a follower. Do it for yourself! If you snowboard for any other reason, step back and ask yourself 'Why ride in the first place?' Then if you really want to snowboard, you will find your own way to ride and have fun. Hopefully the ideas in this chapter will help make your snowboarding experience a sane and safe one.

PHILOSOPHY & PSYCHOLOGY
TRIAL & SUCCESS

People often use the term "trial and error" in reference to learning. This idea infers that if you don't succeed, something is wrong. I believe that if you try something and it does not work, you can evaluate what you did and apply that learned knowledge toward future success. The next time you try the same thing you will "know better" than you did before. By assuming this definition — "trial and success" is the more appropriate term — you are never in error. You learn and grow as a snowboarder from both the successful and unsuccessful experiences. If you fall but keep on trying, chances are, you will eventually succeed. This will make your victory over self and snow and the process of snowboarding all the sweeter. Keep in mind that sometimes you will make the same mistakes over again "knowing better". These are merely the times when you must kick yourself in the butt and scream 'I knew better than that!' Then focus your efforts toward improving the problem areas in each situation. If you continue making mistakes, even though you "know better", take a break and tackle your obstacle with refreshed enthusiasm at a later time.

2

PROGRESSIVE & REGRESSIVE LEARNING

I believe that there are two kinds of learning: progressive and regressive.

Progressive learning (not necessarily successful) is based on trying to succeed. Understand that failure is not a bad thing, rather it is an important part of the learning process. It is part of life. You always begin by trying something new, or improving upon a skill that you have already learned.

Regressive learning (necessarily unsuccessful, making your bad self angry at the cruel world you live in) sets up mental blocks and other negative internal barriers. If you are not having fun and not encountering success, this does not make for a positive experience. When you stop having fun, you stop wanting to learn. Frustration can stifle your desire to improve, and in the worst case might even stop you from wanting to snowboard altogether. It is important to change your approach or even postpone your efforts before reaching the point where all patience is lost. Angry snowboarders make for ugly human beings.

RELAXATION

Relaxation plays a large role in the learning process. We are much more receptive to new information and movement patterns when relaxed, and we are also able to move much more efficiently. Consider a cat. Typically cats are considered to be very relaxed animals. They can lie in one spot for hours upon end, yet when they hear something that interests or frightens them, they move almost instantaneously. When relaxed, muscles can react more quickly and forcefully. There is no need to draw a division between the concepts of ready and relaxed.

Relaxation is a state of being that varies among individuals. Some people are wound up tight all the time so that even when they "relax", they are still a bundle of nerves. Others are relaxed to begin with. When they kick back they become so devoid of stress that they fall asleep. Sometimes when you try to relax, you end up becoming more tense because you are trying so hard to loosen up. I equate relaxation with

"letting go". When I let go of tension I feel it leave my body. This release may be subtle — there may be no visible change — but it is something that can be felt. The exact sensation is specific to each individual. For me it starts in and around the head and then travels throughout my entire body. When I'm relaxed, I can feel my shoulders drop and the rest of my body following suit. Such a slight change compounded throughout my entire body makes a huge difference in the way I interact with the world. As a result my mind is alert and open to everything around me; I'm ready to confront whatever it is that I want to do.

THOUGHT PROCESSES:
PRE-CONSCIOUS, CONSCIOUS & SUPER-CONSCIOUS

There are three kinds of thought processes related to our learning and our subsequent actions: Pre-conscious, Conscious and Super-conscious.

Pre-conscious thoughts are secure internal thoughts. You don't really think about them. You just act and the actions become automatic. Pre-conscious thoughts are acquired only through experience. They may also be referred to as habits. Good habits are great for your riding. Bad habits are extremely difficult to correct or break because they are already "inside" of you. It is not easy to unlearn these pre-conscious thoughts and then immediately learn and internalize new techniques.

Eating while watching television is an example of a pre-conscious thought. For instance, you know where the food is in front of you and you know where your mouth is. Using your hands and utensils, you take the food and place it in your mouth and then proceed to chew it and swallow. All of these actions had to be learned at some point in time, but you can eat without taking your eyes away from the television because the task does not require concentration. You already know how to eat well enough that you can focus your thoughts on other things.

Conscious actions are focused thoughts that become secured through the learning process. Think of something that you must really focus on in order to make it happen. That is a conscious thought. Some thoughts are so intensive that they never transcend into preconscious thought and always require your full attention.

This is a somewhat outrageous demonstration, but it works so...imagine handling a very poisonous snake, the kind that can kill you within seconds after a bite. Other than being scared stiff, you must focus every ounce of mental concentration on the task at hand, or else. This is an extreme example of conscious thoughts.

Super-conscious thoughts are insecure thoughts. When they consume your mind, they make it very difficult to act. Usually such thoughts are linked to excitement and insecurity. Trouble: "Oh my God, I'm going to hit that little tree in the middle of the trail." Vain: "I hope I look cool in these quadruple extra-large jeans and this slalom armor." Fear: "Those skiers are everywhere, I hope they don't lose control and wipe me out — I could get hurt. Maybe I can get the resort management to ban them from the area." You get the idea.

5

THINKING & DOING

At first snowboarding may seem awkward and extremely tough. Eventually the skills and techniques that you learn will become internalized. Active thinking, then doing, takes time. Simply doing takes less time. As you practice snowboarding, complex and complicated techniques turn into habit. You think less about the techniques and more about what you want to do with the hill. Using internalized movement patterns, you proceed to the point where you automatically execute the necessary skills and develop accordingly. In this sense snowboarding is just like walking or eating with a spoon — with practice your thoughts and actions become internalized, another on of those things that you "just know how to do."

Once you have mastered the riding skills at a beginning level, getting better is simply a matter of experience and "turning up the volume."

Here is an example of a progression from a basic skill, the 180 lifetime progression:

◆ A 180-degree turn on flat ground around the learners hill.

◆ Riding and performing a 180-degree turn on a green trail, then on a blue trail and so on.

◆ Riding over a jump and turning a 180-degree turn in the air.

◆ Riding over a jump and turning a 180-degree turn in the air, landing, and riding off down the trail.

◆ Jumping higher, farther, landing it, and riding away.

◆ Putting many 180's into succession, spinning yourself dizzy, landing, and riding away.

◆ Riding the pipe or dropping 30+ foot cliffs and pulling many 180's in succession (few riders ever achieve this level of proficiency). I know I don't ride that well — I just watch and say "that rider is crazy."

Setting goals

As you advance in your riding skills, set a number of goals. This way if you succeed in only one goal, you have still made progress, you have experienced "trial and success." When trying new skills, ride on terrain that you are comfortable with. In some cases riding "easier" terrain allows you to forget the trail and concentrate on the task at hand. When you are ready, go for it until you start to feel frustrated, bored, or Eureka! Success! Repeat the skill to reinforce your success. Enjoy and learn from your experience. When ready, move on to the next goal.

Let's say I'm looking to complete my first fakie 180 mute to forward. To do this trick I must be able to: ride fakie, ride fakie going over a jump, spin 180 to the other direction, grab the board for the mute or perform some other trick, land, and ride away. Here is a good example of multiple goal trial and success.

After scouting out the jump, I take a deep breath, relax, and start toward the jump. I spin around to ride fakie and compress my body in preparation for liftoff. I extend my legs as I hit the jump. In the air I look where I want to go and let my body follow. In the air I grab the board mute. Looking down the hill I ready myself for the landing. When I land, I catch an edge and hit the ground. I am disappointed that I didn't land my jump. However, I was able to do almost everything I set out to do. I am happy with the results of my effort.

Because I've had a good time and I still have one portion of the whole task to complete, I'll give it another try. Even if I was only able to complete one of the many goals I set for myself, I have had success. Now I will try to reinforce my good experience and success with more good experiences and success. By setting multiple goals you give yourself a better chance to have and keep having positive learning experiences. Remember that if you succeed in one of the multiple goals you have set for yourself, or even if you flailed all day and still had the time of your life, you have had a successful day. Look forward to your next one.

Setting goals is an excellent means to improve upon your skills. But don't get too caught up in such goals. The result can be extremely stifling and add a great deal of unnecessary stress to the act of riding. Rememeber, snowboarding is supposed to be fun. Goals are simply markers along the way to progress.

MENTAL FOCUS

The ability to focus your thoughts is the means by which you can use the power of your mind to get your body to do what you want it to do. This is the most powerful and effective resource you can call your own. Mental commitment can be a difficult thing to achieve. There are so many things around to draw your focus elsewhere. In reference to riding, your focus is your direction. Concentrate on where you want to go and what you want to do.

It takes some time to get used to riding with focus and control. There are some people who just do it naturally. They look ahead, and their minds and bodies steer them in the direction in which they wish to travel. Other people cannot manage to guide themselves in any specific direction, and so they just go. Either way works, but there is one big difference. The focused rider is more in control of their riding, more aware of the interaction between body, board, and the surrounding environment; the unfocused rider is not. If you were to ask the latter rider 'How did you get down the trail?' the response would probably be something like, "I dunno, I just did it."

Try this — walk down a crowded street or hallway. Focus on a fixed object further down your path. Remaining focused, go right to it. You will find that if you seriously concentrate, that single object is all you can make out in detail. Everything else is there but not of primary interest. Your peripheral vision gives you the information

you need to guide yourself to the target. Unless you are about to run into something, your mind pays little attention to its surroundings. This selective attention is what you use when you focus your mind. You choose to place your mental resources upon a specific task. Learning how to command this energy is one of the greatest forces you can have in your learning process.

THE ZONE

Sometimes you focus so well that you can achieve anything you set out to accomplish. This is often referred to as "the zone," a state where mind transcends body. When Michael Jordan scored 63 points against the Boston Celtics during the 1986 playoffs, he referred to his state of mind as being within the "zone". Participants in all walks of sport have experienced or witnessed these unbelievable performances, athletes achieving incredible feats. What is this "zone" like? It is amazing — a state where the mind is so focused and the body so in tune with the mind that all you have to do is know what it is you want to accomplish and you follow through successfully.

FEAR

To understand your own learning process, you must understand yourself and how the power of fear affects you. Keep this in mind — fear and excitement are always within us. Fear is simply a negative form of excitement. Depending upon how strong fear affects you, you can be overcome by it. However, you always have the choice (believe it or not) to use or be used by its strength. When in the grips of fear, you may feel your heart race and your mind start to shift focus very quickly. If you are having trouble landing a particular jump or pulling off a new trick, it is usually fear, not technique, holding you back. Dealing with fear is part of snowboarding and part of life in general. Fear is learned. Fear of falling is learned at a very early age. Snowboarding is falling down a mountain with both feet strapped to a plank. Maybe that is why snowboarding is so much fun. To do it well, we have to face and conquer a very basic and primal fear.

Fear is not rational — it does strange things to people. Understand that fear is an emotion relative to each individual. For an experienced rider this could mean a 20-foot drop. For an intermediate rider it could be the first mogul run attempted. And for a beginner, the bunny hill could be as frightening as a charging elephant. Fear is inside of us all. Some are freaked out by fear, others feed on it and are then driven by its power. The important thing is not to allow the feeling of fear to become so powerful that it causes you to lose control of the situation at hand. Teach yourself to recognize this negative excitement. Once recognized, it is possible to train yourself to take the energy and turn it into a positive excitement that can be applied to your riding.

Many times a rider will look at particular terrain and become rigid with fright. There are lots of ways to ride difficult terrain. Most of the "secret riding techniques" are simply descriptions of ways to deal with fear and accept the natural surroundings. Most of the time when people look at terrain they are not comfortable riding down, the initial feeling they experience is fear. This is not a bad thing. I would even call this reaction "normal." Everybody has fears. Someone's ability to ride terrain they fear is directly related to how they are able to deal with the emotion itself. Take the competitors who participate in the extreme championships in Valdez, Alaska, for instance. These competitors acknowledge and understand the role that fear plays in their riding — it keeps them alive. They just happen to be able to take that fear and use it to focus their thoughts on their riding and the dangerous environment that they've placed themselves in. Ultimately, if you are scared you will have much more difficulty learning and executing than someone who is not absorbed by their fear. Fear is the mind killer, and your mind leads your body. If you feel overcome by your feelings...relax, clear your mind, and think about what you want to do. When you're ready to tackle the challenge, do it with positive, controlled energy.

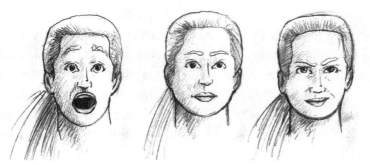

Keep in mind that one of the worst things you can do is disregard your fear altogether. This kind of behavior can have painful results, subjecting you to the mercy of the hill's fall line. In a strange way fear also motivates. It is a wonderful feeling to overcome a long-standing, fear-ridden hurdle. This type of success is usually followed by a long lasting sense of euphoria known as "perma-smile."

ANXIETY

Anxiety is another negative form of excitement that can keep people from accomplishing their goals. Often butterflies or knots in the stomach can prevent people from maintaining focus. If you feel anxious, recognize it and try to turn the negative excitement of fear and anxiety into positive excitement. Then channel that excitement into your riding.

STARTING OUT

LESSONS

A point of advice — take a lesson when you first start snowboarding. This book is by no means a replacement for a trained professional. The first day's lesson may cost you some money, but the initial investment will prove worthwhile. If you were one of the unfortunate souls (like myself) who didn't have the guidance (or the common sense) to start out easy and work your way up, you probably remember the excitement, wonder, and glory of learning something completely new. You will also remember the aches, the pains, and the black and blues. My recommendation is to take lessons, especially early on. You'll gain fewer bad habits and allow yourself the benefit of learning as much as possible, as quickly and painlessly as possible.

Your level of snowboarding ability is built upon those basic skills that are used when you ride. This is why a solid foundation of strong technique and proper habits is as (if not more) important when you first start riding as it is later in your snowboarding life. Think of it as giving yourself training wheels when you try something new. Before long you don't need the training wheels anymore, you just hop on and ride.

THE LEARNING PLATEAU

Later on, if you come to a "learning plateau" where you seem to be riding a great deal but not progressing at all, take a lesson. Riding over an extended period of time without learning or progressing is an indication to seek some help. If you can't "afford" lessons or just don't like to take them, have someone record video of you riding. Then take a good look at the result and be prepared to see things from a new perspective. On video you will probably look nothing like you think you look. Be critical of yourself and search for elements of your riding to work on. When you hit the snow again, go for it with goals for improvement in mind.

It is important to take it easy on yourself when you go out and try something new. Ride and learn what you need first on easier terrain, and then take it to a more difficult environment. Think of it as "training wheels," preparing you for more difficult snowboarding skills. Remember your first day? Your time on the bunny slope might have been hard at first, but it got easier quickly. If you are having difficulty with a specific aspect of your riding or performance on a particular type of terrain, give yourself a break. Go to some less challenging terrain and play around with whatever is bothering you. Before long, you should start to feel what works and what doesn't. When you are ready, go back to the terrain that was troublesome. Now ride using what you have taught yourself. Try over-emphasizing what you have learned. If you are still having trouble, invest in a lesson.

PERFORMANCE PREPARATION

When planning to ride, be good to yourself — eat lots of food, drink lots of water, and get a good night's sleep. Your performance will not be your best without following these simple guidelines. When you are tired, your technique breaks down. Be good to your body, and it will work when you want it to. Bad habits and falls are much more likely to occur when you are physically exhausted and unable to stand upon your own legs. If you are thirsty, stop and get some water. Dehydration, especially at high altitudes, can take a lot out of you. Listen to your body and give it what it needs before it stops working the way that it should. If you are trying to work on technique, do it when you first get to the hill and are fresh and full of energy.

SENSORY DEPRIVATION

Sensory deprivation is a learning technique I stumbled upon one day while teaching a first day's lesson on how to use the falling leaf (See Chapters 8 & 9). Bored with this technique, I closed my eyes during the demonstration. All of a sudden it felt like I was thundering down the hill at an incredible speed. I became intimately aware of my board's edge moving over the snow beneath my feet. As soon as the lesson was over, I rushed to the top of the hill to repeat the blind falling leaf exercise. I started down the hill, opening my eyes after a minute or so of this. I was more aware of the board underneath me as I rode. I was able to carve turns harder than I ever had been before. This accidental discovery gave me a new awareness of my edges and has enabled me to improve my snowboarding tremendously. It can help you as well.

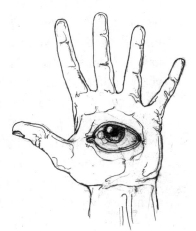

Sight, sound, touch, smell, and taste — these are the five senses we learned in grade school. These are our "connections" to the world around us. What our teacher did not tell us is that we have more than five senses. We have a sense of balance, pressure, heat, cold, pain, hunger and so on. We have all these different ways to observe and learn from the world around us, yet we tend to rely almost solely on our sense of sight to act and react to the world. We take in so much of the surrounding environment that we learn to edit or filter out a great deal of "unnecessary" information. When we block out our sense of sight, we are forced to rely on all other avenues of sensory information, and we perceive the world differently. Because we are using our secondary senses, a great deal of information that we perceive is not filtered out. By closing our eyes we are able to sensitize our body to the board and its interactions with the snow beneath us. This is why sensory deprivation is such a great learning tool. It alters our perspective and forces us to reevaluate our current knowledge of snowboarding.

13

Use sensory deprivation only at low speeds with someone spotting you. Have another person act as your eyes, telling you when to open your own eyes or to stop when necessary. You obviously don't want to hit something or someone else, so do this with a person you trust. This sensation is scary, but try to relax and accept your new perception of snowboarding. When you become comfortable with "riding blind," you will then be able to learn more effectively from your body, your snowboard, and the snow you are riding over. This is what I meant about doing, but not feeling what you are doing. Learning to snowboard well requires you to condition your mind to control very specific body movements. By using sensory deprivation in combination with on-hill and off-hill exercises, you can teach yourself a great deal about how your body works and moves. Ultimately, to realize something we must be able to understand the information we assimilate from all of our senses. Sensory deprivation allows for greater sensory feedback from actions around and inside of us, and their resulting reactions. This kind of body consciousness is necessary for you to realize what you are really doing.

Just try walking across your living room with your eyes closed. Notice how differently you perceive this familiar environment. If you are afraid of bumping into something, move it, or have a friend help you navigate around the environment. Try doing this with movements that you know are used when you ride. Feel how the smallest toe on your foot can affect your whole body and its interaction with the snowboard underneath. Feel the flexion and relaxation of the muscles inside of your body. Sensitize yourself to these stimuli. Efficient technique uses only the necessary amount of muscle strength — maybe a little more here, a little less there, but within a certain minimalist range of effort. You want to work but not overwork the board. Extra effort is wasted effort. Get a feel for how much muscle you need to use, and use no more than that amount. Try to establish a sense of your body in this manner when you are out riding. By doing this we can feel when our body is moving comfortably and efficiently. Try moving in different positions and recognize what feels most natural. If nothing feels quite right, try adjusting your equipment to accommodate your body. That is what good snowboard equipment is supposed to do.

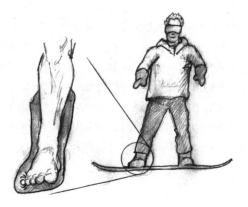

Children are often more agile and therefore able to learn new movements more quickly than adults. As we grow older we develop movement patterns and habits. To learn new patterns of movement we first have to overcome what we have already learned, then accept and develop new ones. Keep in mind that we have also learned fear. Children do not have these sorts of hurdles to deal with. Since they have no old movement patterns to overcome, they simply learn the new movement patterns without ever having to break down old barriers. Sometimes when I am having great difficulty with something I try to think like a child so that I can act with less inhibition and a greater willingness to try and learn new things. I tend to have more fun too!

MENTAL ANTICIPATION

15

Mental anticipation is simply planning what you are going to do further down the hill. As you travel at higher speeds you will need to anticipate more of what is in front of you in order to accommodate the challenge of the speeds you ride. The faster you go the more you want to anticipate the terrain and objects on the hill. The speed of your mind must be faster than the speed of your body and your physical world. As you go faster and the terrain gets steeper, you will need to adjust. The further down the hill you look, the more you will be able to anticipate and plan your descent. Use peripheral vision to sense what is already right in front of you. Though you have already seen immediate obstacles and acted accordingly, it is always good to be aware of your close as well as your distant surroundings.

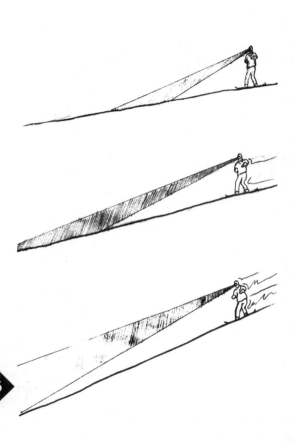

If you can't see where you are going, slow down or stop. Never assume that a trail is going to be in good shape, even if it's your favorite trail at your home resort. There could be a person who has fallen down or a rock that has broken the surface of the melting snow in spring. Perhaps the local wildlife is pausing for a rest...it could be anything. But if it's in your path of travel and you are either moving too fast or simply paying no attention, the result could be life-threatening.

If you are unsure of what you want to do in the process of your descent, STOP. Take a good look at what you are about to ride. Think of the ten-second principle. Know yourself and act accordingly. Pushing your limits and abilities is a good thing; however, if you honestly believe that you are not capable of taking a certain route, it is much better to find another way down. Find another route and hike back up the hill if you must. This is better than hating your run with passion or possibly risking injury to yourself or someone else.

If you watch really good riders go over seriously difficult terrain, they make it look easy. People watching just let their jaws drop and wonder..."What is that person doing that I'm not?" If you ask them they might tell you all the tricks and secrets you are willing to hear. A lot of what they say will relate to anticipating the hill and planning the best possible route to accept and use the terrain.

When riders look particularly "fluid" they are allowing their body and board to pass over the path of least resistance. They are not trying to force any actions. They anticipate what is in front of them, and let the terrain mold their movements. Their body and board accept and conform to the terrain. They flow into the desired direction. When riders look "rough" what they are doing is trying to fight and force the terrain about them. They are not allowing themselves to use the terrain to their own advantage. Trying to push a mountain around doesn't work. Awkward riders often aren't looking more than 10-15 feet ahead. Fear and stress play a big part of their mental process. They let this strain tire them out then get frustrated and wind up looking foolish all at the same time. Once these riders allow themselves to relax, their riding often improves immensely.

Keeping your thoughts further down the hill greatly increases riding options. Think of your eyes as the search lights for your conscious mind. Point your eyes and observe where it is you want to go — your mind will take you there. Rely on peripheral vision to keep you confidently informed of the rest.

It is not always possible to look far down the hill. Going over a jump or pulling a trick requires a great deal of mental concentration. In cases like these, your attention needs to be placed on the task directly in front of you (you don't want to concentrate on your toes or the tip of the board — keep your eyes on your objective). This focused attention is what you need to accomplish such feats.

17

When your mind is not anticipating the terrain in front of you, you are riding in a reactionary fashion, relying on your reflexes and your wits to stay on top of the board. You will know when you are riding like this — feeling like a rag doll, barely hanging on, your snowboard leading you down the hill instead of you guiding it. Mental anticipation is the key, it's what allows you to control and ride your snowboard. As you get better at anticipating, the more you will be able to ride difficult terrain. If you come across some terrain that is exceptionally burly, stop. Take the time to mentally plan out your attack. Then when you're ready, drop in with confidence.

MENTAL VISUALIZATION

Sometimes we all need to sit down and think about what we are going to do. Mental visualization is an extremely important means by which to improve your snowboarding. This technique uses the power of your mind to help you to accomplish what it is that you want to do. By visualizing successful completion of what maneuvers you have planned, you can train yourself without suffering any physical consequences. Because you can alter your mental reality at will, you never have to mess up (more importantly, you never have to pay the painful price for messing up). By using your mind to run "mental movies" of the desired task, you can safely practice the task over and over again.

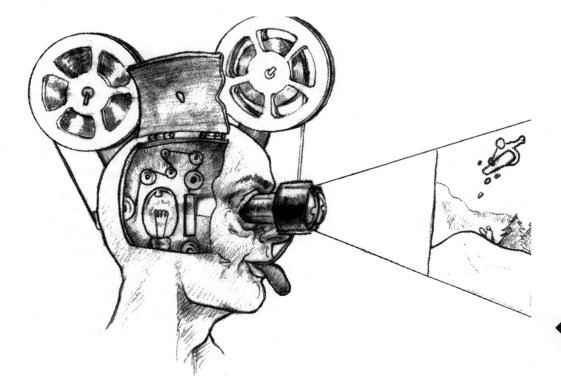

This technique can work for any athlete at any level. If something is giving you trouble and you know it's something that you can do, relax and practice it mentally first. Imagine yourself completing the desired task perfectly. Play this movie over and over, from as many different angles as you can imagine. Then step back into the real world and practice the task physically. Watch a video of a great rider to help out with the process if necessary. Generally speaking, the more difficult the task the more time you will want to spend mentally focusing on it. All the details, no matter how small, require your attention. The more you prepare, the higher your chances of success.

Self-training like this is used by many of the strongest competitors in sports today. By forming a mental picture of themselves riding the perfect race or nailing every trick on the halfpipe run, many riders can improve their chances of success. Their mental movies are often run over and over until they become as natural as breathing. When the time comes to execute the act itself, it is already programmed within.

Using mental movies can help you with specific aspects of your riding. Let's say you're having difficulty transferring from your toeside to heelside turn. You do fine until the actual transfer onto the new edge and BAM!...you're flat out on the snow. You know what it looks like and how it feels to biff on your transfer. Take out the portions of your mental movie that you don't want, and put in those that you do.

Now, imagine yourself finishing a perfect toeside turn, looking down the hill. Your mind is focused down the hill. Now your body starts to smoothly transfer across the board. As you engage the heelside edge you keep on shifting your weight into the new turn. Now you start to pressure the new edge and your new turn is as perfect as you can imagine. Next the new image of the perfect turn is spliced on top of the biff turn. Run this movie over and over. Slow the movie down and pay attention to the smaller details. Slow the movie down even more — look and feel the smallest nuances within your body, in your snowboard, and on the snow. Feel this movie as though it were actually happening. Then go out, repeat as often as necessary, and make it happen.

Combined with video cameras, this method can be extremely powerful. Remember, the preconceived mental image we have of ourselves riding is often quite different from the reality of how we actually interact with the board and the snow.

21

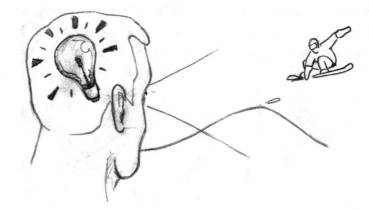

Detailed mental movies can teach your body specific movements without ever having done them. The nervous pathways to your muscles are already known to your mind. Most of our learning travels from the outside-in. You do something, it works, and your mind "remembers" how you did it. Your mind also "remembers" the nervous pathways that were accessed to complete the task. By using mental movies to access and travel those nervous pathways, you can learn from the inside-out. When I use mental movies I sometimes find myself moving around slightly. To me that is an indication that my mind is finding connections to the specific muscles that I am planning to use. When I get back on the hill, I try to feel those connections again and use them.

There is a difference between mental visualization and dreams of grandeur. Mental visualization is a great tool to help you reach attainable goals. Seeing an experienced rider pull a 540 might be a fantasy to a first day rider, but with experience and practice the beginning rider could eventually achieve that goal. Fantasizing about a 150+ foot drop from a helicopter onto a 60-degree slope is just plain crazy. You might just want to leave it at that, a fantastic dream.

A wise man once said that you can tell how well someone is riding by looking at their tracks. This can also be an excellent form of self diagnosis. It is easiest to do this if you can ride a trail just under a chairlift and then check out your tracks as you go up for your next run. Make mental notes to yourself as you ride down the hill. Remember what felt great and what gave you trouble. As you ride up you can see where your turns were sharp and clean. You can also see where your turns sketched out as you rode down the hill. Analysis of your own tracks is best on a flat snow surface. Deeper snow conditions will produce much different tracks than flatter surfaces. If deep snow is available, the last thing on your mind should be technical self-analysis.

When you find a specific aspect of your riding that needs improvement, the exercises and drills in this book can help. Understand that sometimes a drill or an exercise will require the exaggeration of proper form. But sacrificing proper form in one portion of your riding here is designed to achieve proper overall form. For example, a drill that emphasizes rotation may detract from your ability to balance yourself over the board at higher speeds. Don't let yourself become consumed by a single drill. Learn to take the strength of the drill and apply it to your riding — leave the rest of the drill behind.

23

COMMITMENT

Learning is a continual process. Sometimes you have good days, sometimes you don't. If you snowboard continually, you will get better. If you feel as though your riding is in a slump, think about why it is that you feel that way. Whatever the reason may be, if you are not having fun or you are feeling burnt out on snowboarding, do something about it. Take a lesson. Take a break. Take the day off. Try skiing. Then when you are once again ready, you'll go back to your snowboard ready to rip up the hill.

Finally, whenever I have trouble with my riding I think of two words: Relax and Commit. Sometimes it is difficult to ride. Tensing up your entire body puts you in a position where you're fighting your own body in addition to those forces naturally placed against you. Gritting your teeth and tightening up can only make your task more difficult than it needs to be. When you feel this tension overcoming you, relax and allow your body to work naturally. By committing (which is very difficult to do unless you relax) I mean focusing on what you want to do. Everything else around you is secondary information. I don't want you to think like a race horse with blinders on. Rather, think of your eyes as the headlights of a car. Shine your headlights into the direction you want to go. Chances are you will go there. The advanced rider focuses on several turns, sometimes on the entire hill that lies ahead. The greater your horizon the greater your ability to anticipate what you are about to encounter. Look in the direction you want to go. Focus on the difficult tasks you wish to do. Accept rather than fight the terrain you ride. Think of efficiency in your movements, and let your body move the way it was designed to. Becoming an expert rider is a long and interesting process. My definition of an expert rider is someone who can ride any type of terrain under any kind of condition...and make it look easy.

THE PRINCIPLES
OF SNOWBOARDING

All the information discussed in this book can be broken down into general principles. These principles apply to the world in which we live, the snowboard on which we ride, the mind with which we think and the body with which we act. Together, these ideas make up the basic principles of snowboarding.

26

PRINCIPLES & IDEAS

PRINCIPLES OF THE WORLD WE LIVE IN:

◆ Newton was right.

◆ Inertia is the physical law that states: A body in motion, unaffected by anything else, stays in constant motion. A body at rest, unaffected by anything else, stays at rest.

◆ For every action there is an opposite and equal reaction.

◆ Gravity works, as applied to your riding: Whichever end of the snowboard has the most weight over it goes down the hill first.

◆ As you get better you will learn to use the forces you create to make turns that don't rely solely upon gravity. As you get better you will learn to use the forces you create to carry yourself across the hill and into the next turn. The better your technique, the more you will be able to harness these forces and channel them through your board. This way your board can do the work for you.

PRINCIPLES OF THE SNOWBOARD:

◆ Ride a well-tuned snowboard. If you take care of your snowboard, it will take care of you on the hill. The board will also last much longer with proper care.

◆ I like to refer to this principle as the "Golden Rule of Snowboarding". The golden rule states: If you are traveling straight down the hill and you engage the downhill edge, you will trip over the downhill edge and slam, hard. Ouch! Stay on that uphill edge and stay on top of your board. The only time you do not have an uphill and downhill edge is when your board points straight up or down the hill.

27

◆ Speed and direction control is very simple. The faster you want to go, the more you flatten the board to the snow and point it down the hill. The more you want to control your speed and direction, the more you turn your board across the hill and dig your edges into the snow. You can also use the shape of the turn for speed control. The slower you want to go, the shorter the radius and the more frequent the turn. The faster you want to go, the wider the radius and the less frequent the turn.

PRINCIPLES OF THE MIND:

◆ All limitations are self-imposed.

◆ Your mind is the most powerful force you have at your command. If you really want to do something, keep at it. It may take awhile, but you will succeed if you really want to. In other words, don't quit, ever.

◆ The mind leads, the body follows.

28

◆ Think of your eyes as the headlights of the mind. Shine them in the direction you want to go. Look in the direction you want to go, and you will probably go there.

◆ Use the mind to anticipate your physical actions. The faster you travel down the hill, the further you want to look down the hill. Mental anticipation relies on your ability to see what is coming up. When you anticipate the environment around you, your actions will be early. When you fail to anticipate the environment, your actions will be late, and you will be forced to rely solely on reflexes to stay over your board.

I'm Going To Do It!

◆ If you are having trouble with the task at hand, relax and commit. Relax first. Stop and sit down if you have to. Riding with the ordinary forces placed against you is difficult enough, being tense and rigid will only make matters more difficult. It is tough to focus on what you are doing when you feel like this. Relax and let your body work. By committing mentally to what you want to do, you can focus the greatest amount of mental energy and physical power possible. Everything else will seem secondary. This relaxed and focused state of being is an extremely effective means by which to accomplish your desired goals.

◆ The ten-second principle states: If you look at something for ten seconds and it still gives you the willies...look for another way down the hill.

◆ Mental visualization is the act of using your mind to prepare for the task at hand before actually performing the task. It is a way to better prepare yourself and increase the likelihood of your success. I like to think of this thought process as a "mental movie". This movie can be played over and over with attention focused upon specific details. Your mental practice can be perfect every time for the race, pipe run, or first carved turn you have been wanting for so long to execute.

29

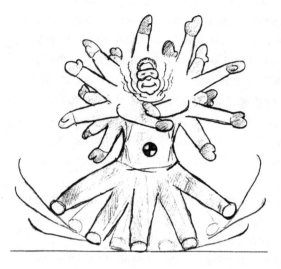

PRINCIPLES OF THE BODY:

◆ Use your body to stay over the board and ride it. Otherwise the board will take you for a ride.

◆ Try to originate movements from your Center of Gravity (COG). This is the most stable part of your body.

◆ The cone of balance represents a "zone of stability" around you. If you stay within the cone, you will be able to balance yourself over the board. If you travel outside of the cone, you will become unstable. Generally speaking the lower and closer you are over the board, the wider your cone of balance and the more stable you will be when you ride. The higher and further you are over the board, the smaller your cone and the less stable you will be. As your cone of balance shrinks, you will have less and less room for error.

30

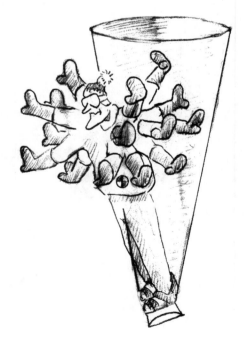

◆ The natural ready stance (the athletic stance) is a position where the body is situated in the way it was meant to work. Everything is easier from this stance. It is your most powerful and flexible body position. The trick is to understand that your body is designed to move in a forward direction — snowboarding moves sideways.

◆ A forward facing stance may be appropriate for riders with high (45+ degree) binding angles on their board. It is twisted but with practice can be worked with in any situation. If you ride with low binding angles and find your body twisting a great deal toward the tip of the board, try to face your head down the hill by turning with your neck rather than with the entire body in order to see where you are going.

◆ The bodyspring uses the elastic properties of your muscles to work to your advantage. Twisting around will build up energy inside the body. By committing to the new direction and relaxing, your body will naturally unwind and release the energy built up throughout your body. Efficient snowboarding technique uses the body's ability to wind and unwind itself to turn the snowboard.

◆ Guiding your board around by using the bodyspring is far more efficient and natural than trying to force the board around. Forcing the board around is known as counter rotation. This occurs when your upper body twists opposite the desired direction of movement to spin the board around into the turn. If you fight your board, your board will fight you back. You may not always win.

31

◆ Partial body flexion is the best way to ride over your snowboard. This way you can flex your legs at will to absorb bumps. You can also extend your legs at will to pressure your ride as you see fit. In this manner your legs act as both the shock absorbers and engine of your snowboarding. Relatively speaking, you want to bend more with the joints that are closest to the ground when using a partially flexed stance. Bend the most with the ankles. Bend a lot at the knees. Bend only enough at the hips to keep your upper body upright.

◆ Riding with fully flexed or fully extended legs is difficult because if you hit even the tiniest bump, you cannot absorb the shock. You get "kicked off" the board. Riding in a fully flexed/extended stance is also dangerous to your knees. When the knee joint is at either end of its range of motion, it becomes vulnerable to the forces placed upon it. Don't ride like a scarecrow or a toad.

◆ The theory of the snake pertains to rotational forces inside of your body. When a snake slithers around on the ground, how does it travel? The head leads, the body follows the head, and the tail follows the body. Believe it or not, humans operate in a similar manner. When we rotate around we lead with our head first, our upper body follows our head, and then our lower body follows the upper body. In this sense we move like snakes. Our snowboard — attached to our lower body — follows as well.

◆ Anatomists divide the human skeleton into two parts. The Axial skeleton is composed of the head and spinal column, and the Peripheral skeleton of the arms and legs. Our Axial skeleton is the Command Center of our body. It houses and protects our brain and spinal nerve cord. Without the Axial skeleton, or the nervous systems that it protects, we could not do much. We would not be able to move our fingers or our toes. We would not be able to bend our arms or our legs. We would just lie there and drool. Let's consider the snake for instance. The skeleton of a snake is composed of a head and a long spinal column with many ribs. If we look at the human axial skeleton without the attachments of the peripheral skeleton, there is just a head, a bunch of vertebrae, and ribs. It kind of looks like a snake. Our peripheral skeleton follows our axial skeleton's lead. What you do with your head and upper body, particularly the spinal column, affects the rest of the body as well.

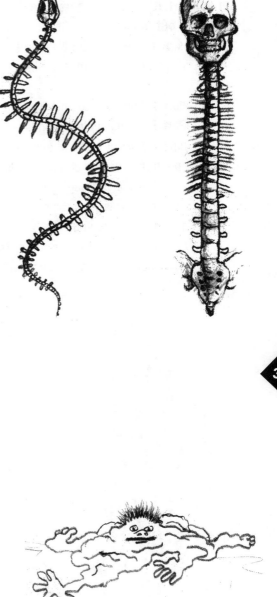

◆ Body separation and angulation: Use the hard structures (bones) of your body for support. It may work to use the soft structures (muscles) for support as well, but it tires you out very quickly. Strong angulation helps you to support yourself as efficiently as possible and still be able to act/react easily to the world around you.

◆ Angulation uses three points of separation with the body when you ride:

Part 1: You want to point your head into the desired direction of travel.

Part 2: To maintain maximum stability, keep your upper body (from the hips up) as upright and quiet as possible. Your head requires a stable platform from which to observe the surrounding world.

Part 3: Make your legs guide and work the board. As I said before, think of your legs as the snowboarding engine as well as the shock absorbers. Drive your knees into the turns and absorb the bumps and forces coming out of the turns. The more work you can do with the lower body the less work you will have to do with the upper body.

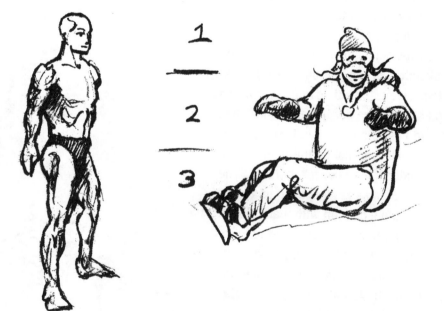

◆ The faster you ride, the more stable you want to be over the board, and the more you want the board to work for you. As you improve you will want to use less rotation and more pressure and angulation to make the turns.

◆ Use all of your senses when riding — body/mind principle.

◆ Flow rather than fight.

◆ Ride as much as you possibly can.

3

THE SCIENCE
OF THE TURN

Knowledge of the forces that affect snowboarding will help you to understand how and why things happen. This is a simplified version of the complex and crazy world in which we live. When learning to execute a proper turn for example, you can serve as your own best teacher by becoming familiar with the physical ideas involved in a turn. But you must learn to teach yourself effectively.

EXECUTING PROPER TURNS

UNDERSTANDING A FORCE

To understand a force we first have to define what a "force" is. My definition of a force is a power that affects any object it encounters. When this power comes into contact with the object, it changes the form, motion, and/or the state of the affected object's being.

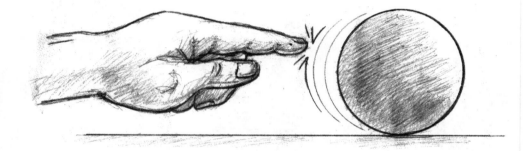

Newton defined the idea of inertia as such: "A body at rest will stay at rest. A body in motion will stay in motion until a force acts upon it." Inertia affects all the other ideas and techniques in this book. When you move, you generate and carry inertial force. You can feel the force of inertia resist you every time you try to change your direction or speed. Try walking around the room and make a quick turn around into the opposite direction. You can feel inertia pull you into your original direction of travel as you turn about.

Newton also said that "For every action, there is an opposite and equal reaction." To hold a turn you have to generate an equal (or more forceful reaction) to the forces being placed against you in a turn. Otherwise you won't be able to hold a turn. This idea also holds true in actions related to balance. Stand upright with both your feet together. Lift one leg out to the side as far as you can. The more you lift your leg, the more the rest of your body has to lean in the other direction to counterbalance the first movement. Understanding this idea and how your movements affect the your whole body is necessary to move and balance yourself well over your board.

EFFECTS OF GRAVITY

A force that we deal with on a daily basis is gravity. Gravity attracts smaller masses to larger masses. Gravity works, all the time. This is why the earth orbits the sun. We are drawn toward the center of the earth. As we ride down the mountain, our descent toward the center of the earth is modified by the terrain we ride over. We can  alter this descent even more by using our snowboard. Becoming a good snowboarder is directly linked to how well you can work with gravity and with your environment.

The fall line is the most direct path down the hill. Imagine a stream traveling down the hill in front of you, which way does it go? Your body will move down the hill in the same direction if you let it. If you want find the fall line, stand with your board flat to the snow. Shift your weight tipward and feel gravity take over. You start to move down the hill in a specific direction, almost as it you were metal being drawn to a magnet. If you want to control your direction and speed, you will need to learn how to use your board to resist the forces of gravity and inertia in the fall line.

Since gravity draws us toward the center of the earth, we wind up taking the most direct route down the hill — straight down the fall line. We have to apply force using our own body and board to alter our path and speed. The forces that we create to hold a turn will be referred to as centripetal force. Using your board and this energy, you can place force toward the center of your turn. Opposing centrifugal forces pull you away from the center of your turn. Centrifugal forces are the combined forces of inertia and gravity.

CENTRIPETAL & CENTRIFUGAL FORCES

When the board is placed upon its edge, it lets you place centripetal force through the board onto the snow. Centripetal and centrifugal forces work against each other to through your snowboard. The result is a turn. Your ability to resist centrifugal forces and hold a turn is directly related to the edge angle of the board. The lower the edge angle, the wider the turn and the more likely the turn will skid. The higher the edge angle of the turn, the shorter the turn and the more likely the turn will carve. If the board does not have a high enough edge angle upon it, the board will lose its grip on the snow and centrifugal forces will take over.

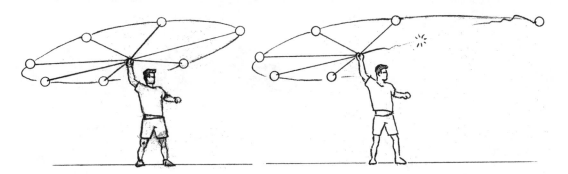

A simple image that can illustrate the above ideas is to think of swinging a ball at the end of a rope. The rope represents centripetal force and the edge of your board. This holds the ball in a circular flight path over your head. Centrifugal forces are the forces that are pulling the ball away from the path; centripetal forces are holding the ball in the circular flight path. The faster the ball spins, the stronger the rope needs to be. If the rope breaks, the ball takes a different flight path, one that is dictated by inertia and gravity. The reason why you feel more pressure at the end of the turn is due to the combination of centripetal forces and gravity placed against the rider.

39

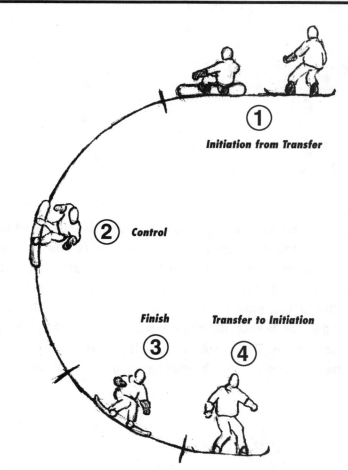

① **Initiation from Transfer**

② **Control**

③ **Finish**

④ **Transfer to Initiation**

PHASES OF A TURN:
INITIATION, CONTROL, FINISH & TRANSFER

The Association of American Snowboard Instructors (AASI) teach that a turn can be broken down into 4 phases: 1) initiation, 2) control, 3) finish and 4) transfer.

The initiation phase of a turn takes place the moment the new edge is engaged. This is the setup for the turn. The aggressiveness of the initiation defines the turn. The more aggressive the ignition of the turn is the quicker the turn itself will be.

The control phase of a turn is the actual "work" of the turn itself. This is when the edge is raised and it digs into the snow. The board "decambers" and builds energy inside of it. Pressuring techniques can also be added to the board to increase flexion and edge hold. This work determines the size, shape and direction of the turn.

The finish phase of the turn releases of the energy inside the board and prepares for the transfer into the next turn. Pressures inside the board release as the board "recambers" into its original shape. This release of energy can used to accelerate or decelerate the board. The more the board points down the hill during the finish of a turn the more the board shoots the rider down the hill, adding to your speed. The more the board points across the hill at the finish phase of the turn, the more the board shoots you across the hill and slows you down.

The transfer phase of a turn is simply your COG (center of gravity) transferring to over the other edge of the board. As the COG transfers, the edges transfer and a new turn is initiated. And so on, and so on all the way down the hill.

All four phases of the turn are linked together. If one of the phases is altered, the whole turn is affected. Riding well uses all four phases effectively as the terrain dictates. Different types of terrain require different types of turns. Sometimes different phases are emphasized and others become less important to the turn. However they are always present, even in the smallest amounts.

TURN SHAPES

The shape of the tracks that you make in the snow can tell you a great deal about how you are manipulating your board. These are the three types of turns that you can make. Sometimes you can combine more than one type of turn in the same arc, but this is built upon at least two staggered and incomplete turns. Not an efficient turn, but sometimes that what you need to do to accommodate for the mountain you are passing over.

41

J-TURNS

J-Turns place the most pressure on the board at the end of the turn where the board recambers and shoots you across the hill. This kind of turn is a decelerating turn. It slows you down. It feels like a great deal of forces are against you. After all, you are resisting both centrifugal forces and gravity at the end of the turn which is why you feel so much pressure.

J-Turn

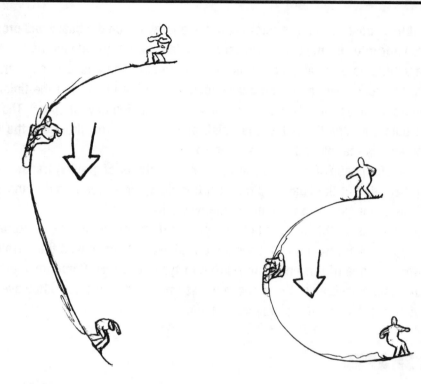

Comma Turn   *Apex Turn*

42

COMMA TURNS

Comma turns place a great deal of pressure at the start of the turn but do not turn across the hill. This shows very little control over the board once it enters the fall line. Too many of these turns on steeper terrain will quickly lead to a bombing run.

APEX TURNS

Apex turns place the most pressure upon the board in the middle of the turn. These are the fastest turns you can make. When done properly, the board recambers as it points down the fall line which will shoot you down the hill and add to your speed. This turn uses the board most efficiently and uses those forces built up inside the board along with gravity to increase your speed as you travel down the hill, accelerating from turn to turn.

In theory that is what this book is about — learning how to change your rate of descent down the side of the earth on a snowboard while enjoying the time of your life doing so. With this knowledge, the rest of this book will make sense.

chapter 4

THE ANATOMY
OF A RIDER

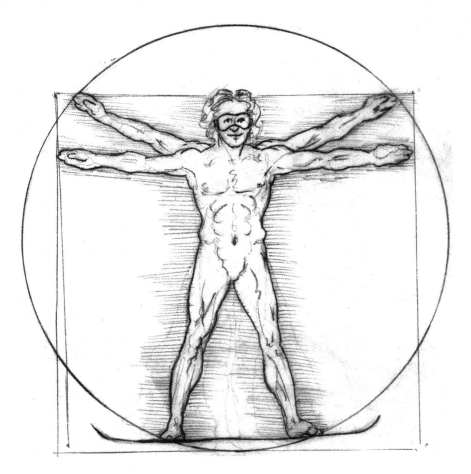

Specific terms are used throughout this book to describe the rider's body and positioning on a snowboard. In this section those working terms will be related to the process of snowboarding so that they may be of practical use in the learning process. If there are further questions about any of the words, refer to the glossary in the back of this book.

SNOWBOARDING PHYSIOLOGY

RIDING TERMS

Leading body part: If you split your body vertically between the eyes, the leading half is the half of the body going down the hill first.

Trailing body part: If you split your body vertically between the eyes, the trailing half of your body is the half of the body going down the hill last.

Toeside: The side of the board that your toes are closest to. A toeside turn is right turn for regular, left turn for goofy.

Heelside: The side of the board that your heels are closest to. A heelside turn is left turn for regular, right turn for goofy.

44

Center of Gravity (COG): The center of your entire physical body in relation to height, width, and depth. Every person has a body unique in its size and shape. Every body has a different center of gravity.

Cone of Balance: A visual representation of how the body balances itself. The cone represents the area of the board over which you are balanced. If your COG starts to travel outside of the cone, you will start to feel wobbly. If your COG passes all the way out of the cone, you will become unbalanced and proceed to meet mother earth.

BALANCE & STABILITY

ORIGINATING MOVEMENT FROM CENTER

Moving from your center is an unusual concept for many. Most people center their movements around their head. Again we defer to Newton who said: "For every action there is an opposite and equal reaction." A centered and relaxed state does not compromise your ability to act/react. Rather, it gives you the ability to act/react to your world in the most efficient manner. There is also the matter of spreading your body out to achieve balance. Think of balancing yourself on a stool. Other than sitting on it, which is easier — to balance on your head or to lay down on your back or stomach?

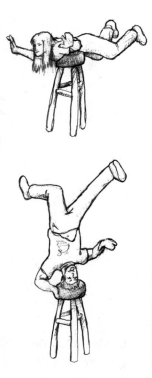

If you intitiate all movements by first moving your head, your body can become easily unbalanced. On the other hand, when you lead with your mind and originate movements from your center of gravity, the entire body moves more easily and more efficiently. That is not to mention that your head has a more stable platform upon which to move. Moving from your center allows you to create a more dynamic and balanced state of being.

46

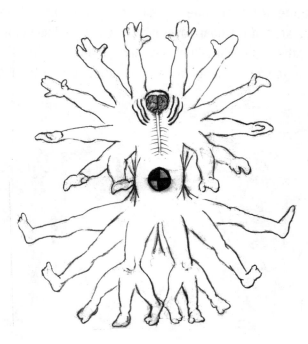

If you have ever seen film of a cheetah or any other high speed predator, they all share one quality when they move. Their heads remain steady and focused on the prey at all times. Legs, tail, and body can be moving in all sorts of crazy directions, but the head is quiet, the predator is fixed upon the direction it wants to go. The head rides and leads on top of a stable body.

To ride your snowboard board you need to project your body and board into different directions to hold and link your turns, even in the gentlest of terrain. Balance is essential. Your board and body do not travel the same path down the hill. The board is guided outside to hold your body inside the turn and above the snow.

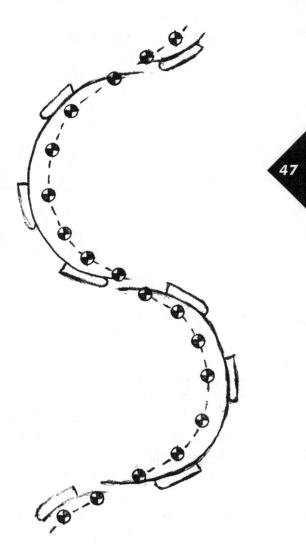

47

CONTROLLING COUNTER ROTATION

When you walk around, your body alternates the arms with the legs when you step. As you put your left leg forward your left arm swings back and vice versa. Your body counters the movement of the leg with the opposite arm. This is how your body is designed to move forward. Try walking around in a pattern of left leg and arm, right leg and arm. When your body does not counterbalance itself it swings all over the place. Now, try putting your hands on your waist and walking around. Notice what it feels like to move like this? Feel it even more by increasing the bend at your ankles and knees as much as you can and just skim your feet over the ground. Focus on keeping the height of your hips over the ground as constant as possible. Take your time with this exercise. It is not always easy to feel and realize. When you do this your whole body moves more as a single unit. There is little counter swing in the motions you make. When I do this I sometimes feel like I am floating.

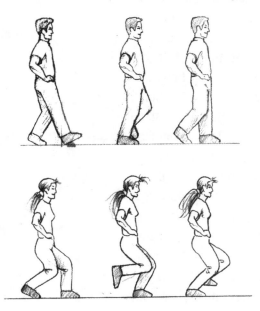

Close your eyes and use sensory deprivation to accentuate this feeling. As you move more in this manner, your movements will start to change. They will start to emanate from your waist (close to your center) outwards. Your mind still leads your body, but the movements are more fluid and you are using less energy. Feel this as much as you can. It may feel strange at first, but try not to resist it, accept it. Soon you will find yourself traveling very quickly and wondering...How did I get that way? All you are doing is allowing your body to work the way it was designed. The reason we want to try to move this way is because snowboarding is again a sideways sport. These flexing and floating movements will help you to resist the upright counter-rotating movements and help you to move sideways as naturally as possible.

FINDING THE NATURAL READY POSITION

Here's a game you can play to increase your awareness of balance, agility, and proper movement from center. Your goal is to find your natural ready postion, a stance from which you can react quickly and forcefully in all directions. Have a friend face you and place their hands against yours. The object is to unbalance your friend and make them move their feet. Initially whoever shoves the hardest first wins. Before too long, however, both players should learn to move and flex, to accept and absorb the energy projected toward them without moving their COG. Eventually, whoever maintains stability will win the contest as the shover ends up throwing themselves off balance, lacking the resistance to hold themselves up. Your arms will move back and forth. Your legs will move in the opposite direction around the center. Don't try to think too hard with this game, just relax, let go, and you will find that your body will start to move about effortlessly.

PARTIALLY-FLEXED VS. FULLY-EXTENDED

Now it's time to perceive balance, stability, and movement on the snowboard. Your center of gravity must now be kept within a certain area, referred to as the cone of balance. First, you will want to realize that a lower and partially-flexed stance is easier to ride with than a higher, fully-extended stance. A higher, extended stance raises your COG and narrows the cone of balance. When this happens you become less stable. By flexing your legs and keeping the upper body as upright as possible, the cone of balance widens over the board and stability is increased. When your position is lower and closer to the board, you widen the cone and give yourself the maximum amount of balance and room for error. By flexing your ankles, knees and hips you can ride lower and closer to the board. This helps to widen the cone of balance. You may further extend the cone by stretching your arms out to your sides like a tightrope walker. Now you have more room to play — back and forth, side to side, and so on.

MIKE KILDEVALD

Leverage works. Tall people will have more and therefore be able to pressure the board more. Tall people are also less stable due to their higher center of gravity.

FACTORS AFFECTING THE CONE OF BALANCE

There are other factors that affect your cone of balance. For instance, it's not only your stance, but also way that you move over the board. Then there's the snow conditions that you face. When the snow is softer, it provides a platform to ride over — the softer and deeper the snow, the wider the platform. Harder snow conditions, on the other hand, leave a much smaller contact area with the snow, leaving very little room for error.

Finally, the forces of each turn will project the cone into the turn. If you are moving at slow speeds, the cone does not deviate too far to the side. Blazing down the hill as fast as possible, the cone drops much closer to the snow.

51

ESTABLISH A RIDING POSITION

REGULAR VS. GOOFY

How do you determine whether you are a regular or a goofy rider? Only you can answer this question. Do you have a preference from skating, surfing, water-skiing, or some other sideways aligned sport? If not...how do you step up to the plate when you hit a baseball? Which way do you swing a golf club? How would you instinctively shoot a bow and arrow, or a rifle? Stand on the board in a similar way. Which foot do you kick a ball with? The foot that stays on the ground as you kick the ball should be your leading foot. If you are still having trouble figuring it out, put the question to rest by following a time tested method...experiment and find out for yourself.

STANCE ANGLES

This is the way I like to tell people how to figure out their foot angles for riding. Close your eyes and jump as high as you can. When you land, open your eyes and take a look at your feet. Do your toes point in, out, or toward the same direction? Now imagine yourself standing on the board. This is a good indication of the angles you will want to ride with. Usually this will be toes out with about 5-15 degrees of difference between the feet. Set up your snowboard with this binding angle difference for a natural custom stance. If your stance angles deviate more than 40 degrees between, the difference can put a great deal of strain on the knees and might even lead to injury. Try and work with a stance that has less than a 40-degree deviation between both feet.

40°

STANCE WIDTH

The best I way I have found to measure your own personal stance width is to take a tape measure and record the distance between the bottom of your heel and the middle of your knee. This distance is a good stance for both carving and stability. Racing/alpine stances will be a little less than this measurement to allow the board to flex and carve more easily. A freestyle/pipe stance will be a little more than this measurement as a wider stance gives more rotational control and a bit more stability when landing jumps. If you are riding with a wide stance and your knees are giving you pain when and after you ride, try riding with a narrower stance for the health of your knees.

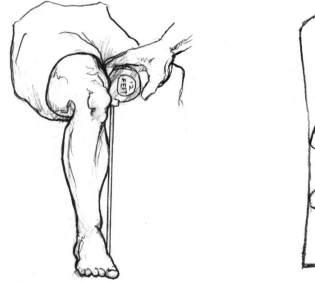
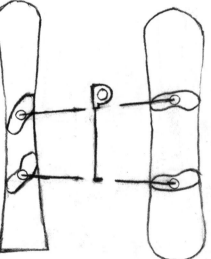

KERRI HANNON-MARSH

To find your stance, take a hop and land as if someone was trying to push you over. Set that width and resulting foot angles to your board. Stance width and foot angles are different for every person, so don't just let a shop hand you a board — make sure it's set to your individual needs.

MIKE KILDEVALD

Foot angles on a snowboard are totally relative to your feet and the board you ride. People who say that you have got to use this and that binding angle and no other angles have no idea what they are talking about. Put your feet on the board. Stand with your body and legs straight on. Stand tall like a skier. Place and turn your feet so that your toes are directly over your toeside edge, and your heels are directly over your heelside edge — that should be your stance for that particular board.

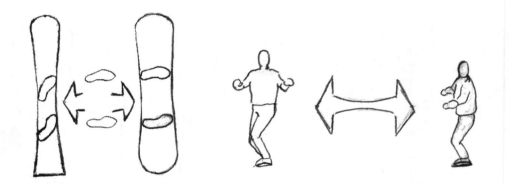

54

SHIFTING ACROSS THE BOARD

Once you have established your working stance, it's time to focus on moving while on the board. The efficiency of shifting across the board is determined by three things. First is the manner in which you actually shift your body across the board. Second is the shape and design of the board you are riding. And third is the binding angles that are placed upon the board itself.

The best way to figure out how you shift across the board is to ride different boards with different shapes and different binding angles. Then decide what works best for you. Some people shift using a twisted body position that forces their upper body to face downhill. Other people shift across the board in the direction of the angles in which their feet are placed upon the board. Some riders transfer straight across the board by leaning straight across from one side to the next. Every rider uses a varied combination of these techniques to complete the turns they wish to make.

Symmetrical boards are designed to work best with either low binding angles (0-25 degrees) or or very high binding angles (45+ degrees). It is important to note that each angle type requires its own unique style of riding. Different body movements and techniques are required to transfer your weight straight across the board, and these movements are greatly influenced by the binding angle. Low binding angle transfer is like (Asym)metrical shifting — you shift according to the direction of your feet. Shifting with high binding angles is accomplished by forcing your upper body to face the direction of travel. Once this is accomplished, weight transfer travels across the board from side to side.

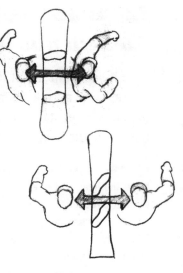

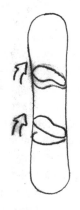

Shifting across the board with low binding angles is easy to do. However, many riders make it much more difficult than it needs to be by twisting the upper body around to face downhill. This in turn straightens out the leading leg and places all of your weight onto the back leg. There are two ways to beat this. Try turning the binding angles tipward. If you like your binding angles, try flexing your ankles more and riding in a sideways stance. Traveling down the hill shoulder first can be a bit scary so make sure to turn your head in the direction of travel. Moving with your chin touching your shoulder might feel unusual at first, but it allows for a much more natural body position for low binding angle riding. You are riding with a twisted neck rather than a twisted body.

Asym boards usually work best with high (25-50 degree) binding angles. Some people have described this transfer as falling forward and toward the tip of the board for toeside turns, and falling or sitting down toward the tail of the board for heelside turns. If you have difficulty finishing or you tend to wash out of most of your heelside turns riding an asym board, try a symmetrical design.

Everyone shifts over the board differently. This is a matter of personal preference, so take the time to experiment and feel what works best for you. Ultimately, it is up to you to realize how you ride most comfortably. Find out what works best for you and go with it.

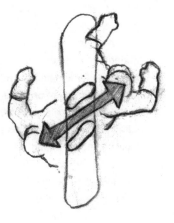

55

THE HUMAN BODY

ANATOMICAL TERMS (MUSCLES)

If you want to get the most out your body when riding, you should be aware of how specific muscles affect your snowboarding experience. In the event that you wish to pursue a regiment of training, this knowledge will also help you to tailor your activities/workouts to your own snowboarding goals.

1 — Trapezius, Sternocliedomastoid: Stabilize the head and direct its movements into the desired direction.

2 — Upper body and back: Hold the entire body over the board, especially important at speed and over unpredictable terrain conditions.

3 — Rhomboids, Latissimus Dorsi, Deltoids, Pectorals: Stabilize the upperbody and manipulate the arms. Bench presses, pull downs, or any other upper body intensive activity keep these muscles in shape.

4 — Abdominal Obliques: Bend the body from side to side, as well as twist the body around — necessary for general upper body stability. Side sit-ups work these muscles (try to pinch the ribs and hips together, or do sit-ups with one leg crossed over the other).

5 — Abdominals: Provide upper body stability and shock absorption of terrain. Work this muscle group with bent-leg crunch sit-ups.

6 — Leg Abductors: Pull the legs out in a sideward direction, a motion necessary when standing on top of the board. Also, aid in recovering when landing jumps. Sports like inline skating and skateboarding keep these muscles toned as do side-pulls with machines or surgical tubing.

7 — Quadriceps: Bear the primary burden of a standing position. This group of muscles is responsible for keeping the rider upright and necessary for exertion of pressure upon the board. Also, assist other muscle groups in shock absorption resulting from terrain. Exercise these muscles by biking, running, or hiking.

8 — Anterior Tibias: Lifts the toes to help the rider get the board on its heelside edge. Also helps flex the ankles to get the rider in a lower position. How do you exercise this muscle? Try pointing the toes upward and holding the stretch. Repeat as often as necessary. If you can touch your kneecaps, you're doing great.

9 — Erector Spinae, lower back muscle group: Keeps the back upright — crucial to upper body equilibrium. When thrown forward, for example, these muscles pull the back upright. Exercise with squats or reverse sit-ups (back curls).

10 — Glutei muscle group: Helps the rider stand upright, also very important in absorbing shock from terrain. If your bum is out of shape you will probably find yourself looking down at your toes. And one last thing — a really fit bum is great for attracting sexy people to ride with. Exercises such as squats, skating, and running are all great for getting a bum into better shape.

11 — Leg Adductors: Pull the legs together, necessary to keep the body over the board and also help in recovering from jumps or falls. Exercise them by skating or using adductor weight machines.

12 — Leg Biceps/Hamstrings: Flex the legs, assist in balance, and absorb shock from the terrain passed over. Quite often these muscles are under-emphasized. Since they must counteract the quadriceps, they must be strong. Exercise the hamstrings by riding a bike, running, or using a leg curl machine.

13 — Calves, Soleus: Help establish balance and important when it comes to the endurance required to ride all day long. Also used to dig the toeside edge into the snow. Exercising the calves is easy. Simply jump around as much as possible or try trail/stair running and calf rises with weights.

(*) — Face: Keeps you smiling. How do you work these muscles? Keep on riding and you will keep on smiling.

56

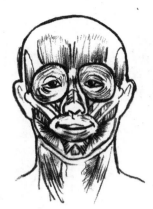

(*) Face

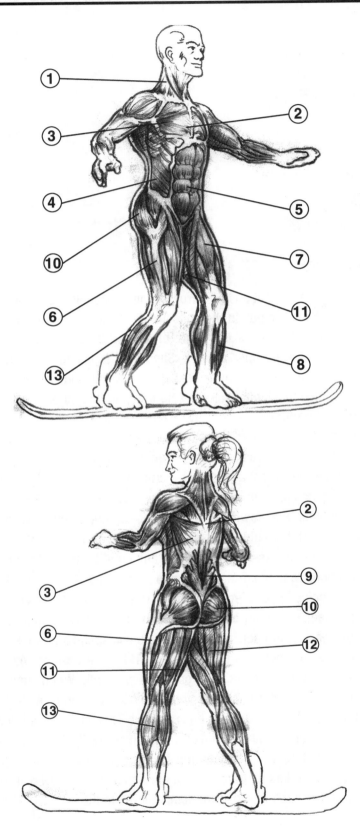

57

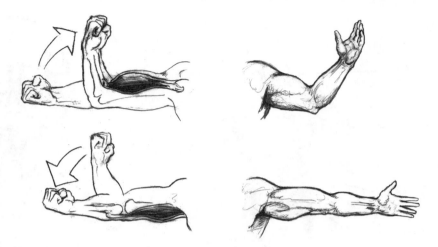

MUSCULAR CO-CONTRACTION

Muscles only contract, they do not push. To create a pushing movement, muscles use the bones and joints as levers to pull in the opposite direction. Flexion decreases the angle of a joint. Extension increases the angle of a joint. Whenever there is a movement there are two (or more) muscles at work. Shoulders, hips and ankles move in more than two directions but the same principle applies. If your muscles move in one direction, there will be an opposing muscle/muscle group on the other side of the limb to pull in the opposite direction.

Strong technique makes the most efficient use of your body's resources. Weak technique uses more energy than necessary and is counter-productive to your goals. One big reason for this is that weak technique often requires the over-use of co-contraction. Co-contraction is what happens when both of the muscles of a joint are pulling their own way. Working your way down the mountain is difficult enough. Working against your own body on top of that only serves to increase the difficulty of the task.

Muscular co-contraction is necessary for balance and equilibrium. In fact, most movements and body positions require co-contraction to be possible. For you to stand up straight, most of the muscles in your legs, abdomen, torso, and neck are working with/against each other to keep your body balanced and upright. If the abdominals are not countered by the muscles in your back, chances are you will spend a great deal of time looking at your toes. Going down the hill you are working with forces that are more powerful than, say, when you are standing on a flat sidewalk. When traveling down the hill you must also use the muscles of your body to counteract additional forces naturally encountered in the surrounding environment. This can be amplified if you add more resistance with your own body. You can actually make the journey down the hill far more difficult than it needs to be. Learning how much "muscle" is necessary is not an easy task — it takes a great deal of time and effort to become an efficient rider. There is no real substitute for experience in this matter.

Here's a demonstration of the use and overuse of co-contraction. Hold your hand out in front of your shoulder. Tighten up all the muscles in your arm as much as you can. Have a friend say "Go!" and touch your shoulder with your hand as quickly and as forcefully as possible. Now relax and shake all the tension out of your arm. Hold your hand in the same position and have your friend start you again. Touch your shoulder, and notice how much quicker and stronger your reaction was.

MUSCULAR RELAXATION

Relaxed muscles act much more quickly and powerfully than tense ones do. The most efficient use of muscles is generally achieved when one set of muscles acts powerfully and the opposite muscle barely resists. Even at full flexion and extension there are minute opposing forces working against the direction of movement.

Think of flexing your arm as much as you can using your biceps. Then focus on your triceps. Try to relax your triceps as much as possible. Can you feel your arm move a little bit more because you relaxed the opposing muscle? However slight, this kind of control is what will allow you to move fluidly. Imagine what the muscles are doing when you're riding. Focus on those muscles being used. This should be pretty easy. The trick is trying to feel the muscles *not* being used. The more aware we are of our total body, the more we can accomplish with it.

What does it mean to ride comfortably? I would describe it as a relaxed state of balance, with just enough co-contraction to keep stabilized but no more than necessary. I know that I am riding like this when I find myself moving both quickly and forcefully — comfortable, stable and absolutely in control. It is a wonderful sensation, a relaxed and focused reality both in the mental and physical sense. When I am having trouble with my riding I often find that I'm reminding myself (when I can) to relax and concentrate. But it is difficult to focus when you are gritting the fillings out of your teeth. So let yourself relax. Let yourself concentrate. Then go do what you want to do.

QUALITY OF MOVEMENT

Judging quality of movement is difficult to put into words, so it's best to use an image. Think of a really great athlete doing whatever it is he or she does best. The athlete moves gracefully and powerfully with absolute efficiency. Often one can tell how efficient someone is just by watching them move. Effective movements are smooth and flowing. On a snowboard, the rider seems relaxed, traveling effortlessly. That is because the "fluid" rider uses their muscles only as much as necessary. This also helps the rider to accept rather than battle the terrain. If you try you fight the mountain with your board, you will lose. Eventually the mountain will wear you down, and then you will have to either stop or fall from exhaustion.

A visible mark of efficient motion is this element of smoothness. Smooth movements are comprised of constant gradual motions. Inefficient movements usually stand out because they appear as jerky, staggered actions. This is a huge waste of energy. Each time you start a movement, a great deal of energy is used. Kind of like a car. You actually use more gas by starting the car than by letting the engine run for a minute or two. The fewer breaks between movements in your riding technique, the more efficient the technique will be. You will burn less energy in this case, and be able to ride longer as a result. Just remember that smooth and committed movements are far more effective than wild, erratic, energy-wasting movements.

Do not try and force actions or movements. Try letting the action dictate its own course. Allow your movements (whatever they may be) to occur naturally. Consciously forcing a movement adds unnecessary tension and stress to the action. Ready and relaxed is quicker and stronger than ready and clenching your fists in anticipation.

BREATHING

How can breathing technique help your riding? Simple, when people get uptight and tense it takes over their entire body. I know that I am strung out when I feel myself holding my breath. Many people concentrate their efforts by doing the same. But when you exert yourself, holding breath in merely blocks the flow of oxygen to the lungs. This is not a good thing. Your blood pressure can rise considerably, and an unnecessary strain is placed upon the whole body as a result. Try breathing from the bottom of the chest. Relax the muscles of the face, head and neck. Let your body work. By breathing naturally you can relax and get back to thinking about riding rather than falling.

Another area where breathing helps is with the accentuation of extension. This is the case in karate, where the punch or kick is emphasized by a shout. The act of forcing out the breath contracts a great deal of the muscles inside the chest and the trunk. From the inside out, this serves to stabilize the upper body and trunk. It involves the muscles of the whole body, not just the limbs in the action of the turn. Think of hitting a punching bag. If you use only arm muscles, you won't be able to apply much force to the strike. If you use your whole body accentuated by forceful exhalation, you can move the bag around quite a bit (a case of lovetaps vs. the Rocky Balboa uppercut!). Using this breathing technique, you can add rhythm and power to your turns. Focus forceful breathing when you pressure the board. This will create a vacuum in your chest cavity so that all you have to do is relax the chest and your lungs will fill with air quickly without any muscular contraction. By concentrating on forceful exhalation you will expel more carbon dioxide out of your lungs and allow more room for oxygen. Karate students also use the intimidating sound to scare their opponents. And even though you may not be able to scare the snow into making turns easier for you, a vocal burst feels good, it sounds cool, and it psyches you up for the next turn. So grunt like a bull. Bark like a dog. Squeal like a pig. Whatever helps out your riding.

PHYSIOLOGICAL FACTORS

FEEDING THE MACHINE

Riding a snowboard is energy intensive. You should drink lots of liquids before and throughout the day. Feeding yourself well is important, otherwise you can run out of gas in which case you won't be able to do much riding at all. Sugars and carbos provide quick energy. Proteins and fats give longer-lasting energy that is depleted at a slower rate. Carry an energy bar with you when riding. I also recommend a snack such as Gorp™ which is made of mixed dried fruits, nuts, coconut, carob, and other treats. This will give you a combination of all the above types of energy, and it tastes really good too!

Muscle movements are fed by chemical reactions at the cellular lever. These reactions consume energy and generate heat. Inefficient movements use much more energy and generate much more heat than necessary. When using muscles, you also generate cellular waste and lose water through sweat and exhaled breath.

Being in good physical shape can only benefit your riding by enhancing performance and making you less prone to injury. Sports that use short bursts of concentrated energy are best for off season training. Participate in sports that are challenging both physically and mentally such as rock climbing, trail running, basketball, racquetball, tennis, inline skating, mountain biking, skateboarding, and whatever else fits the profile. As long as you are out there exercising and enjoying yourself, you are in training — there's no need to hire a personal trainer. Just dedicate a couple of days a week of your favorite activity and you are well on your way to getting into shape for the winter.

If you feel your muscles seize while riding, your body is telling you that the muscles are being overworked. Shakes and cramps can be attributed to a lack of oxygen, food, or an overabundance of wastes inside the muscles. If you feel this happening, take a break. Gently flex and massage any troublesome areas. Stretch after a day like this to prevent cellular wastes in the muscles from building up and taking hold. This will help to avoid stiffness the next morning. Failure to care for muscles in this fashion may cause you to wake up feeling like the tin man from the *Wizard of Oz*.

If you are consistently in pain when riding, your body is telling you something. Listen to it or face the possibility of injuring yourself and watching the season pass you by from a set of crutches. It's hard to ride if you can't even walk. Be good to yourself and you will grow to be a happy old snowboarder.

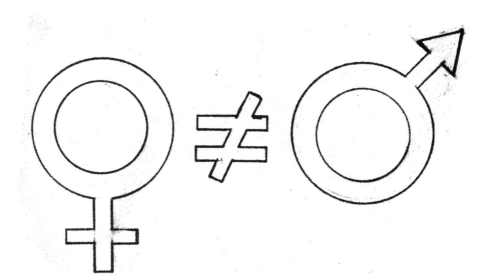

WOMEN & MEN & RIDING

Women and men differ from one another in a variety of ways. Each perceives the world from a unique perspective and experiences subtle differences in their senses, movements, interactions and relationships with other people. Volumes have been written on the subject. We'll limit ourselves to dealing with just those physical aspects that affect snowboarding.

Understand that these descriptions are generalizations and not absolutes. Race, environment, diet, and other factors can lead to substantial changes in the way someone develops and grows. Each individual's "build" differs from those around them. Here are the related factors that are know to affect riding.

The physiological differences between men and women can be more specifically defined. Our consciously activated muscle category is divided into two specialized forms, red/slow twitch muscle and white/fast twitch muscle. Red/slow twitch muscle is iron and oxygen heavy and capable of operating for long periods of time before becoming fatigued. White/fast twitch muscle is very dense and power oriented, but it fatigues much more quickly than red muscle. Proportionally, men have a greater total amount of muscle in their body than women. For men there is a greater ratio of white muscle to red muscle, so the emphasis is on power and strength. Women, on the other hand, have a greater red muscle to white muscle ratio, and their bodies have an advantage in terms of stamina.

Women have a wider pelvis than men, and they are also more flexible at their joints. Men have a narrow pelvis by comparison and a more developed upper body. The width of the pelvis affects the angle that the head of the thigh bone (femur) moves inside the hip socket. As a result, women stand, move and snowboard differently than men do. Men can use upper body strength to muscle themselves about. Women are more flexible and therefore angulate more easily. Men drive into turns primarily with their knees. Women drive into turns putting more of an emphasis on their hips.

The width of the hips can also lead to a heelside turn anomaly known as girlie hip. Turns where the hips are projected sideways into the heelside turn often make the finish of the turn difficult. This can be realigned by overemphasizing the driving action of the knees into the heelside turns in order to bring the hips over the board once again.

Men have a different distribution of weight throughout their bodies than do women. Therefore a man and a woman of equal weight and height will have different COG's. It is lower in women, and higher in men. This difference is not considerable, but the effects can be magnified as additional forces are placed against the rider. Due to their higher COG, men tend to be more unstable than women. With good technique, however, men can learn to use their higher center to place leverage against the board. Since women have less mass in their upper bodies to be controlled, their riding tends to be more stable and consistent.

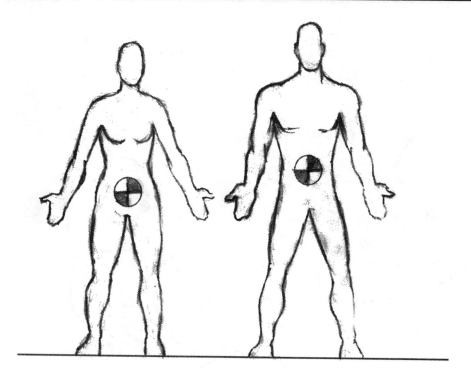

Chemically speaking, the testosterone effect influences aggressiveness. Men tend to go bigger and faster and also tend to suffer more injuries than women. Men use brute force, sometimes referred to as "balls". Women have less testosterone in their blood than men and tend to think and feel more when they ride.

If you are interested in a book that is devoted to the female body in the alpine environment, look for *Ski Woman's Way* by Elissa Slanger (Summit Books). It is an excellent resource that deals with the female body on skis and the differences in comparison to the male body in relation to skiing. Many of the ideas transfer very well to snowboarding.

SHANNON DUNN

Know yourself and how you learn. If you're (a girl and) intimidated by riding with the guys, go ride with the girls. If you feel that you're not being pushed as a rider, go ride with the guys. Remember that the key is to have fun and ride with the people with whom you have the most fun.

THE ANATOMY OF
SNOWBOARD EQUIPMENT

A snowboard's riding behavior is determined by several independent aspects of its design. A variety of components must work together to achieve the optimum performance for a board's designed purpose. Features such as length, width, sidecut, flex patterns, camber and the materials used in construction together dictate the board's behavior on the snow. By looking at each of these independent features you will become familiar with snowboard performance in general. The purpose of this chapter is to help you recognize and understand these general and specific terms that are used to describe the features and components of a snowboard.

DESIGN FEATURES OF A SNOWBOARD
LENGTH

WHAT IS IT? Overall length is the snowboard's length from tip to tail. The running length is the length of the snowboard in contact with the snow when the board is running flat.

WHAT DOES IT DO? Longer overall lengths have greater surface area. This leads to an increased ability for the board to float over the snow and also results in directional stability. Longer running lengths provide more effective edge contact with the snow which also creates greater stability. Longer boards are more stable while landing large jumps and taking on greater speed. Shorter running lengths create less edge contact and allow more rotational maneuverability.

Length also affects turning quickness. Generally speaking, the longer the board, the longer the turns. The shorter the board, the quicker the turns.

WHAT CAN I DO WITH IT? Freestyle and halfpipe boards are generally shorter. Big mountain, alpine, and race boards are generally longer. Specialized powder boards will have a long nose, adding to their ability to rise over the snow.

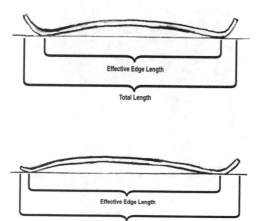

EFFECTIVE EDGE LENGTH

WHAT IS IT? Effective edge length is the length of the edge which contacts the snow when the board is being ridden. This is also referred to as contact length.

WHAT DOES IT DO? The edge length is directly related to the ability of the board to hold on to the snow. The more edge contact, the more stable the board acts on the snow. This happens because all the pressure applied upon the board gets spread along a longer length. A shorter edge length translates into a board that can be manipulated more quickly in and out of turns. The longer the edge length, the more stable the board will be. The shorter the edge length, the quicker the resulting turns.

WHAT CAN I DO WITH IT? Freestyle and halfpipe boards usually have shorter running lengths. Big mountain, alpine, and race boards usually have longer running lengths. If you want to turn quickly and are happy at slow to medium speeds, a board with a shorter edge length is for you. If you want to go fast and be stable at speed, look for a board with a longer effective edge length.

WIDTH

WHAT IS IT? Width is considered to be the distance straight across the board. Because snowboards have a sidecut, they are thicker at the tip and the tail, and thinner in the middle.

WHAT DOES IT DO? Narrow boards are quicker to transfer from edge to edge. Wider boards are slower edge to edge, but have a larger surface area under them that can help them float in deeper snow.

WHAT CAN I DO WITH IT? Narrow boards are better for riding with higher binding angles and are generally associated with alpine and race riding. Wider boards are better for low binding angles and designed to accommodate big feet and floating in deep snow (yea!).

SIDECUT

WHAT IS IT? Sidecut is the amount of curve in the contact edge of a board. Sidecut depth is expressed as the radius of a circle measured in meters. This radius is the turning radius the board is designed to make. The sidecut depth is determined by the difference between the nose and tail width and the waist width. This can best be seen when the board is stood on edge upon a flat surface.

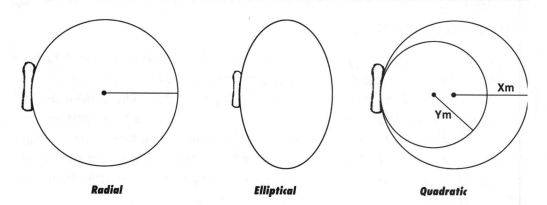

Radial   *Elliptical*   *Quadratic*

There are several types of sidecuts:

◆   **Radial:** This sidecut would be a portion of a perfect circle since it has a curve with a constant radius. A board with this kind of a sidecut makes a turn that is characterized by a constant turn entrance, turn, and turn exit.

◆   **Elliptical:** This type of sidecut is part of a large ellipse. The sidecut makes a turn that is gradual at the start and the end.

◆   **Quadratic:** This type of sidecut is deeper in the center, more drawn out in the tip and tail. It has a curve with compound radial and/or elliptical design. It is not constant. This kind of sidecut provides a more gradual entry and exit out of turns with a deeper carving sidecut radius in the center.

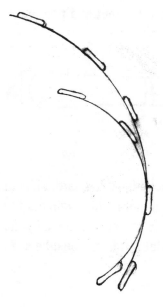

WHAT DOES IT DO? The sidecut of the board directly affects the width of turns. The wider the sidecut radius, the wider the resulting turns. The shorter the radius of the sidecut, the narrower the turn. A shorter sidecut radius will make the turns quicker and increase the board's turning response on the snow.

WHAT CAN I DO WITH IT? For a board that is meant for sliding, pipe riding, or performing tricks, a shallow sidecut is more appropriate. An aggressive carving machine will more likely have a very deep sidecut. Big mountain riders will probably opt for a deep elliptical sidecut for maximum stability at speed. Each manufacturer designs its boards differently. Check with your shop to see how your prospective board is designed to turn.

Long(itudinal) flex

What is it? Longitudinal or long flex is the resistance with which a board bends along its length.

What does it do? Soft longitudinal flex allows for easy turn initiation, easy low-speed landings, and overall maneuverability. However, a board like this is not very stable at high speeds, on hard conditions, or landing big airs. Stiff long flex patterns allow for greater stability at higher speeds and better performance on harder conditions. A stiff board will edge well and plow through adverse conditions better than a softer board. However, it's not as maneuverable as a softer board, especially at lower speeds.

What can I do with it? When testing a prospective board in the shop, make sure the flex pattern is smooth and consistent. Any board you are considering buying should flex evenly. There should be no soft spots or kinks in the board as you bend it. A board that flexes more is more forgiving of pilot error. A pipe or a trick board should flex a great deal throughout its entire length. Most alpine, big mountain, and race boards have stiffer flex patterns.

Take into account that different people flex the board differently. A PeeWee Herman will not flex the board in the same way as a Grizzly Adams. Most boards are softer in the tip and tail; you want that. What you don't want is a sudden soft or stiff spot in the board. A good test is to put it on in the store and bounce around the carpet. Try to feel for any unusual flexion beneath your feet.

TORSIONAL FLEX

WHAT IS IT? Torsional flex is the resistance to twisting a board has along its length.

WHAT DOES IT DO? The softer a board is torsionally, the more forgiving it will be and the less edge grip it will have. The stiffer a board is torsionally, the better the edge grip it will have.

WHAT CAN I DO WITH IT? A board with less torsional stiffness will be better for someone just starting out. This kind of board is made for the freestyle rider who is in the pipe, sliding or whipping the board around doing tricks. A board with greater torsional stiffness will hold an edge better in the snow. A board like this is more effective in freeriding, alpine, and racing applications. Most boards are designed to be torsionally softer at the tip and tail, and stiffer beneath the feet. This is for ease of initiation into and exit out of turns. The beefy flex pattern underneath the feet holds the edge for carving at speed. Alpine/race boards are a bit softer in the tip, and stiffer in the center and tail. They are designed to slip easily into their turns, hold, and snap into the next one.

CAMBER

WHAT IS IT? When a board has camber the ends of the board's base touch on the flat ground, and the center of the board rises off the ground. That distance is the measurable amount of camber the board has.

72

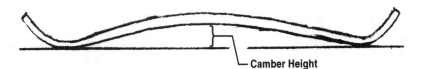

Camber Height

WHAT DOES IT DO? It affects the responsiveness of the board. A board with a lot of camber will have a lot of "snap." The more camber a board has, the greater the edge pressure that can be generated upon the snow. Some boards have more camber (alpine/race boards) and some have less (freestyle and halfpipe boards). Too much camber will impact your ability to slide around because the edge will always be grabbing onto the snow.

WHAT CAN I DO WITH IT? By flexing the board and harnessing the energy created inside of your ride, you can increase speed with each turn. This build-up of energy occurs when the board flexes and decambers. The resulting energy is released by the board as it returns to its original shape. This can sometimes kick the board off the ground altogether, lifting the rider off the snow and into the next turn. If this is the kind of riding you want to do, get a race board with lots of camber and a super stiff core. If you want to slide down logs and ride pipes, camber is not as important to the style of riding.

73

STANCE

WHAT IS IT? A regular stance is when someone rides with the left foot forward. A goofy stance is when the right foot is forward. The name goofy is taken from a surfing term for someone who rides with the right foot forward. It's nothing personal.

The width of the stance is the distance between the centers of both feet on the board. Stance angles relate to the direction that the feet point across the board.

WHAT DOES IT DO? It's a matter of comfort. Some people are left handed, some are right handed. The same goes for people's feet. Whichever way you feel most comfortable going down the hill, that's the stance you should choose.

Goofy   *Regular*

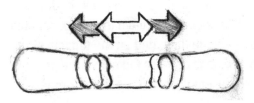

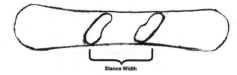
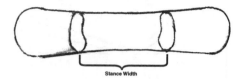

A narrow stance allows the board to flex more easily. A wider stance gives the rider a wider platform to ride upon and allows for more rotational maneuverability.

High stance angles let the rider face more tipward and can help reduce toe/heel drag. Low stance angles allow for more lateral stability and aid in bi-directional riding.

WHAT CAN I DO WITH IT? If you buy a board with a symmetrical designed sidecut, you can adjust your bindings to a regular or goofy stance. If you prefer asymmetrical designs, you will have to buy a board made specifically for your regular or goofy riding.

If you race, a more narrow stance should help you transfer the edges of the board as quickly as possible. If you're a tricky spinner, a wider stance should help you widen your cone of balance. Narrow stances increase the binding angles and help to keep your heels and toes from dragging in the snow. Wider stances use lower angles to make trick riding and spinning easier.

SIDECUT/STANCE CENTER

WHAT IS IT? Sidecut/stance center is the point where the center of the board's sidecut occurs. It represents the narrowest portion of the board.

WHAT DOES IT DO? The sidecut/stance center determines where the center of your stance should be, where to ride on your board.

WHAT CAN I DO WITH IT? This is how you measure your stance out (from the center of the sidecut) over the board. Usually the manufacturer will help you out with this one. Either the board will have inserts or binding marks will be indicated on the topskin of the board. If none of these indicators are present, have a pro look at your board before you let someone take a drill to your sweet ride.

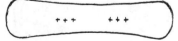

74

SIDECUT OFFSET

WHAT IS IT? Sidecut offset is the measurement of the shift of the board's sidecut toward the tail. If your sidecut is tailward, you have a directional board. If it is tipward, your board is set up backward — you never want a tipward set sidecut. If it is in the center you have a twintip board.

WHAT DOES IT DO? In many freestyle, alpine, and race boards, an offset characteristic helps the board to travel better in one direction than the other. Many times a snowboard will have a sidecut, shape, and a core that is offset toward the tail of the board. Race and powder boards in particular have easily discernible offset features.

WHAT CAN I DO WITH IT? You can specialize your riding style with boards that are created with offset design. This is usually terrain- and snow-condition specific.

High Swing Weight   **Low Swing Weight**

SWING WEIGHT

WHAT IS IT? Swing weight is the board's resistance to changing its direction.

WHAT DOES IT DO? A board with a high swing weight (lots of weight in the tip and tail) is difficult to turn around. A board with a low swing weight (little weight in the tip and tail) is easy to turn around.

WHAT CAN I DO WITH IT? A snowboard that has a low swing weight is easier to use for freestyle applications (spin, spin, spin). A snowboard that has a high swing weight will want to go straight (zoom, zoom, zoom).

CORE

WHAT IS IT? Basically the core can be considered the "guts" of the board. The core is the material inside of the board which dictates most of the board's riding characteristics. Most cores contain fiberglass and other similar materials. Some have space-age materials like carbon fiber, kevlar, and even boron. Still, the definition of the core falls into a few simple categories. Wood, foam, and composite are the three major core types.

WHAT DOES IT DO? The "stuff" inside the board determines how the board will act/react on the snow. The first thing to understand is that both the quality and the material of the core's construction will determine the performance as well as the lifespan of a snowboard. Certain materials are characterized as having longer lifespans than others.

Core types and how they react to extended use:

◆ **Foam Core:** Very snappy stuff, very quick to react. The board's total weight will be lighter with a foam core. However, foam cores are known to break down quickly and lose their liveliness. Depending on the quality of construction, this can happen in as few as 20 days of riding. Foam core boards (especially older used ones) should be checked out thoroughly before purchase.

◆ **Wood Core:** In the early days, all you had was a flat wood plank with bindings placed on top. Some even came with metal fins or edges on the side (deluxe cruiser). Now, the wood core is on the inside of the board. Wood cores have a very long life and hold up their camber very well. Wood cores are damper than foam core boards (meaning less flexible/less lively).

◆ **Composite cores:** The idea behind composite core constructions is to gain the positive characteristics of different materials and produce the ultimate ride. As an increasing number of new materials are tested, the science of snowboard design advances. Each year lighter and more durable designs hit the market. If you are not sure exactly what is in a board, check the manufacturer and applicable warranties before you buy. The metal/wood core, for example, has a sheet(s) of metal placed inside the board along with layers of wood. Such a core results in a durable board that is very damp, great for shock absorption and long lived. However, if the metal in the core bends, it stays bent. So if you buy a board with a metal core, try to stay out of the bumps if possible.

WHAT CAN I DO WITH IT? Some people will say that this core stinks and that core is the way to go. For me, the superiority of wood versus foam core is not as big of an issue as the overall quality of the board's construction. The best advice — look for a reputable manufacturer that stands behind their product (check that warranty!).

Many new snowboard designs use caps over the top of the board to increase strength and lighten the board at the same time. The idea here is that the outside of the board acts as a partial core to help define the board's performance. In effect, you need less on the inside to get the same (if not better) characteristics as a board built with traditional construction. But if there is a drawback to this type of design, it would be that such a board is very difficult to repair. If you damage the outer cap of the snowboard, you can drastically alter the performance of the ride.

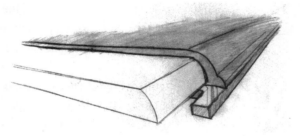

BOARD TYPES

(ASYM)METRIC

WHAT IS IT? The theory of asymmetry is based upon the fact that turning on your toeside edge is different than turning on your heelside edge. This also means that you shift from one side differently than the other. To accommodate for this, manufacturers adapt the equipment to the body's movements. In theory this should work, and it does, for some people. Other people have figured out ways to move differently from one side to the other. Essentially these "other" people have merely adapted their body's movements to the equipment.

To change the shape of a board from symmetrical to asymmetrical, there needs to be a shift in the sidecut. This is done by moving the midpoint of the heelside edge sidecut further toward the tail. In some cases the heelside sidecut is also deeper. Some manufacturers believe that the core must be designed asymmetrically to properly work with the sidecut. This is expensive since two designs (regular and goofy) must be produced for a single sidecut-shifted model. There are some asymmetrical boards that look like symmetrical boards. There is no shift forward or backward of either sidecut. However, there is deeper sidecut on the heelside of the board.

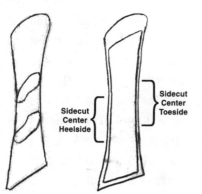

Sidecut
Center
Heelside

Sidecut
Center
Toeside

(X)m.   (Y)m.

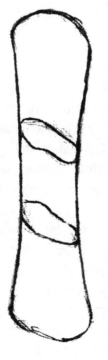

78

WHAT DOES IT DO?

◆ **Asymmetrical Shape:** Sidecuts are shifted to accommodate diagonal shifting across the board. This is partially determined by the foot angles. The idea is to compensate for the body's tipward shifts during toeside turns and aftward shifts when a heelside turn is made. The shape of the board accommodates the weight transfer over the board.

◆ **Asymmetrical Sidecut:** The toeside and heelside sidecuts of the board are different radii. A larger radii of sidecut leads to larger radii of turn shape. Usually, the toeside has a larger radii and the heelside a smaller radii. This is to accommodate for a lower degree of leverage on the heelside turns.

◆ **Asymmetrical Core:** The core of the board can also be designed to flex asymmetrically.

WHAT CAN I DO WITH IT? An asymmetrical board is built upon the idea that the rider shifts their weight diagonally across the board. Some people ride like this, some do not. Designers have found shifting the sidecut and core forward on toe side and back on heel side enables the board to achieve optimum asym performance.

If there is a drawback with asymmetry it lies with the slow diagonal shift from heelside to toeside. The more extreme the diagonal shift, the further you have to travel and the slower the transition from heelside edge to toeside edge. Some riders feel like they become locked into their heel. This is due to the extreme shift of the rider's COG toward the tail on heel side. Shifting from toe to heel is very easy. However, the transition from heel to toe requires a long forward diagonal shift to initiate the toeside turn. Other notable problems include the tendency for the board to drift to one side when running over flat terrain. Also, an asymmetrical nose and tail do not move as efficiently over the snow.

SYMMETRIC

WHAT IS IT? A symmetrical board is a type constructed in a manner so that both edges and/or tips are shaped and will act identical to one another.

WHAT DOES IT DO? Symmetrical boards allow you to make the fastest possible transition across the board. For any snowboarder, this is accomplished by shifting the COG straight across the board. Snowboards that have an identical tip and tail are known as twintip boards.

WHAT CAN I DO WITH IT? If you know that you shift symmetrically, buy a symmetrical board. If you shift asymmetrically, get an asym board. If you don't know how you shift...the best way to find out is to ride them both. When I first started riding, I rode a symmetrical board. Then I used only asym equipment. On the suggestion of a friend I tried symmetrical equipment again and now I only ride symmetricals. I'm sure if I really wanted to, I could go back to asyms. But I don't want to, and I couldn't afford it even if I did. The moral of the story is: If you aren't sure, give it a try. Ride one of each type for a day or so. When you decide which one you like better, go with it. Remember, everyone's body moves differently and caters to different styles. Take the time to find out how your body works best.

Twintip boards are boards that are symmetrical lengthwise. These are best suited for people who like to ride down the hill in both manners. Either way, the board acts the same.

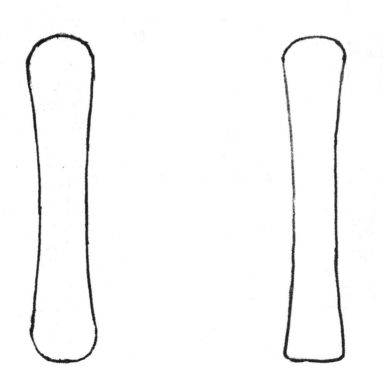

CUSTOM RIDES

Some snowboard are designed for specific purposes or for use in specific conditions. For instance, race boards do not travel backward very well and powder boards have difficulty holding their edge on ice. Other boards do a combination of things well. Freestyle and freeriding designs are quite capable to handle just about any task. Try out as many different types of boards as you can before making a purchase choice.

◆ **Freestyle Board:** A freestyle board has a soft to medium all around flex pattern, and both tips are upturned. It is of short to medium overall length and has a centered or close-to-centered stance. Usually mounted with soft bindings and a boot system, it is a good all around snowboard and often stiff enough to carve until you reach high speeds. A freestyle snowboard is a great initial investment into the sport and is usually less expensive than a specialty board.

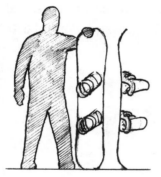

◆ **Freeride Board:** A do-everything board, the freeride has a soft to medium-stiff flex pattern. Both tips are upturned with a definite tip and tail. It can be mounted with hard or soft bindings. This is a great first board that can go anywhere. These boards can carve, go big, and still be maneuverable enough to ride into bump fields.

◆ **Alpine/Race Board:** These boards are made to do one thing — go as fast as possible in one direction. If this is what you desire, take a look into a board of this breed. With stiff flex and sleek design, there's little kick at the tip of the board and even less or no kick on the tail. Sidecuts are shifted toward the tail of the board and there's very long edge contact with the snow for carving capability. They are usually mounted with a hard binding/boot system. However, some of the best riders in the world ride and win in soft boots — Craig Kelly and Ashild Loftus, who've been world champions many times over, ride exclusively in soft boots. They ride in soft boots because it allows for greater sensitivity to the snow.

Snowboard subspecies include: Halfpipe, big mountain, twintip and powder. These specialty boards designed for special applications are usually mounted with a soft boot/binding combination.

◆ **Halfpipe:** A freestyle board with a soft flex pattern, these boards are characterized by a low swing and overall weight for rotational and aerial maneuverability.

◆ **Big mountain:** A large freeriding board. These boards are stiffer, to accommodate the higher speeds and bigger terrain they are designed to ride over.

◆ **Twintip:** Twintip boards are produced so that riding fakie is the same as riding normal. This is accomplished with a centered symmetrical sidecut, a stance that is placed over the center of the board, and a set of symmetric tips. Hence the name twintip. If you cut a board like this in half at the waist, both ends would look exactly like each other. The flex pattern of boards like these are usually a bit softer than other boards.

◆ **Powder:** A very wide, sometimes spoonlike board. This board is designed to rise over deep snow. The stance is set toward the rear of the board. Some are specialized to the point of having a swallowtail, having the tail split. I think these boards resemble goldfish.

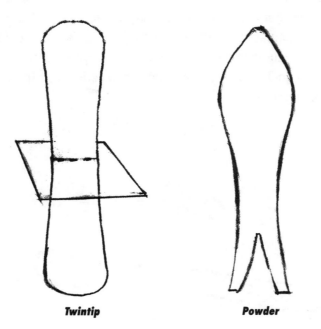

Twintip   *Powder*

COMPONENTS OF A SNOWBOARD

BINDINGS

WHAT IS IT? Bindings are the connections between rider and snowboard.

WHAT DOES IT DO? The bindings are the hardware parts that keep you attached and in control of the board.

WHAT CAN I DO WITH IT? Bindings allow you to ride on top of a snowboard. The setup should be comfortable, fitting properly and allowing you freedom to move in the manner you want to move.

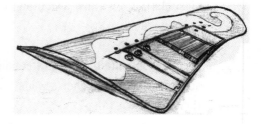

BINDING/BOARD CONNECTIONS

Inserts: These are little T-nuts (very strong) built right into the board. If the bindings do rip out of the board, the manufacturer will usually replace the board and chalk it up as a defect. Using the T-nuts that came inside the board, just set your stance, screw the binding in, and ride off.

Some snowboards do not have insert patterns in them. This means that you have to drill the board to mount your bindings. You have to know how wide you want your stance and at what angles. Make sure that you know exactly where you want your feet on the board before you start poking holes in it. Talk to the local shop tech if you are having trouble. With any alteration of a boot, binding, board, or snowboard product you must check with the manufacturer before you alter it. As I've said before, in many cases alterations of product void all warranty policies. If you are sure that an alteration is the only way to go, take it to a shop that has experience in this matter before doing something you might regret.

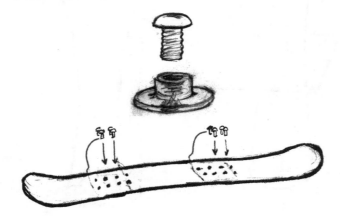

Drilling: If the board has no inserts, the only way to go is to drill the board. The only downside is that this does not always allow for a great amount of variation in stance widths/angles. Something to remember is that when you drill your board, you are weakening it. Make sure you get it right the first time and be wary of any snowboard that looks like someone took a machine gun to it. A board that has lots of holes close to each other is very weak in that area. If you try to drill close to those holes, you can almost expect the bindings to rip out of the board. T-nut the board if you are unsure of the stability of the deck.

Retention plates: These are the plates in the board that hold the screws that hold the bindings in place. These can alter the flex pattern of the board. But in this case it is a small price to pay for your safety. Make sure that both plate systems have plates that are large enough to hold all the screws drilled into the board. You don't want to drill into a part of the board that does not have the plate inside of it.

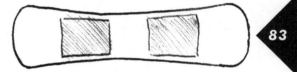

83

BOARD TOP HARDWARE

Hard boot/bindings offer instant reactions. Such a system is all about control, particularly edge control. It is worn mostly by racers, alpine riders, and free carvers and offers quick entry/exit with a bail or even a step-in system. Hard boots have a small range of ankle flexibility, and there is very little feel for the snow through the plastic sole of the boot. Because this system is so unforgiving, it does not work well with tricks.

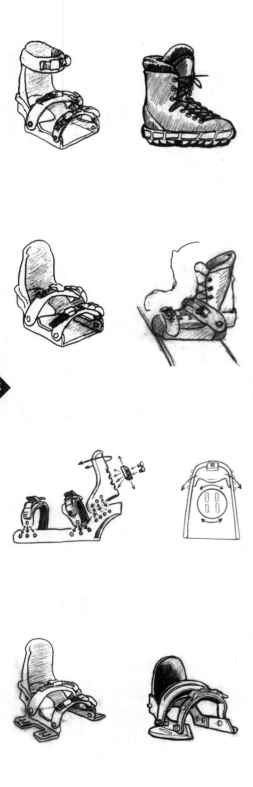

The 3-strap soft binding is designed to give quicker reactions than a traditional soft boot/binding system. It's a soft binding with a third strap that wraps around the calf. Although it takes a little longer to get into because there are so many straps, this type of boot/binding system gives maximum soft boot support and hard boot-like edge-to-edge reactions with a soft boot feel of the snow through the board.

The highback soft binding boot is the most common boot/binding system. It has two straps around the ankle and the toe. Highbacks can offer varying degrees of flexibility and support. The higher the highback, the more support you will get in your heelside turns. The lower (or absence of) the highback, the more flexible the binding.

You can also adjust binding performance with the straps and alter your ability to flex your ankles in the bindings by adjusting the ankle strap attachments to the binding's baseplate. The higher you attach the ankle strap over the ankles and the more directly you place the toestrap over the toes, the more control you will be able to exert over edge angles. The lower you place the ankle strap over the ankles and the further back you place the toestrap over the arch of the foot, the more you are able to flex your foot and the more flexibility you will have with your feet and ankles for tricks.

Baseless bindings are highback bindings without a base on them. The idea behind this design is that a binding like this does not produce a "dead spot" in the flex pattern of the board beneath it. This means the board should flex the way it was meant to, without interruption from the binding on top of the board. Some people have experienced tiring of the feet caused from the flexion of the board and a looser fit with the binding straps.

ALLAN CLARKE

You need good equipment and real snowboarding boots and bindings with higher highbacks. Your feet should hang just over each edge, if your board is too wide it will be difficult to turn your board around.

There is also a new theory of design in snowboard bindings. Step-in bindings represent the newest addition in the evolution of snowboarding technology. The basic idea behind this type of board/rider interface involves doing away with the burden of strapping/locking yourself into the binding. In this case all you have to do is step into the binding and off you go. When you want you can turn a switch or a latch to get out, similar to a ski binding. Some systems are designed to work with hard boots, others with soft boots. Some of these systems require special boots that work only with their special brand of bindings. Step-in technology is still very young. So if you are shopping for a step-in system, try before you buy. Some bindings release upon impact (Miller releasable bindings), but this type of binding has only found a limited market with the speed boarders.

If the toes or heels of your boots stick far over the edges of the board, they will drag in the snow. This overdrag will slow you down, maybe even catch and throw you off the board. You want to shift and rotate the bindings on the board so that there is as little toe and heel drag in the snow as possible. You can also place foam rubber lifts underneath the toes and heels of your boots. A more extreme measure is to grind off the excess toe and heel of your boot. But be careful with this one. If you grind too far,

85

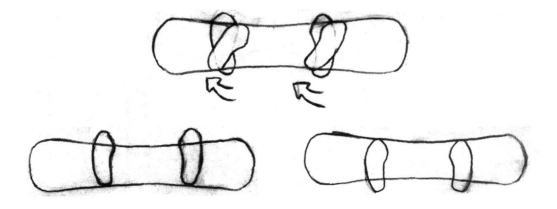

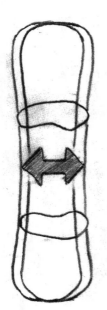

you can ruin the boots. Altering the product in such a manner is another reason for boot manufacturers to void all warranty on their product. If you are sure that you want to do this, take it to a reputable shop with an experienced grinder and see if they can help. You may also try riding a wider board designed for riders with longer feet.

Underdrag happens when your toes and/or heels are over the board, but too far away from the edge. This foot placement makes it very difficult to place leverage on the edge underneath, or to feel the snow you are riding over. This problem can be easily fixed by shifting the binding toward the edge in question. If your board is just too wide, get a more narrow shaped board.

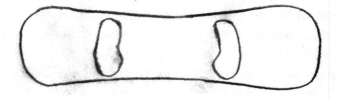

86

Boots

Soft/Snowboard Boots: Great for doing whatever you want, soft boots allow for a large amount of movement in just about any direction — a must for pulling tricks. This is the most functionally flexible choice you can make. There are many different types of boots being manufactured as well. If you enjoy traveling at very high speeds, softer boots can be shaky. But this is usually not a problem. You can reinforce soft boots with a stiffer binding, and soft boots are comfortable enough to walk around town or even drive your car in.

Hard/Ski Boots: Designed for precise control, these boots are best for higher speeds and immediate response from the board. Hard boots are usually not as flexible as soft ones, so make sure you can flex the boot forward easily and smoothly in the shop before you buy it. If the boot's flex is not smooth, it may give you trouble during transitions. If you already own ski boots and they flex easily, try using them to save some money.

Pack boots with ski boot liners. This is what I used for my first snowboard boots. Some people can put boots like this together really well. But though you may save money, this type of boot can be a sacrifice both in terms of comfort and functionality.

To check the fit of your boots, put them on and stand on your toes. The heel of the boot should rise off the ground. If you can feel your heel rise inside the boot and the boot does not lift, it isn't a proper fit. When you put on a hard boot you should feel minimal toe movement. When you put on a soft boot you should feel some toe movement. If the boot does not feel right, try another or the same boot in a different size. Get your local pro boot fitter to help you out here.

So, should you ride in hard or soft boots? That is totally up to you. Go out and try both. I ride both. I can honestly say that my hard boot riding is stronger because I also ride soft boots and vice versa. Hard boot systems work best in harder snow conditions, soft boot systems in softer conditions. I often find myself starting out the day riding in hard boots, then switching to soft boots as the day gets warmer.

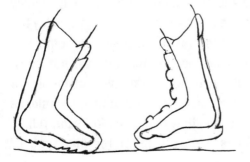

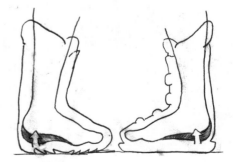

LARRY HOUCHEN

Daily boot care is extremely important. Now that you have invested all this money in footwear, you want it to stick around. Hard plastic has a memory. If you leave your boots open when you are not in them, your boots will "remember" being open. Once your boots "remember" being open, they will retain their new "open" shape. You want your hard boots to "remember" their closed form. So keep the buckles closed so your hard boots do not go "flat." Pull the bladders out after a day of riding, and leave them near a mild heat source. Do not put your boots over a heating vent. This will deform the hard plastic of hard boots and crack the leather of soft boots.

88

SAFETY LEASH

WHAT IS IT? A safety leash is a non-releasing strap that attaches to your leading leg.

WHAT DOES IT DO? A leash is designed to keep your board attached to you in case of a binding release. This prevents the board from becoming an alpine projectile.

WHAT CAN I DO WITH IT? The leash is wrapped around the leading leg to keep the snowboard from accidentally getting away. Snowboards can accelerate very quickly because of their large P-tex base surface area. Whether you like them or not, insurance companies will not allow snowboard companies to sell boards without them. For this reason, resorts will not allow you to ride their slopes without wearing one. And they're not just for resort riding. Wearing a leash is a safety must for any type of snowboarding, anywhere.

"BIRTH OF A SNOWBOARD"

The "birth" of a snowboard starts with the industrial design and engineering — the plans for a board's construction. Next comes collection of all the parts necessary to create the board. This includes the core material, metal edges, a P-tex base, tip and tail material, sidewalls, topskin, epoxy glue to hold the whole thing together, and either inserts or retention plates for the binding interface. These parts are made of a variety of materials. The important thing is that the manufacturer knows how to put them together so they'll stay together.

The first step in production is to prepare the parts to be bound together. Many parts need to be cleaned first so that the epoxy binds properly to them. The core of the board needs to be drilled to accommodate the board's insert pattern (if it has one). Once the pattern is drilled, the t-nut inserts are placed into the core. Then the metal edges are bound to the perimeter of the P-tex base with glue, and the prepped parts are sent to the presses.

90

The assembled base and prepped parts are placed over each other in a metal template. These parts are smothered with a two part epoxy glue. This template is placed in a heated press at high temperature for a very specific amount of time. This bonds and shapes the profile of the board. When the board has been cooked, it is removed from the press and allowed to cool.

The excess material is cut from the sides of the board. The sidewalls are milled and the bases are ground flat. Then the base is textured with a base grinder, and finally cleaned and waxed.

Before the board is let out of the factory, it is carefully scrutinized to meet quality control standards. If it passes inspection, the board is marked with a serial number and shipped out to the stores and eagerly awaiting customers.

CHOOSING YOUR EQUIPMENT

What type of snowboard setup is right for you? This section of the book is dedicated to helping you acquire a setup that maximizes your riding preferences without limiting you to one type of riding. A more educated rider generally knows what type of board they want and how it can be expected to perform. But what if you are about to purchase your first board or find yourself confused by the various board and equipment options. I hope that the following information helps you to see through the haze of choices and makes the selection of your ride an enjoyable process.

INVESTING IN EQUIPMENT

WHAT TO LOOK FOR

The first thing to remember when purchasing snowboarding equipment is this —how do you intend to ride? Do you want to ride the mountain or the pipe? Do you want to focus on learning tricks or going fast. There are many such considerations. Ride for the rider you want to become, not for the rider you already are. With each passing year snowboard equipment evolves into more and more specialized designs and construction. If you know what kind of riding you want to do, ask for a board that is specifically designed to ride in that manner. A good shop will have a wide selection and a knowledgeable staff to help you find what you're looking for.

When considering a purchase, it is better to get a board that you can grow into and enjoy. Start by renting or borrowing. Your first trials will probably be on a freestyle/freeriding board. Generally speaking, the lighter the better. Modern construction materials for boards weigh less yet offer greater strength, durability and maneuverability. Avoid a board that is too long for your riding ability. Unless you weigh over 200 pounds, for example, a 170+cm board will be difficult on those first days. If you have trouble bending a board in the shop, chances are that you are going to have trouble bending it at low speeds on the learner's hill. Your first day is the one day you really want to get a board that is easy to turn. As you get better you might want a board that is "beefier." But until you are a beefy rider, a noodle board will do just fine.

When you are finally ready to invest in your own snowboard equipment, take the time to make responsible choices. At upwards of $500+ for a retail board, binding, boot and clothing setup, most people cannot afford to own more than one board. In other words, don't settle for second best. Boards are now being manufactured more like skis both in design and materials. Be wary of cheap plastic boards. You will get what you pay for by cutting corners. Look into a used board in good condition rather than a cheap new plastic board. If you do opt for the cheaper new board, be sure that it has metal edges if you plan to ride at a resort. Resorts won't let you ride their hill on a board that does not have metal edges.

Shop with a friend who knows a bit about snowboards. A trustworthy second opinion will prove helpful in these situations, and there is safety in numbers. Besides, it's more fun to get your friends in on the excitement of purchasing a new ride.

There are a lot of things to consider when buying a snowboard. Some people choose their board for the graphics. Some people get the same type of board all their friends ride or buy for whomever's name is printed on it. These reasons are great for the manufacturers with money who can put the coolest images on their boards and hire big names to endorse them. In fact, there are some manufacturers who rely solely on these kinds of marketing strategies to sell their product. The bottom line is that this usually translates into higher priced equipment as the manufacturer must cover the costs of high end graphics and professional endorsements.

This in no way detracts from the quality of the board. Ultimately, you will want to buy a board for what it does for your riding rather than your image. Buy a board because it does what you want it to. The best way to choose a board that works for you is to ride as many boards as you can, then make your own decisions about what works best. If it happens that you find a snowboard you really like to ride but just can't stand looking at, you can always change the graphics after you buy it (See Chapter 11).

93

WHERE TO BUY

Buy your board from a reputable dealer who is knowledgeable about the product. Usually a specialty snowboard shop run by people who have been snowboarding for a long time can assist you best. Always ask how long the dealer has been selling snowboards. This is often linked to overall snowboard knowledge. Don't be afraid to ask questions. Sometimes intimidating salesmen from shops can vibe you; but remember, you are about to spend a lot of cash on a board so assert your right to be picky and take your time. It is your privilege to buy a board. Your salesperson caters to you, not the other way around.

There are some shops that pay their employees a flat wage, but most also pay some form of commission. Commissioned salespeople make money when they sell product. Obviously, the more product they sell, the more money they make. If you go into a shop that pays on commission, that particular workplace is more conducive to pressure. Pressure for the salesperson to sell can translate to pressure applied to the customer to buy the product. If you feel like you are being pressured, let your salesperson know about it. When a salesperson is giving you the squeeze play, put that person in their place. Sometimes this happens as a matter of habit. Then if you do tell your salesperson how you feel and they still don't change their sales strategy, find another salesperson or move on to another store.

Shop around for the best price, but also consider the service ability of your dealer. A snowboard is a technical product which needs servicing to assure the best performance. You will want someone who can easily and efficiently help you with board modifications, tune-ups, and repairs. Many shops have a maintenance package to sell you upon the purchase of a board. This should last for at least one calendar year. Some dealers sell boards with service packages incorporated into the total price. The service of your board is a consideration that should not be overlooked.

How to Recognize Quality

Inspect the board's adjustability of stance. This way you can change your stance from time to time or sell the board more easily when you are ready for a different board. In addition, check out the interchangeability of different bindings. Not all hole patterns fit all types of bindings, and not all snowboard manufacturers make bindings.

Check the reputation of the board manufacturer. How has the product held up in the past with people that you know? How long have they been making boards? What is the warranty policy of the board? You need to know these things. If the dealer and the manufacturer stand behind their product with a solid warranty, then chances are high that the quality is good. It's also a good idea to buy a board and binding from the same company. If you choose to mix products, be aware that many snowboard companies do not take responsibility or guarantee compatibility for their products when they are used with other companies' products. With any modification of a boot, binding, board, or other snowboard product, check with the manufacturer before you act. In many cases, the alteration of product voids all warranty on the product. If you are sure that an alteration is the only way to go, take the equipment to a shop that has experience in this matter before doing something you might regret.

95

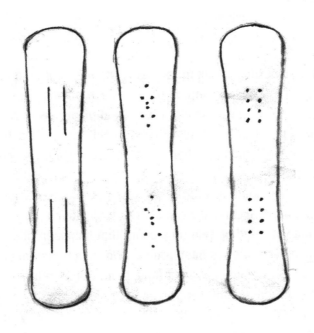

PUTTING EQUIPMENT TO THE TEST

CHECKPOINTS FOR QUALITY

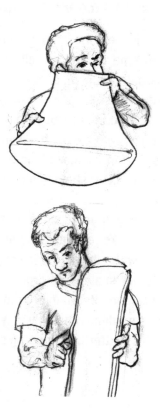

There are some things that you can use as indicators of a board's construction quality. Look at the edges on the board. If you see any gaps or crooked parts, look at another board. Check out the sidewalls — do they go all the way to the tip and tail? Flex the board a few times. If you hear pops or cracks, there are air bubbles inside the board that may shorten its longevity. Line up the horizons of the tip and tail of the board. If they are at different angles, the board is twisted from the core. (Do not buy a board such as this — it has either been constructed poorly or it has been damaged.) These checkpoints are all helpful in assuring that your purchase is a good one. But regardless your degree of expertise, keep in mind that it is hard to tell if a board is constructed well or poorly just by looking at it. The only true test is to go out and ride the board.

TRY THEN BUY

For your first day of riding, look for a board that is designed to be forgiving. Try to rent a freeriding, freestyle, or halfpipe board. These planks are constructed in a manner that will allow the rider to make mistakes and "get away with them". Look for a board that is light and flexes easily. This should be a good first time rental board. If you have trouble bending it when you hold it up on one end, chances are it is too stiff for you to learn on.

When you do rent a board, ask for the newest equipment possible that fits your needs. Sometimes shops will carry the same stock for as long as it will hold together. This could mean that you wind up renting a board that has been ridden almost every day for however many years it has been around. Worn, outdated equipment will not make your task any easier. If you can't get equipment from a rental shop that is less than one season old, I recommend going to another shop.

Buying a used snowboard is another option and a good way to find a quality board at a reasonable price. If you are not sure what to do, make it easy on yourself. Go to a shop with a good reputation. Again, try and take along a friend who knows what to look out for. Of course it helps when you already know what style you plan to ride. This is simply insurance against those shops who are out for the quick sell. You don't want to be left stranded with a board that is not what you really wanted.

What is the right board for you? This is not an easy question to answer. There are so many different styles of riding, so many different riders, so many boards to accommodate riders and their style of riding. As we've learned, a snowboard is a significant investment. Remain mindful that borrowing or renting different styles of equipment is often the best way to find out what serves your specific needs. Many shops have a "try then buy" system. In this case you pay a small fee to ride the board for a day; then, when you're ready to take the big plunge, the cost of the rental is deducted from the final purchase price. This is a win-win situation that allows you to try many types of boot/board combinations from different manufacturers. If you buy a well-constructed board that is in good shape, you should expect a superior ride. You cannot expect good performance from yourself without good equipment. Investing in the best equipment you can afford is truly investing in yourself.

FINE TUNING YOUR BOARD PURCHASE

Sizing a board's length is fairly simple. Hold the board up. Place one end by your toes. The other end should come up to a certain height — from just beneath your collarbone up to right beneath your nose. If you want to do lots of tricks, you might try something shorter. If you want to reach warp speeds, get a snowboard that towers over you.

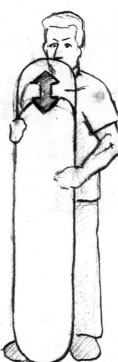

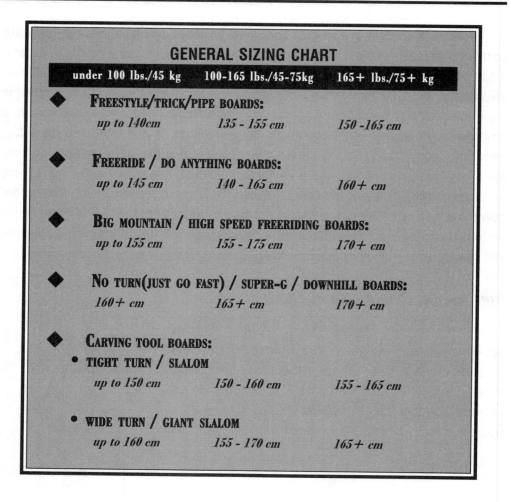

GENERAL SIZING CHART		
under 100 lbs./45 kg	100-165 lbs./45-75kg	165+ lbs./75+ kg
◆ FREESTYLE/TRICK/PIPE BOARDS:		
up to 140cm	135 - 155 cm	150 -165 cm
◆ FREERIDE / DO ANYTHING BOARDS:		
up to 145 cm	140 - 165 cm	160+ cm
◆ BIG MOUNTAIN / HIGH SPEED FREERIDING BOARDS:		
up to 155 cm	155 - 175 cm	170+ cm
◆ NO TURN(JUST GO FAST) / SUPER-G / DOWNHILL BOARDS:		
160+ cm	165+ cm	170+ cm
◆ CARVING TOOL BOARDS:		
• TIGHT TURN / SLALOM		
up to 150 cm	150 - 160 cm	155 - 165 cm
• WIDE TURN / GIANT SLALOM		
up to 160 cm	155 - 170 cm	165+ cm

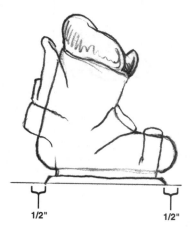

1/2"   1/2"

Many riders early on in their snowboarding careers often make the mistake of not paying close attention to their board's width. Ideally you want no more than a 1/2 inch of toe and heel overhang over each edge. Alpine and race boards are narrower and will dictate the binding angles you need to ride them with. If you don't like the foot angles on your board, look into a different board.

The best way to figure this out is to stand on the board with your boots on and get into your riding stance. Your toes and heels should be right over their respective edges. If this isn't the case, find a board that fits your feet.

FEET ON BOARD SIZING CHART	WIDTH OF BOARD AT THE WAIST
◆ **LITTLE FEET:**	
US Men's 5 / US Women's 6.5 (or less)	*23 cm /*
Mondopoint 23 (or less)	*9 in. (or less)*
◆ **MIDDLE FEET:**	
US Men's 5.5 - 9 / US Women's 7 - 10.5	*23 - 26 cm /*
Mondopoint 23.5 - 27.5	*9 - 10 in.*
◆ **BIG FEET:**	
US Men's 9.5 / US Women's 10.5 (or more)	*26 cm /*
Mondopoint 28 (or more)	*10 in. (or more)*

ADDITIONAL EQUIPMENT

Boots

With any boot, soft or hard, buy the pair that fit your feet best. Otherwise you will be in pain and out of control when you ride.

Get your hard boots as comfortably small and snug as possible. You want the boot to hold your whole foot. Your foot should not slide around, especially in the heel and arch areas. When you first buy hard boots they will be as small as they are ever going to be. The soft liners inside the plastic shell will "pack in" over time. This means that the boot will get "bigger" as it gets older. You may want to down size from your normal shoe size. If you can't flex the boots in the store, you won't be able to flex them out in the cold on the hill. Plastic gets stiffer as it gets colder.

LARRY HOUCHEN

When you want to buy boots, go see a pro. Your local boot fitter knows how to center your stance inside the boots. You want a thin stiff insole. This is good for support when you are standing in the boot. Get custom footbeds if you can afford them — they are power steering for snowboard boots. Once you try them you may wonder how you ever did without them. Custom insoles may look bigger, but because of the more accurate fit, your boots will feel bigger and more comfortable.

100

Buy the right size soft boots to start with. Strange as it may seem, soft boots are much less likely to pack in than hard boots. They are also much more accommodating than hard boots as they will mold and stretch around the shape of your foot better.

The most important indication of a good fit is the heel holding power of the boot. The heel holding power in hard boots is defined by the hard outer shell. If your heel floats in a hard boot, try a smaller size or another brand. In soft boots, heel holding is determined by the bladder inside the boot. If your heel still lifts inside of your soft boot, try an ankle strap. This little device wraps outside of your boot to drive your heel into the cup of your boot.

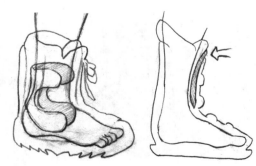

Minor adjustments can be made with the boots and/or the bindings to give you the best possible fit. Butterfly wrap around the ankle bones is a great cure to prevent the heels from lifting inside your boots. Also, a tongue pad placed on the inside of the boot's tongue will help to push your heel back down into the heel cup of the boot.

Boots are not the only equipment that can be adjusted. Some foot/leg problems can benefit from binding adjustments. Wedges/bevels/cants can help with excessive pronation (knock knees) or supination (bowlegged). Adjustments like these will improve comfort, reduce fatigue, and produce more efficient power transmission into the board from your feet through the boot and binding.

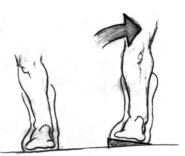

When purchasing bindings, you need to consider two criteria:

◆ the bindings should mold to your feet and board and should not offer movement other than a bit of flexion from the binding material itself. In other words, your feet should not spin or "float" inside of the binding.

◆ the bindings should be comfortable. If they hurt, they are not fitting you correctly. Make it a point to get bindings that fit or else look into customizing with additional pads or duct tape to ease any pain. Be aware that if you cut or alter the bindings you will likely void any warranty. Therefore give serious consideration before carrying out any such actions.

CLOTHING

When choosing your snowboard clothing, take four factors into consideration:
◆ fit
◆ quality of material and construction
◆ style
◆ $ costs involved. Buying snowboard clothing (or equipment for that matter) is a seasonal market. Picking your stuff up in the off season will afford you much more buying power. The tradeoff is that the selection may be somewhat more limited.

101

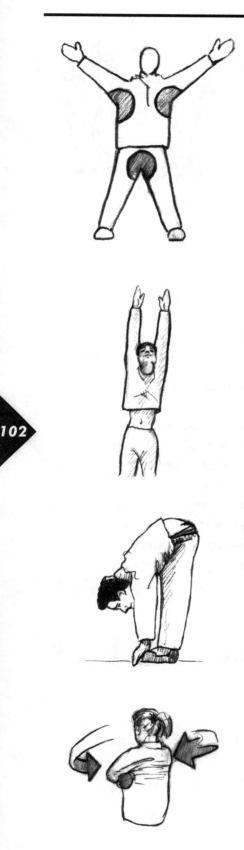

When you ride you use a great range of motion, especially starting out. Therefore you will need clothes that keep you warm and dry but also permit movement in all directions. Clothes should fit comfortably but allow a little extra room to layer up in. Put your prospective threads on in the store, move and stretch about using your full range of motion. Areas of clothing constraint to be aware of include the crotch, armpits, waist and middle of the back. Lifting your arms, make sure your waist is covered; touching your toes, make sure you are not to mooning everyone. If either test fails, you need a longer jacket. Cross your arms in front — you should be able to do this freely. If your sleeves hike up toward your elbows or you feel tightness behind your back, get a larger size jacket. Pants are usually roomy, but the one area to look for pinching is in the crotch. If you can feel the pinch, get a roomier pair.

Clothing styles vary with the manufacturer. Shop around, pick the ones you like with the features you want. Light clothes are just that, light. They are not very protective against harsh weather but are often very warm and easily layered. Technical clothes are often already layered up and have all sorts of pockets and breathing zippers. These are great but usually more expensive.

The quality of construction for snowboarding equipment really can't be discovered until you beat such equipment up and find out the hard way. Fortunately, most manufacturers have at least a year's worth of warranty to stand up to. Ask around for the reputation of the manufacturer.

So there you go. With the information in this chapter and the information in the "Anatomy of a Snowboard" chapter, you should have a strong idea of what to look for in your snowboarding purchases.

PREPARING FOR A DAY
OF SNOWBOARDING

It is important to make sure that you start out with good equipment. Borrow a board and boots that fit you, from a friend, if possible. If you can't borrow the stuff, rent a board and boots. Then get a lesson and a lift ticket. Most resorts have a "learn to" package that will consist of all the above. You may have to pay for it, but good equipment and instruction on your first day will make a world of difference.

GETTING READY TO RIDE

EQUIPMENT CHECK

First, inspect the board. There should be no cracks, breaks, or missing sections of the edge along either side of the board. Sharp edges make turning more precise and predictable. If the edges appear rusty or dull, sharpen them. Look for gouges or foreign objects in the base of the board. The base should be clean and slick. If you put the board base down on the snow and it has snow stuck to it when you pull it back up, the base needs to be waxed.

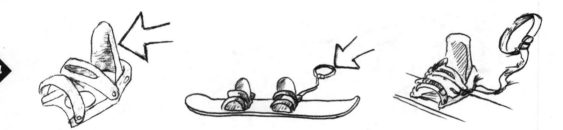

Are your bindings securely fastened to the board? Do the buckles adjust and hold properly? Make sure you have high backs on the bindings if you are using soft bindings. Look for loose screws, breaks, cracks, and other signs of wear. Verify that the leash is in good shape and is not frayed or partially ripped; check to see that it is securely attached to the board. Inspect the buckle/catch and make sure it works and stays around your leg.

Check boots for broken laces, loose stitches, cracks in buckles, and anything else that might compromise a tight fit around your feet. Stuff the laces in your liners to prevent loose ends from getting tangled up. Worn or broken equipment will probably detract from your ability to ride and might even be dangerous. Do not ride with such equipment. If you are not sure, ask someone who knows (i.e., shop tech). If something is wrong with the equipment, it is wise to find other hardware to use.

WINTER ATTIRE

Dress for the weather. What I mean by that is dress for weather that is going to be colder than what the weather man (being the eternal optimist) predicts. It's much better to remove a layer or two of clothing in order to cool off on a warmer day than it is to freeze when an unexpected storm front settles in.

Exposed skin is the most direct avenue for the body's heat to escape. Mitts are the best way to keep fingers warm. Put on a neck gaiter to keep body heat in your jacket. If your jacket has a hood, use it. I don't care for neoprene face masks which seem to just collect sweat, snot, and spit all over the inside. Then they freeze. You can turn them inside out to put the dry (but cold) side to your face, but then everyone gets to see what a mess you have accumulated. Some people like the masks, though I'd rather cover my face with a scarf. Wear a hat on colder days. You can lose up to 90% of your body's total heat through the top of your head. Putting a lid on your cranium is excellent protection against the cold.

Weather is a chaotic reality. By dressing in layers you can tailor your wardrobe to the environment. Try to layer up in loose clothing. Believe it or not, air is an excellent insulator. Cotton fibers press and stay pressed together, leaving no air pockets for insulation. Try to wear materials that resist compression, like down feathers or look into some of the new age materials available for protection against the elements.

Keep in mind that you can also over-do the insulation. You will know that you have made this mistake when you can't stop sweating. This feels nasty and certainly smells worse. It can really make your day miserable — too hot riding down the mountain then too cold riding back up. You go from overheated during normal exertion to freezing as you sit motionless on the chairlift exposed to Mother Nature. This can lead to a freeze/thaw cycle which will make you very cold very quickly.

Don't wear denim jeans, especially on the first day. You will be spending a lot of time either on your bum or your knees. The snow will melt and soak into the denim, then freeze, then melt again, then freeze again — the cycle repeating over and over until you get inside and dry yourself off thoroughly. Cold and wet is not a good way to learn, warm and dry is. Now if you are really concerned about impact to your rear and your knees, wear pads. You may even want to try and get a pair of pants with pads built in to protect these areas.

Try wearing goggles instead of glasses. The sun's effect upon your skin increases as altitude increases. The higher you go, the more protection (higher SPF) you will need. With eyewear, always check for UV protection. Dark shades without UV protection can actually be more harmful than good. Dark lenses will cause your pupils to open more but still allow the harmful radiation in. If you are serious about protecting your eyes, look into wearing goggles or alpine glasses that protect the sides of the eyes as well as the direct path of light into them. I once hiked up Mary's Glacier wearing only a hat. That night after the hike I couldn't sleep. I had sunburnt my eyes. It felt like hot pokers were being stuffed into my head. I could not open my eyes for four days. My vision was blurred for three weeks after that. Although I have not suffered any real permanent damage, I certainly could have. I do not want to risk becoming "sunblinded" again. So please, don't make the same mistake I did — don't learn (and burn) the hard way.

LAYERING YOUR CLOTHES

One idea for warm, dry riding is the three-layered system used by many mountaineers and alpinists. This simple concept allows you to cater your outfit to the temper of Mother Nature. Most importantly, it gives you freedom to wear whatever you are most comfortable and warm in.

The underlayer is meant to keep you warm and dry. Space age wicking materials that draw moisture away from the body as well as keep you warm are the best. They can cost some serious cash, but they are a worthy investment. Wool combinations also work well, but you need to have a high itch tolerance to remain comfortable in them. Cotton gets wet, compacts, and stays wet, so try to stay away from it if possible.

Underlayer (wicking):
◆ Warm long-sleeved undershirt/T-neck shirt
◆ Thermo-funky polypropylene long underwear
◆ Polypropylene socks

107

The insulation layer is the middle layer. It is made of materials designed to hold warm air next to your body as you ride. On warmer days it can double as the outer layer of protection as well. Wool and fleece are the best materials to use here.

Insulation layer:
◆ Wool/fleece sweater
◆ Fleece leggings/vests/long-sleeved tops
◆ Glove liners are a great aid for keeping the fingers warm. A good idea is to have a glove liner inside of a mitt shell for both outer and inner warmth. When you need individual finger dexterity, remove the shell and keep the liner on.
◆ Neck gaiter to retain the heat inside your jacket.

The overlayer is the barrier between you and the elements. A breathable, waterproof layer is the best material for dealing with the winter mountain environment. With all of your heat inside the inner two layers, the overlayer should allow moisture vapor out and still maintain an affective barrier keeping snow and water out.

108

Overlayer:

◆ You will also need to protect your skin and eyes. Make sure to get skin protection with the necessary amount of UV protection and SPF rating. Regardless of what you wear over your eyes, always check for UV protection. Shades are worn for protection and style. Some shades are better at blocking out wind than others. Wraparound shades are great, John Lennon wireframes are not. Everybody falls, so it's wise to invest in croakies or some other type of frame holder to avoid losing or pancaking your favorite shades. Sunglasses are best worn without a hat. They can give you a more even facial tan, and, of course, you can wear them off the hill and look cool.

◆ Goggles are designed for functionality — full eye wind/UV protection that won't fly off when you fall. They can be placed over a hat and fastened onto your head. Warning! Goggles can cause raccoon eye syndrome. It's hard to wear them off the hill and look cool.

◆ Pants, waterproofed riding pants with pads in the knees and rear. If you must ride in jeans, there are waterproofed jeans specially designed for snowboarding.

◆ Water repellent/breathable fabric jacket.

◆ Wear a hat of some sort, up to 90% of body heat can be lost through the head. Those with the little earflaps are best.

◆ Gloves/mitts, preferably designed for snowboarding. Gauntlet style gloves are great for keeping the snow on the outside of your cuffs. Gloves — easy use for the hands but they can be cold. Mitts — warm, with little dexterity. Trigger mitts — a nice compromise. If the index finger gets cold, put it in with the other fingers.

◆ Snowboard boots.

◆ Wrist guards are optional — a precaution but not a guarantee against all upper body injuries.

JONATHON B. SMITH

Stretch out and warm up with a not so challenging trail. Bombing the steepest run at the start of the day opens you to sprains, pulls and ligament injuries.

GETTING LOOSE

Stretch before and after riding. This will benefit performance and help to lessen the wear and tear resulting from a hard day of riding. Warm, loose, stretched muscles act and react more quickly & powerfully than cold, tight muscles. They are also much less susceptible to injury. When you stretch you want to feel the stretch but not pain, especially not the type of pain that feels like a cloth or rag tearing. If you feel like this when you stretch, talk to your doctor about what would work best for you.

When you stretch, use stretches that affect opposing muscle groups. If you are stretching your abdominals, for example, then you need to stretch out your back as well. The same goes for the legs, arms, neck — any part of the body. If a part of your body moves in one direction, it moves in the other direction as well.

I try to stretch out at least three times a week for at least ten minutes and always at the beginning and end of any day of riding. If you stretch out after a hard day of play, your muscles will be warm and more flexible. You will also be able to work out a great deal of the acids and other waste products that your muscles produce and store. This will help curb the stiffness and aching that is often felt the following day.

There have been studies showing that regular stretching increases range of motion in the joints and helps the body to secrete its own natural muscular lubricants. Yes it can feel uncomfortable at times, but like any other workout you will certainly feel better afterwards.

Warming up with jumping jacks or similar exercises will help to get the blood flowing so it makes sense do them just before and after you stretch. Some people think that this stuff makes them look silly — well, not quite as silly as being towed down the hill in the ski patrol bucket.

Here are some examples of stretches that work well to prepare you for and cool down after a day of snowboarding:

109

Side splits

The hero (booty stretch)

110

Butterfly

Pretzel stretch

Lower abdominal quad stretch

Legs over the head

Side bend   **Toe touch**   **Quad stretch**

Calf stretch

111

Windmill

FIRST DAY FORMULA
TAKE A LESSON

LEARN TO SNOWBOARD HERE.

I'll say it again, take a lesson on your first day out. An initial lesson is important because many basic errors are made the first day. People often start to snowboard on their own, or with the help of a friend who happens to snowboard. A "can do" attitude is a great thing to have, but a lot of people wind up learning by the crash-and-burn method of snowboarding. This can have two negative effects. First, it can make the entire experience more painful than necessary. Second, learning the "hard" way can start you out with potentially bad habits that later can prove very difficult to break.

Instruction from a trained professional may be slower and more expensive at first, but it is worthwhile. Strong techniques, especially when learned from the start, are the foundation for solid riding. The well-trained eye of the instructor will recognize weak body positions and improper technique and then help you correct them before they grow into habit. I've also heard of many a horror story that starts off like this: "I went with my friends. They took me straight to the top of the mountain and then they rode off." The rest is predictable. Unfortunately this is the kind of experience that can turn someone away from snowboarding for life. Just another reason I strongly recommend at least a first-day's lesson.

The first day is always the toughest so expect to fall a lot and prepare to be sore and exhausted by the end of the day. Snowboarding introduces you to a new sense of balance and coordination. When you fall, your body will send you a message, and the message usually comes with a return address of pain.

Help yourself by wearing protective gear. Elbow, knee, and butt pads provide great relief for the joints. Helmets are excellent insurance for your head. Protection like this is not a cop out, and it doesn't mean that you are a wimp. It does mean that you are concerned enough about yourself to protect your body. Wimpy? More like smart. Almost all of the top racers in the world wear helmets and protective race armor when they train and compete. They realize that it is hard to go as fast as you can and perform your best when you are in pain.

There is a difference between soreness and real pain. Soreness can be cured with a massage or a hot tub. You should realize when you're in real pain, but in the case you are not sure what message your body is giving you, go see a trained medical professional. Patrollers in particular are trained to give medical treatment in the alpine environment. If you think you are hurt, or you think you might be hurt, go see them. They will help you out.

Drink like a racehorse — I mean it, drink a lot of water. You will be working hard and the high altitudes will further add to the stresses upon your body. The body cannot operate properly without sufficient amounts of water. If you feel thirsty, you are already dehydrated and then it's too late. So drink more water than you think you should before going out, then keep on drinking more throughout the day. It's important to give the body more than an adequate amount of water to assure proper functioning.

113

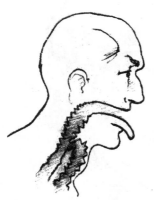

Dehydration is a serious concern for anyone in a winter environment. Cold, dry air can suck the moisture right out of the respiratory passages. Remember running in the snow as a kid and that feeling in the back of your throat? It felt like cracked leather. Consider this a good sign that you need more water in your body. A power drink or Sooper Gulp 96 oz. blue Slurpee (instant ice cream headache) will keep your body working the way it was meant to. Drink lots and lots of water before you feel thirsty, and remember to wear a scarf over your face as protection from the dry winter air.

Also, keep in mind that alcohol does you no good, in fact it dehydrates the body. Riding under the influence of alcohol or drugs makes you an extreme danger to yourself and to anyone around you. Such activity is grounds for expulsion from any resort and possible conviction after that. If there is an accident and you are chemically impaired, the aftermath could be a nightmare. Ride sober or don't ride at all.

PLAN AHEAD

Prepare yourself to encounter obstacles — this includes trees, rocks, other people and a variety of other possibilities. Pack everything you think you'll need, and then bring along some extra money if possible. Something will always be forgotten that you just may need. If you are traveling to a resort, give yourself lots of extra time (at least an hour) to take care of everything you'll need to do when you arrive. This includes fitting rental equipment to your body, changing into riding gear, and waiting in line for rentals and a lift ticket. If you are planning to rent a package during the busy days of the resort's schedule, see if you can reserve a board and boots by calling in advance. Understand that most rental shops have a first come, first serve policy. Are you sure you want to get up before the sun does? That is what you may need to do to get your rental equipment squared away.

MONITOR YOUR BODY & SURROUNDING ENVIRONMENT

The alpine environment is not a friendly one. High altitudes combined with very low temperatures make for a chaotic and potentially hazardous world. Here are some points to be aware of and some suggestions on how to take better care of yourself in case of overexposure to the elements.

If you start to feel cold, move around. When this doesn't seem to help, get into a warmer environment. If you are riding with a bunch of people, or you're involved in a lesson, don't hesitate to tell your friends/instructor that you are cold. It's hard to learn anything when you are uncomfortable. Don't feel wimpy if you are in a group. Say it out loud — chances are if you're cold there are others in the group who feel the same way. Maybe they'll even join you to warm up in the lodge.

Hypothermia and frostbite are two of the most dangerous risks of winter sports. Hypothermia is what occurs when your core body temperature drops below its normal baseline temperature. This means the core temperature deep inside the body, not at an extremity or near the body's surface. A drop in the total temperature of the body's core affects the entire body, including all of its internal systems. The result can be lethal.

Frostbite is the actual freezing of body tissues. It is a side effect of the body's effort to prevent hypothermia by centralizing the body's total heat. In this case the body reduces the circulation to your extremities. This keeps your core temperature up, but leaves the hands, feet, and face at risk from the cold. Frostbitten body parts have no feeling. The skin becomes hard and turns a whitish color. The face, ears, fingers and toes are the portions of the body in greatest danger of frostbite. This is the result of exposure to the elements and the distant location of such body parts from the heart.

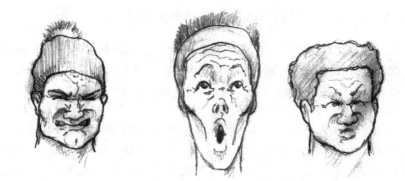

The best way to avoid frostbite is to monitor the body regularly and warm up frequently. If your face is cold...make crazy faces to warm it up. If you are riding with others, look at their faces frequently, too. Be on the lookout for whitish skin, numbness, and lack of reaction in affected tissues. Be sure to have fellow riders check you out as well.

If you or someone you are with shows signs of frostbite, get out of the cold and get warm. Do not try to warm up frostbitten tissue by rubbing it. This will only serve to damage frozen tissues which will no longer be pliable. If you have to warm up quickly, place your hand or other mild heat source upon the frostbitten area. Thawing out takes a minimum of 30 minutes — after warming up, keep in mind that the frozen area is even more vulnerable to freezing again. So if you find yourself or a riding buddy showing any signs of frostbite, get inside and consider calling it a day.

People shiver when they are cold, but this is not a direct sign of hypothermia. Shivering combined with signs of muscular weakness, however, is something to watch for. Pale skin or shivering that takes place even when the person is exhausted are signs of hypothermia. Severe internal cooling can affect a person's motor coordination and mental state. Ask the cold person a simple question like "What is your name?" or "What day is today?" If they look dazed or it takes longer than it should for them to answer, then it's time to warm them up. For a person in this condition, the day is over.

Treating hypothermia requires bringing the body's core temperature back to the proper level. First, get the affected person inside. Try to change them into warm, dry clothes. A sugar drink will help to rehydrate and pump some quick energy into the body's system. Look into a text devoted to this subject for a more intensive solution (See Bibliography). With hypothermia and frostbite, prevention is the best medicine. Learn to dress yourself appropriately for colder weather.

Mountain sickness can occur when a person rises quickly to higher elevations. Oxygen levels at higher altitudes are not as saturated as they are at lower altitudes. When the body receives less oxygen than the amount that it's used to...strange things can happen.

People react differently to climate and atmospheric changes. Some of the more common signs of altitude sickness are headaches, loss of balance, fatigue, shortness of breath, loss of appetite, dizziness, and even insomnia. If your body is telling you that something is wrong, listen, and take care of yourself. Drink lots of water, avoid alcohol, and get enough rest to allow the body adequate time to adjust to its new environment.

If you are planning a trip to higher altitudes, plan for the change. Take a day or two in the new environment to adjust, if possible, before exerting yourself. Most of us will want to jump into the new playground right away (I know I'm like this). But if you've got the option, consider the adjustment a wise move. Perhaps you will want to talk to your doctor before your alpine adventure. He may find it helpful to prescribe you some medicine to help the body cope with the increased altitude.

A general rule for the harsh alpine environment — the higher you go the more the change in environment will affect you. Oxygen becomes thinner at high altitudes, temperature generally drops lower. Solar radiation has more of an effect in the thinner atmosphere. The weather is much more chaotic and prone to quick and drastic changes several times in any given day. In these conditions, be aware that young ones are much more susceptible to these changes than older riders. Be especially sensitive to the needs of the younger members of your snowboarding party.

117

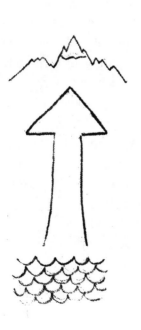  

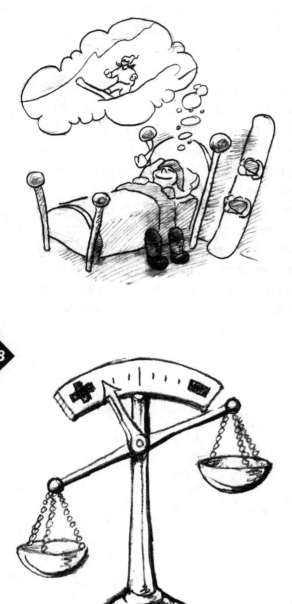

GET PREPARED

To prepare for a day of riding, inspect your equipment and make any necessary repairs. Eat good food and get a good night's sleep. Drink lots of water, then drink some more. Make it a point to keep yourself hydrated throughout the day. Be good to your body by stretching before as well as after a day of hard play. Dress for success and safety. Check the weather forecast and plan for temperatures to be a bit colder than what is predicted. Remember that you can always remove extra layers if necessary. Ride with people you trust —there is safety in numbers. Whether it's scouting a new jump, encountering difficult terrain, or dealing with a possible injury, riding with friends is always a good idea and more fun than riding alone. Play hard and play smart when you ride.

If you prepare well for a day of riding, chances are you will be rewarded. Well-maintained equipment will only enhance your riding. If you prepare your own body in the same manner, it will also work at its optimum potential and you will be more likely to have a strong day of riding. This is not a guarantee or a written law. Precautions like these will simply cut down the variables that might add up to a bad experience. By preparing both board and body for your day of riding, though, you are putting the odds of a good experience in your favor.

NOVICE
TECHNIQUES

Welcome to your first days of snowboarding. These initial trials will provide some of the most challenging and exhaustive experiences you may ever encounter. Don't worry though, it's worth it. As soon as you get past them you will find that the learning curve goes straight through the roof. Once you link your first turns, you're snowboarding. Put aside your worries, we're going to use our bodies and boards to start with. That is what you are going to learn about in this chapter — the foundational techniques to snowboarding and how to turn.

GETTING STARTED

What to expect

Everybody's perspective of this sport is individual. To some first timers the bunny hill may look like a 60-degree slope. The mach nine speeds they envision could blow them away. Relax; this is simply a matter of perspective and circumstance. You will probably see people out there riding effortlessly like it's no big deal, and then you may feel like it shouldn't be for you either. The most important thing you need to do is be ready to learn. Relax and concentrate on what you are doing.

When starting out, learn first on gentle terrain. If you know how to skateboard or surf, you will already have a good idea of how to move on a snowboard. But keep in mind that it's not the same thing, you are dealing with different equipment on a different riding surface. Once on the learning hill, be aware that you will not need to counteract the large amounts of force that you could expect when riding down steep slope at high speeds. Most of the movements you will create are slight (even though they may not feel slight) and gentle. You are not going to be scraping your knees on the snow quite yet, however, the principles of riding are the same as those used in advanced riding technique. Start out easy and build upon these.

A quick reminder to those new to the sport; you will be using groups of muscles that you're not used to exercising either in the specific manner or to the degree you will be exercising them. Expect to be sore at the end of your first day. To reduce the strain on your body, make sure to stretch out before. Later, if you are tired or feel a muscle cramp coming on, take a break. Come back when you are ready.

Bryan Iguchi

Take your time when you learn to ride. Respect the mountain and the resort environment you ride in. Marked signs are there for a reason. Respect them as well.

120

Quick guide to the trail maps (U.S.)

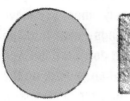  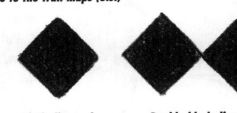

| Green circle **EASY** | Blue square **INTERMEDIATE** | Black diamond **ADVANCED** | Double black diamond **EXPERT** |

*Red markers are designated for out of bounds or danger warnings.
These are posted by the patrol for good reason. Heed the warnings.

When it comes to carrying your board about, you can tie the leash between both bindings and sling it, bindings toward your body, over your shoulder, kind of like a back pack. Some people hold it to one side, like a book. Others hold it behind the body, like a fireman's carry. You may want to walk the dog if you're really tired. If you have to carry your board a long distance, make sure to hold and/or wrap the leash around your wrist. Just in case the board does slip from your grip, you still have a way to stop your ride from running away from you. I try to skate around on the flats as much as much as I can, but when this is not possible, I carry my board with me wherever I go.

121

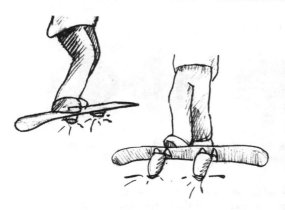

When you are not attached to your board, you want it to stay where you leave it. Put the board bindings down into the snow, high backs facing down the hill. You should always do this when you are on the hill and not leashed to your snowboard. Snowboards don't have a brake system like skis do, and they accelerate even more quickly than skis due to the large surface area of P-tex underneath.

Sometimes you have to leave your board alone. Here are some good ideas to keep your board secure. Buy a lock and use it. If you don't have your own lock, share one with a buddy. If you are going to leave your board at the base, put it where it is easily visible from wherever you are. If you have no other option, tie your leash and buckle your bindings to whatever you are leaning the board against. This isn't much protection but forces a thief to spend more time trying to get your board. This can allow you precious seconds when it comes to stopping a would be perpetrator. Thieves are especially prevalent during the start of the season. So stay as close to your board as you can. If a mad dash becomes necessary, make sure it is as short as possible.

FOUNDATIONAL SKILLS

FALLING

Before you even step on a board you need to know how to fall. Falling is inevitable. Every snowboarder, no matter how great or unskilled, has fallen and will likely do so again. Since this is the most common cause of injury, it is important to understand how to fall as safely as possible. Your first day of snowboarding will probably include a great deal of falling. Expect it.

When we fall we need to train ourselves to react in a specific way. Relax when you feel a fall coming on. It sounds funny but if you can train yourself to relax when you reach "the point of no return," you can significantly reduce the chances of injury. Fully relax the entire body, bobble and bounce about with the fall. I like to think of an on/off switch for my muscles. I'm on while I'm riding. Then, OOPS, I'm falling — I turn the switch off and completely relax through the fall. During a fall, a tense body is much more likely to strain, sprain, and suffer injury than a fluid, relaxed, flowing body.

123

Practice falling and relaxing. Falling safely is one skill that you want to internalize from the get go. You can practice falling at a gym with a gymnastics or a wrestling mat. Learn how to relax and shoulder roll to both sides. Learn to fall toward your face and your bum and turn it into a rollover. Practice falling from a standing position, then try running forward into a shoulder roll and backward into a bum roll. This will give you a great introduction to the feel of a fall on snow.

124

Falling practice techniques

Ride with your hands in a loose fist. This will help to prevent injuring your digits in the event of a fall. Make it a habit to bring your arms to your body by giving yourself a hug, one arm over the other. Most falls happen very quickly, so hugging yourself is not always possible. However, the closer you can get your arms toward your body, the less likely you are to injure yourself. It is estimated that approximately 60+ percent of all snowboard injuries occur from the hands, through the shoulders and collarbone. With this in mind DO NOT try to break your fall by sticking your hands out in front or behind you. Don't be convinced that wrist guards will shield you from upper body injuries. All that happens when equipped with such guards is that the forces of the fall pass over the wrist and are then transmitted to the next joint in the arm. The chances of shoulder dislocation, in fact, are much higher for someone falling onto outstretched hands when wearing wrist guards. Additional safety wear like helmets and protective elbow, knee, and bum pads can provide an extra precaution against injury, but they are not a guarantee against injuries.

125

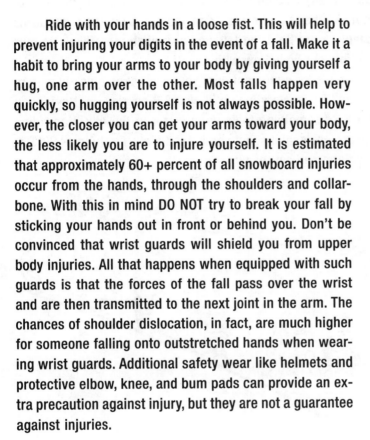

The degree of potential injury is generally determined by two factors. First, the terrain: Is it steep, gentle, smooth, rocky, or full of trees? Granted you will be falling on snow. However, snow is not always soft (ice for instance). Second, the actions of the rider during the fall: We can't really change the terrain you fall on (until you hit it of course). However, you can make the fall a lot easier on yourself by getting your arms in and relaxing before impact. If you fight the fall, you are much more likely to hurt yourself than if you learn to let your body flow with it.

After the fall, try not to move for a moment until you have taken quick inventory of your body. Is there any pain? Does everything still work? If so, ride on. Now if you feel that something is wrong, or something feels wrong later in the day, stop riding and have a trained medical professional inspect you immediately. First Aid or Ski Patrol will be your most immediate medical resources.

If you are moving at high speeds when you fall, or you feel like your board is getting in your way, try to get the board off the snow and slide on your back. This will prevent the board from catching the snow and lofting you down the hill. When you have slowed down sufficiently, get the board down and stand up. In some cases (extremely steep terrain) this is not recommended due to the possibility of an "uncontrollable slide."

There is no shame in falling. Some people even view falling as positive because often it means that they are pushing their physical and mental abilities. When you ride and push yourself, falling can be a good indicator of how much you are pushing yourself. If you fall a lot doing the same thing, maybe you are pushing yourself too hard. Or maybe you need to step back and work on the problem on less challenging terrain. If you think you are going to hit someone or something, falling and stopping might be a good option to avoid a collision.

126

ROB CANDELARIA

With large falls , you DO NOT want to fall flat on your stomach. Try to twist and shoulder roll if at all possible. Accept as much of the momentum as possible. Injuries almost always occur from trying to stop a fall. Don't try to immediately regain control, let the fall run itself out before you try to get back up. A proper fall is a learned skill, so practice falling until it becomes a reflex. Falls often happen so quickly that there is no time to think, only time to react. Tuck it before you land, flip it before you face it.

Practice your falling technique on a gentle slope by simply somersaulting with your arms in and your board on your feet. Do this toward both your toe and heelsides. You can displace the force of a heelside fall against your head by bringing your arms up and behind your head.

BODY POSITION: THE NATURAL READY STANCE

Solid riding is built upon a foundation of strong body position. Good body positioning allows the rider to stay on top of the board at all times. This is the Natural Ready Stance (Athletic Ready Position). From this body position, you are ready for just about anything that the mountain puts before you. This position should be comfortable and relaxed at all times, allowing for all the movements necessary to ride well. You can create fluid, easy, forceful motions in any direction, and your board can be easily manipulated. Your center of gravity is over the center of the board which is especially important for stability. If you are not "riding" over the board, chances are the board will ride off out from underneath you. Strong body position is not difficult to achieve. Once acquired, other riding skills become easier to learn.

Finding your own natural ready stance is easy — just allow your body to act naturally. I recommend using sensory deprivation to help you find your own natural ready position. Stand on a flat section of the hill with your feet about shoulder width apart, close your eyes and jump. When you touch mother earth again, try to feel what your body does. Feel how your body balances itself and then relaxes after it has absorbed the impact. Repeat this until you can instantly relax upon landing. When you feel relaxed upon touchdown, hold it. Try to fix yourself in that position. Now extend your upper body to the point that it feels upright. When your upper body feels upright, open your eyes and look at your body position.

This is a little different for each individual, but almost everyone will find themselves bending a lot at the ankles and the knees. Your upper body will be relatively upright. Your head will face forward with arms out to the sides, slightly bent, and hands are in front of your body. Try bouncing up and down. Jump and leave the ground a couple more times to really work in the "feel" of this body position. This should feel comfortable. From this stance you are ready to move in just about any direction. This is the position we are going to start to build your snowboarding skills upon.

If you have tried this and the body position you wind up in feels funny, relax. If you cannot be comfortable in your riding position, you will probably not be comfortable riding. Try using a different boot setup. Try bending more or less with your legs. Try different stance widths. Everyone's body is unique. Take the time and find out how your own body operates most comfortably.

MICHELLE TAGGART

Come out with a good attitude. Your first day will be difficult, but progress comes quickly. Concentrate on bending your legs and keeping your arms out for balance. It will feel odd at first, but it will help you to enjoy the experience.

BALANCE & MOVEMENT

An important thing to understand about snowboarding is that you are dealing with a new sense of balance and movement. Even really good skaters and surfers will have to get used to the feeling of having both feet bound to the board. The natural ready body position allows you to use your body in the manner it was designed, not twisted or contorted. You will want to move easily from your center outwards. This ideal position is a little different for everyone. But it will have:

◆ **Flexion at the ankles:** You should feel your shins pressing against the tongues of your boots. You can bend only at your knees very easily. It is very difficult to bend at the ankles without also bending at your knees. If you are having trouble getting lower when you ride, focus on bending with your ankles. (If you are in hard boots, try to make sure you are flexing them at least a little.)

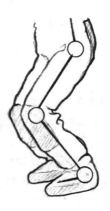

◆ **Flexion at the knees:** This will help you to act/react quickly and forcefully. As you get better you will learn to drive into your turns with your knees. Excessive forces placed on the knees when they are "locked straight" are especially dangerous. An injury to this joint can hurt you badly enough to halt riding, much less walking, for some time.

◆ **Flexion at the hips:** You want to ride with just enough flexion in the hips to keep your upper body upright. This will help you to stabilize the upper body over the board and direct your body into the turn. Too much flexion at the hips and waist can lead to "stinky" riding, a situation where the butt sticks way out to one side of the board.

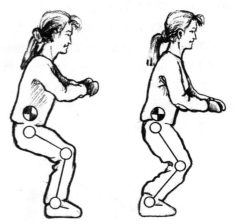

129

A good demonstration of proper body stance is to stand tall with your legs locked straight and then have a friend try to push you over. Then, get into your ready position and have your friend try to push you over. It's a lot tougher for someone to push you over when you can absorb their efforts and then push them back.

Think of the body in three sections. First, the head looks into the desired direction of travel. Second, the upper body stays upright in a relaxed and centered position over the board. Third, the lower body is relaxed, ready and moderately flexed overall with a bit more flexion at the ankles and a bit less at the hips.

The reason you want to bend more further down the ladder than higher up is because the joints that are closer to the ground affect your stance more than those that are further from the ground. Try this out, lean as far as you can in every direction by bending only with the ankles. Note how far you can get before you move outside of your cone of balance and how much you bend at the ankle joint. Then try to do the same thing by bending over only at the waist. Feel how much more you had to bend at the waist to achieve the same amount of distance from vertical over the board. Also note how much more muscle strength it took to bend over at the waist. You have a great deal more muscle mass around your waist than you do in your lower leg. The more you can move with the joint closer to the ground, the more you can manipulate your board while using less energy.

ALEX BIRCH

Riding with straight legs is bad karma, you can hurt yourself this way. Bend at your knees and ankles. Try not to twist your body around more than necessary.

Most people who ride with straight legs tend to compensate by bending at the waist. Although the rider is closer to the ground, this stance is awkward and puts the rider out of balance. If you ride like this and go over a bump, you will be unable to absorb the force of the impact and will likely be thrown even further off balance than before. Riding in such a manner is unstable, especially as speed increases. Riding stinky is both straight legged (boned) and uncentered with low binding angles — not a good combination.

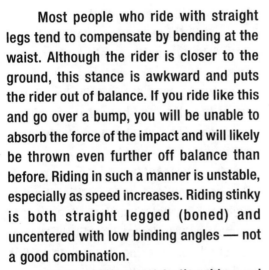

131

Hold your arms out to the sides and forward for good balance. Your hands and arms are indicators of what our upper body is doing. If you can see both your hands when you ride, your weight should be tipward and over the board. If you can't see your hands, chances are your weight is tailward. Like a tightrope walker, the further out you hold your arms the easier it is to balance yourself as you ride. Keeping your arms at a partially flexed position allows for a quick reaction with your arms. Find out what works best for you and go with what feels most comfortable.

NATURAL READY STANCE VARIATIONS

Here are some variations on this natural ready stance. They may seem extreme, but the way they relate to your riding skills is very important.

◆ **Total skeletal support:** A full extended body position relies upon the bones and takes almost no energy to hold. However, because you are relying on your skeleton and fully extended to the end of the range of motion limit, you have no ability to react to the environment.

◆ **Total muscular support:** A fully flexed body position relies upon your muscles for support and takes a great deal of energy to hold. When fully flexed, you are at the other end of your range of motion; once again you have no ability to react to the environment.

◆ **Skeletal/muscular support:** This compromised body position (partial skeletal & partial muscular) allows you to support and act/react effectively to your surroundings, making it possible to flex and extend your body as necessary.

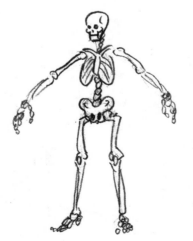

When you ride, don't think of your posture as being straight. This implies a static state of being. Snowboarding is not static, it is fluid. Think of your legs as bending. Reading this book does not require you to think. Reading this book requires thinking. It is an active process. Ride with legs that are actively flexing at all times, even to the smallest degree. Do this so you can absorb the terrain by bending your legs, pressure the board by extending your legs, and prepare for jumps and rugged terrain by so readying your legs. Imagine your legs as both the engine and the shock absorption system of the body. You absorb the terrain. You pressure the board. You maneuver over variations in terrain riding fluidly and safely.

The natural body position is one that is easily contorted. Many riders turn their body around to face their direction of travel. This may work to a rider's advantage or disadvantage, depending upon the binding angle ridden.

A forward facing twisted body position can be more effective than a sideways facing stance if you are riding with higher binding angles (45 degree + with both feet). Some riders use very high binding angles on their boards. From this stance they can twist their bodies into a forward facing position without much effort. When I ride my raceboard I use 60 degree + angles with both of my feet. With this setup a tipward facing position works extremely well. It still shifts and twists around a bit as I move, but so does my sideways facing stance. This also works for many alpine riders and racers. This kind of style gives exceptional lateral stability and balance with each arm stretched out to the side.

If you are riding with lower binding angles, however, a forward facing body position often results in an extremely twisted body position. Riders can generally get away with this on gentle terrain and in softer conditions; but on tougher terrain, the technique doesn't hold up. It fully straightens the front leg, places all of the weight over the rear foot, and winds the rider's body up in one direction. This can make for a number of difficulties when riding — trouble initiating turns, excess stress on the trailing leg, blowing out of the heelside turns, instability in bumpy, uneven terrain, and so on. Many of these problems can be traced to riding with a forced, twisted body position. So if you ride with low binding angles, ride in a relaxed, natural position rather than a forced one.

All right, you're going to find out a little bit about yourself. With your feet unbound, find your natural ready stance and jump as high as you can. Remember how this feels and how high you leapt. Now try to jump as high as you can from a twisted body position. How high did you get from the ground? Which position were you able to jump higher from? I'd put money on the fact that you jumped higher from your natural position. If you jumped hard enough from your twisted position, you probably even unwound a bit when you jumped.

Ride up a rope tow. Let it pull you up the hill. If you feel strain on your body's muscles from your forced, twisted body position try to move around to a more comfortable position. Listen to your body when it tells you something like this. Ride in a position of strength that places as little stress upon the body as possible.

A twisted position is weaker than a natural one. The way to beat it is to go back to a more natural body position. This means riding more sideways. Imagine yourself riding your snowboard. Look into the desired direction of travel, not with your whole body, just by turning your neck. Touch your chin to your leading shoulder. This may feel strange at first, but it is necessary to maintain a more natural body position when riding. You will get used to such a position over time.

Now, you are going to add a weighting element to your natural ready position. One of the principles of riding states: Whichever end of the board has the most weight over it goes down the hill first. Modify your stance by shifting your weight (using your legs, not a twist or a lean) toward the tip of your board, so the tip goes down the hill first. A good way to tell if your weight is forward is to look straight down toward the board. If you can see the toe of your leading boot just past your knee, you are there. If you look down and see your trailing foot underneath your head or you have to look down at an angle to see this, then you need to shift your weight further forward. Try and achieve a weight distribution over the board of 2/3 over the leading foot, 1/3 over the trailing foot. The best way to do this is to drive the trailing hand and knee forward. When you do this, the rest of your body will be shifted forward from the knees upward. You want individual motion with your legs and your knees should not be locked together (remember, this is supposed to be comfortable). Both hands should be forward as well, ideally you should see both hands in your field of vision when riding. With this weight distribution, the leading foot becomes a pivot point. The trailing foot can be used to guide the board around the pivot point into a new direction. By using your body in this manner you can turn and stay over your snowboard in a controlled fashion.

STRAPPING ON THE BOARD
BINDINGS

Now that you have a strong natural ready body position to work with, it's time to strap on the board. Putting your boots into your bindings can be difficult at first. Once you get the hang of it, though, it too will become easy. Some people can even do this as they start to ride down the hill.

◆ Soft boot/ binding system: Make sure the boot is snug and comfortable with as close a fit as possible. Remove all snow from between the boot and binding. Snow can build up, pack into ice, and make a binding less safe than it should be. Step in and place the leading boot inside the binding, and the heel as far back into the cup of the binding as possible to minimize heel lift. Control of the board starts at the ankle so it is necessary to reduce as much "float" in the rider/board interface as possible. The ankle strap is the most important strap in a soft binding system. Start by tightening it. Remember, you want to be comfortable and in control. When you have a snug fit there, put on the toe strap. If you are still uncomfortable, loosen up the binding and mess around with it until it feels right.

137

◆ Hard boot/binding system: Make sure your boots fit comfortably. There should be no heel lift, and the boot buckles should be closed. When you're ready, clear the snow out of the binding and place the boot into the end of the binding which does not have a latch on it. Put your foot down into the binding and lift the bail over the other end. Pull the bail and latch into a secure position over the boot. Once in this "locked" position, the boot should not lift from the binding or wiggle side to side. If there is movement between your boot and binding, adjust the binding. A loose binding adds to the risk of unwanted binding release. Make sure the fit is tight and secure.

SAFETY LEASH

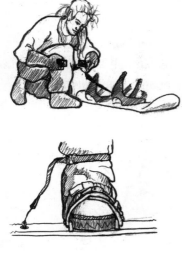

Before attempting to strap yourself to your board, always remember to first attach the safety leash. Start by putting your leash on the leading leg (leading foot is left for regular, right for goofy). This will keep the board from running from you if you should accidentally kick it away. Resort areas require a leash (retention device in legal terms) to be worn when you are riding. If you can, try to attach the leash directly to the board rather than to the binding in case of binding release. There are some people who don't take leashes seriously. However, losing your board in the trees, seeing your board disintegrate against a boulder, or worst of all, facing a lawsuit from an injured person hit by your runaway board, should each be more than enough reason to take a leash very seriously.

TURNING & LIFTING THE BOARD

Now that you are securely attached to the board with one foot, lift the entire board from the ground. Feel the weight and the imbalance of the weight with only one foot bound. Counter that imbalance by pushing with the side of your foot. Rotate the board about by twisting the bound foot around from one side to the next. Practice turning yourself around while the board is off the ground.

138

Once strapped to your board and able to turn and lift it, you are ready to get moving. Walk around taking little steps at first. If the angle of the foot feels awkward at first that's okay, try bending more at the ankle and knee. Take little steps and keep your unbound foot and the board relatively close to prevent the Baryshnikov split from taking place. Walk in one direction. Stop, spin the board about and walk in a new direction. Try skipping along. This works best leading with the unbound foot and catching up with the bound foot and board. The trick is not to catch the heel of the unbound foot with the toeside edge of the board. Again, this is a process that becomes easier over time.

139

SKATING ON THE FLATS

Skating on a snowboard is a lot like getting around on a skateboard. Skating is a good way to get around the flats. Doing it well can be difficult though. There are two ways to skate. You can skate with your weight over the board (in control), or you can skate with your weight over the snow (i.e. goofball). Just like riding, you want to skate with your weight over the board. This way you can guide the board into the desired direction. If someone tries to skate and their weight is not over the board, the board will travel away from the intended direction. The unbound foot will be pushed aside in the opposite direction from the bound foot and board and the result will be a very awkward rider traveling in two directions at once.

This can be easily overcome by keeping all of the weight on the leading foot, over the board. Try pushing sideways with your foot if you ride with lower angles. If this feels funny, try pushing yourself around with the foot on the other side of the board. Go with the way that feels most comfortable. If this is done well it will look like you are pushing a skateboard along.

Think of holding your COG over the center of the board then pushing off toward your destination. Start out by taking little pushes. The pushing foot pushes along side the board into the desired direction. Keep your body over the board. Bend your ankles and your knees. This will help keep your bum and your COG over the board. Practice by skating around in a figure eight. This will help you to get used to going straight and turning around in both directions. When you are ready, take bigger steps and go faster. Try to keep the board as flat as possible as this will keep the greatest amount of P-tex on the snow and keep you moving quickly. In this way you can glide easily between steps. If you are traveling across a slight incline, a bit of edge hold will be necessary to travel in the desired direction. Before too long you will get enough speed going so that you can put your other foot on the board and just glide along. Trailing foot placement is best in between both bindings, pressing against the outside of the trailing binding.

141

You can try to skate up to an incline, however, the steeper the ascent, the more difficult this becomes. Try pointing the board across the hill, below the unbound foot. Take one step with the unbound foot up the hill first, and follow it up with the other foot and the snowboard. The skipping technique mentioned earlier also works great for this. Going down a slight decline is easy. Simply put the unbound foot onto the board — a stomp pad helps here to prevent your trailing foot from slipping.

Knowing how to stop with one foot bound is surprisingly useful. This is especially helpful in a lift line with a slight downgrade. Start by getting your weight over the bound foot. Place the heel of the trailing foot into the snow by the leading foot. Flex your legs a bit to accept the shock. Then place the unbound heel just to the side of the leading foot by the board. Dig it in a bit for best results. If the heel digs in too far back from the nose, you'll do the splits. If you dig in too far to the side, you're going to go for a spin. If you execute the move properly, however, you'll slow down quickly without losing control. If you have built up a lot of speed, many short heelstops in a row should do the trick.

Moving around with one foot in and one foot out is great for low speed travel. If your speed increases past walking speed it is advisable to stop and buckle both feet to the board.

INTRODUCTION TO DOWNHILL MOVEMENT

STRAIGHT RUN

The straight run is your introduction to downhill movement. Find a gentle portion of the learners hill with a flat runout at the bottom. Hike/skip about 20-30 feet up the hill. Adjust this hike to fit your comfort level for both the way up and the way down. You can keep from sliding down before you want by placing the heel of your trailing foot on the board, keeping your toes on the snow. Point the board down the hill and place your body into the "ready" position. When you are ready to go, just slide your foot all the way onto the board. Look down the hill and press your unbound foot on the board pressing against the inside of the rear binding for stability. As mentioned before, whichever end of the snowboard has the most weight over it will go down the hill first. Commit to keeping your body position forward and over the board. Relax and accept the sensation of flying down the bunny hill and let the board run out its own speed. If you need to, use the heel stop mentioned earlier. Repeat as many times as necessary until comfortable with the prospect of the straight run.

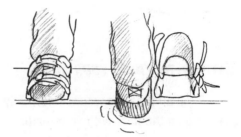

143

GETTING TO KNOW YOUR EDGES

Back on the flats, you will formally introduce yourself to the edges of your board. Standing on the flats with your leading foot bound and your trailing foot unbound, find your natural ready position. To get your board up on the toeside edge: push down on your toes and pull up with your heels. To get your board up on your heelside edge: push down with your heels and pull up with your toes. Lean over the board from side to side. See how far you can go before feeling unbalanced. Try to hold it as close to the point just before being unbalanced as possible. Now try doing this with your eyes closed. Feel the force of gravity pulling your body out away from the board and toward the ground. You will find that this gets a lot easier the more you bend your legs while keeping your body upright. Many people react to being unbalanced by standing straight up. This is not the best thing to do. By standing up, your body's center of gravity rises, taking your entire mass higher up and further away from the board. The result — you become less stable. The lower and closer you are to the board, the wider your cone of balance.

Something else happens when you find yourself unbalanced — your instincts force you to place your unbound foot on the snow to keep from falling down. Notice how high the edge in which your board rises when you do this. To get your board high on edge, you must get your weight into the turn. Edge transfer can be practiced with one foot in and one foot out. This is best demonstrated on the flats by simply stepping over one side to the next. Back and forth. Feel how easily the board rises and rolls from edge to edge. This is an important idea to understand as you begin to connect turns. Your weight must travel over the board from one side to the next as you transfer turns.

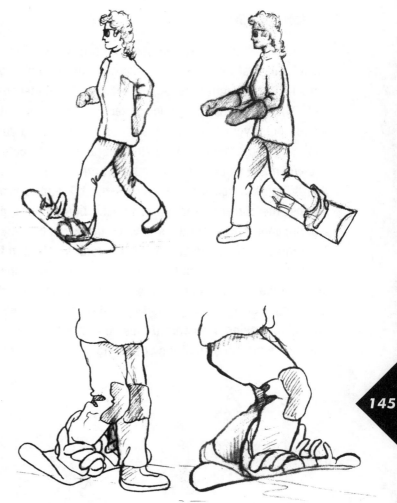

145

INITIATING TURNS

All right, now that you are comfortable with the straight run, you're ready to make your first turns. Go to the gentle learners hill and take a little hike just like we did with our straight runs. Maybe hike a little higher than you did before.

The wonderful thing about direction control is that it is also gives speed control. As you point your board across the fall line and dig your edges in the snow, you are changing two aspects of your riding: speed and direction. When you first start to ride you will make skidded turns. You use both legs to guide the board into the new direction. When the board points across the hill and is brought onto its edge it reflects against the current direction of travel. The more you point the board across the hill and dig your edges into the snow, the more you will change your speed and direction. The more you point the board down the hill and flatten the board to the snow, the less you will resist gravity and the faster you will move down the hill. If you find yourself pointing the board straight across or even up the hill and you're still not slowing down, try using a bit more edge angle to bite into the snow. If you find yourself spinning around or moving backward (unless that is what you want to do), you can get back in the saddle simply by shifting your weight tipward and keeping it there.

SHANNON DUNN

The key is bending your legs and you always want to look where you're going. It won't work if you try to complete a turn without also turning your head.

Turns are easier with both feet bound to the board. However, hiking up the hill, putting on your board, standing up for each short run, taking off your board, and doing this over and over again can take a great deal of energy. I recommend hiking up the gentlest section of the learners hill and turning with the trailing foot unbound, just like you did before with the straight run.

You are going to turn with your leading foot bound and your trailing foot out of its binding. When you get to a comfortable height up the slope, stop and turn your board across the hill. Let the foot on the snow and the snowboard's edge together support your weight. When ready, turn your board so it points down the hill. As with your straight runs you can hold your position by placing the toe of your trailing foot in the snow. When you put your other foot on the board, find your stance. Toeside turns are easier for most people, so try turning in that direction first. Once you are comfortable with toeside turns, go for heelside turns.

FIRST TURNS

Now it is time to attempt your first turns having both feet bound to the board. There are three parts of a turn:

◆ **First:** Gain a little bit of speed so your board can flex and work on top of the snow. Walking speed should be fast enough. If you don't have enough speed on the board when you start to turn, it will be difficult to turn the board around. When you feel that you have enough speed, go for your turn.

◆ **Second:** Look into the desired direction of travel. Look into the direction you wish to turn for your heelside turns. Now that your mind is leading your body in the direction you wish to travel you will have an easier time using your body to get there.

◆ **Third:** Use your body. Start turning your upper body into the desired direction and commit to the turn. Keep looking and turning your upper body into the new direction. Put both hands over the side of the board you want to turn to. As you slide over the snow, your body will begin to unwind. Rotation relies upon the principle of the bodyspring. Think of your body as a spring. When you wind up and commit to a turn, you are building energy inside to put toward the turn. Now, this energy has to be released. As you slide over the snow, your body unwinds and releases that energy. The lower body aligns itself with the upper body. Since the board is bound to your feet, it changes its direction as well. Now with the board pointing in a new direction, you can add a bit of edge angle bite into the snow. To get the board up on edge, push/pull with your toes and heels on the board, and lean slightly into the turn. This will bring the board on edge and help guide it into the new turn.

147

ALEX BIRCH

Take your trailing hand and point into the direction you want to go. This will help you to drive your weight forward and rotate your upper body into the new direction.

GUIDED TURNS

This combination of turning your body and getting your board up on its edge is all you will need to guide the board around. A guided turn is subtle and uses very little physical energy. This strong technique allows you to harness the energy inside your body and the board, and use both to propel you down the hill. The real trick is to be patient with your first turns. These first turns will be gradual changes of direction, not immediate ones. Once your bodyspring has released its energy, your body is unwound and ready to be wound up once again into another turn. Repeat until you are comfortable with one turn, then try turning into the other direction. Get tricky and go for both turns in a single run, one right after the other. If you can you're doing great!

What you have just done is created a guided turn. Guided turns are a natural sideways movement pattern that originates from your natural ready position. You do not have to work hard to make your body move the way it was designed to function. Your natural ready stance is not broken in as dramatic a fashion as with a forced turn and balance is preserved. Guided turns are very efficient — they do not require a great deal of energy to be effective. Guiding movement patterns may require more mental determination at first. Yet once you are comfortable with this kind of a turn, you will quickly become an efficient and fluid rider. With this in mind, you want to concentrate and commit to your turns. Committing to guided turns is the difference between smooth, efficient turns and forced, energy-intensive ones. Gradually guide rather than force the board around whenever possible. This will help you to steer the board across the hill with both feet. Ignore the temptation to spin or twist your upper body for the instant reaction.

149

There are disadvantages to this type of turn. It takes some time and practice to learn to do it well. Also, it is not an immediate turn when you are first starting out. This will change as your riding skills improve, and when done well it will allow for much more efficient riding.

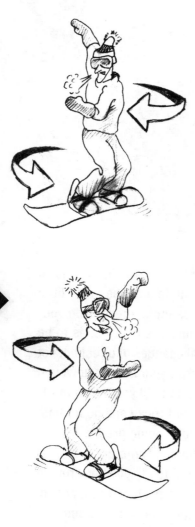

COUNTER-ROTATED TURNS

Forcing the board around is accomplished by twisting the upper body opposite to the direction of the new turn. I refer to this as a counter-rotated turn. It works, however it works with penalties. Although the goal of turning the board into the new direction is achieved, you end up throwing your back into your turns, and it is difficult to see where you are going through the back of your head. Counter-rotated turns are also very energy expensive — they will tire you out more quickly than guided turns. When you force the board around, the board will fight you back, and you may not always win. In a sense, you are playing a game of catch-up all the way down the hill. When you guide your turns, you can ride more forcefully and for a longer period of time before tiring out. Forced turns also look strange, and no one wants to look like a funny bird flying down the hill. There is one advantage to this kind of a turn, it is immediate. When something, or someone pops up right in front of you and you need to stop NOW!!!, then you have a need for this kind of a turn.

IMPROVING GROUND SKILLS

ROLLING OVER

When you are comfortable turning in both directions and are making smooth toeside and heelside turns with one foot in and one foot out, hike up the hill again. Sit down and put both feet into your bindings. Before we start to cut the hill up, though, let's work on a few more ground skills. Since you are already sitting down you are going to start with rolling over from sitting down on the snow, to lying face down on the snow. Shift your weight up onto your shoulders by lying on the snow looking up at the sky. Now using the muscles in your legs and abdominals, lift the board off the ground. If you are having trouble lifting the board, try wrapping both your hands around the knee you will lift off the ground when you roll. Roll over, leading with your shoulders — do this in both directions. Keep in mind that rolling from your stomach to your back is easier than rolling from your back to your stomach. Lift the board up off the ground by bending your knees. Roll over with your body, leading with your shoulder as before. Do this both ways in both directions.

151

GETTING INTO POSITION

Now we are going to learn how to get up from the ground. Start by placing your board further down the hill from your body. Getting up on your toe side is a cake walk — just walk yourself up with your hands and ride away. Getting up onto your heel side can be a bit of a trick, but once you figure it out it isn't that tough to do, especially on steeper slopes where you have gravity and the slope angle helping you out. Scootch your bum up to the board. This will make it easier for you to roll forward. Take one hand and grab the board by the toeside edge. Put your other hand on the ground next to your bum and get ready to push off the ground. Now you're ready to roll forward. As you do so, push with your leading hand against the ground and pull with your trailing hand on the board. This works best if you coordinate it into one motion. When you roll your body over the board, stand up. If you haven't rolled far enough forward or if you stand up too quickly, you will fall back down to where you started. Some people will try to stand up without being over their board many times, only to fall down again and again. You have got to be over the board before you try to stand up. If you are having lots of trouble getting up on your heel side, keep trying. If you begin to get frustrated, roll over, get on your toeside edge, turn around and ride away.

SIDE-SLIPPING

Now that you can roll over and stand up on your board, start using the snowboard to control your descent. An easy exercise to introduce edge awareness and control is called side-slipping. Side-slipping is simply turning your board across the hill and using your uphill edge to control your downward descent. Another one of the principles of snowboarding states: "The more edge angle you use, the more you can resist gravity and the slower you travel down the hill." If you use enough edge angle, you don't move at all. As soon as your edge angle drops below a certain degree, the forces of gravity will overcome the resistance you create with your edge and you will start to slide down the hill. The less edge angle you use, the faster you will be able to travel down the hill. Once you stand up, gradually release the edge so that the board starts sliding down the hill. This will be tricky at first, but that's okay. Just go with it, keep your body position over the board and relax. Stick with it until you can smoothly descend using just enough edge to slide down the hill at a slow, consistent speed without any sudden stops.

153

You don't want the board to go flat to the snow because of the 'Golden Rule of Snowboarding' which states: "If you are traveling down the hill and you engage the downhill edge, you will trip over the downhill edge and down you'll go." Ouch! Practice your side-slipping on both the toeside and the heelside of the board. Looking down the hill on your heelside edge, bring the board's edge angle up by pushing down with your heels and pulling up with your toes. Looking up the hill on your toeside edge, push down with your toes and pull up with your heels. Stay on that uphill edge and stay on top of your board.

154

THE FALLING LEAF

The falling leaf drill adds directional control to your side-slip. This is extremely easy to do. Whichever end of the board has the most weight upon it goes down the hill first. Start out by side-slipping down the hill. Shift your weight over one end of the board. You will find that the board will start to travel in the same direction of your weight shift. Shift your weight to the other end of the board. Now your direction of travel will change as well. You can go back and forth down the hill on one edge like this if you have to. This is a good skill to have for traveling down scary terrain when you feel it is too difficult to turn both ways.

THE 180

Now you're going to learn how to manipulate the board beneath you — specifically, learn how to change direction when standing up on the board. First, bind both feet to your board again on the flats. You will immediately notice that it is very difficult to move around this way without a decline. When you bind both your feet to the board you become a slave to gravity. If you find yourself sliding around unintentionally, go to another area that looks as flat as a parking lot.

The manuever to work on here is better known as the 180. All we are going to do is jump into the air and spin around so that we face the opposite direction. I like to use the mental image of a discus thrower, the body-spring being loaded by downward twisting forces. Upon release, all of this stored energy releases upwards and twists opposite the original direction of movement. Find your natural ready position. Set yourself up with the combined movement of compressing the body, especially the lower body, and winding the body around in one direction (just like that discus thrower). Start your 180 by leading with your head and hands into the new direction. Forcefully extend your body upwards and unwind into the new direction. As you extend your body you will leave the ground. At this point your whole body will be twisted about, the upper body almost facing the new direction. Now that you are airborne, pull your legs up to your body and let your lower body wind around to face the same direction as the upper body. Now with your entire body and board facing the new direction, let your legs extend and ready yourself for touchdown. Absorb the impact and smile. You just pulled off your first 180. Congratulations!

155

THE SCOOTCH

It is time to learn how to muscle the snowboard beneath your body. I call this exercise "The Scootch." You are going to slide your board from side to side underneath your body. This way you can move the board around when you ride rather than play catch up with your body and the board underneath you. Start out by pushing the board out to one side. If you do this far enough, your entire body will be over one end of the board. Try pushing this so far that the end of the board your body isn't over starts to lift off the ground. Be sure to use your leg muscles when you do this — you don't want your legs to noodle or collapse into a pile beneath you. Try to keep your upper body as upright as possible so you are not bending over at the waist toward your toes. Now do the same thing over the other end of the board. Shift your board back and forth beneath you, from one end to the other. Try and establish a rhythm, back and forth (notice how stable your upper body is over the board when all the work is being done by the legs). Turn it up, you can really lift the ends of the board off the ground. Stay on top of it. When you wheelie, you can also learn to use the energy that you have built up to transfer and loft you into the air and onto the other end of the board.

Once you have figured this exercise out, try doing the falling leaf, but now use your legs to push your board about instead of leaning from side to side. You can also use this technique in a direction as you travel down the hill. It's lots of fun.

Which of the following is it safe to assume is lighter — your body or your snowboard? Unless you are starving and weigh next to nothing, it should have become quite apparent that your board is much lighter. The scootch works on the assumption that the snowboard weighs less than the body on it. If for some reason your board is too heavy, get another one that you can move around more easily.

157

CONTROLLED DESCENT

TRAVERSING

Now we are going to work at moving in a direction down the hill with both feet bound to the board. We are going to start out by working on controlled slow speed descent. The easiest way to do this is to traverse. This means that you will be traveling more across than down the hill. By traversing across the hill you can get used to traveling as you would on your board. Start by getting both feet into the bindings. Stand up with the board pointing across the hill. Look in the desired direction (focusing on a fixed landmark helps). Try not to look straight across the hill, rather, look across and down the hill just a bit. Get your weight tipward and let the board slide beneath you. Be patient and keep with it. If you are not moving in the desired direction try to bend your ankles and shift your weight over the tip more. If you are moving too quickly, guide the board across the hill and work your edges into the snow. When you get to one side of the trail, change your board's direction. Stand up and travel down and across the hill in your new direction.

GARLANDS

Next we are going to try garlands which are staggered, continuous turns. Garlands are a good way to get used to pointing the board down the hill to increase speed. You can control speed by pointing the board across the fall line. This is all done riding in a single direction across the hill. Start with the board pointing across the hill. When ready, shift your weight forward to get the board to travel down the hill. As you pick up speed, look across the hill and then turn your body across the hill. Commit to pointing your board across the fall line. Try to get your board to point straight down the hill and then turn. Turn so that you can control your speed almost to a complete stop, then look down the hill, shift your weight tipward, and gently, gradually let go of your edges and turn again. When you point your board down the hill, see how long you can stick with it and then recover your control turning across the hill once more. When you are satisfied with your speed and direction control it's time to make it all come together.

159

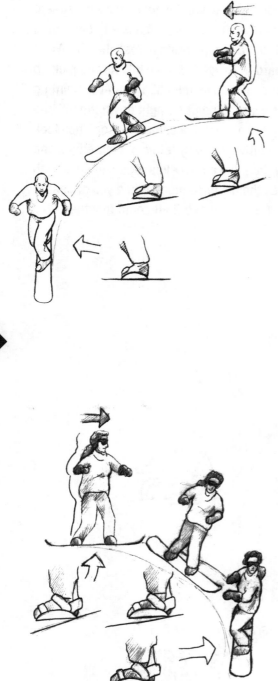

CONNECTING TURNS

Next you need to learn how to make and connect your turns with both feet bound to the board. Connecting your turns in both directions with both feet bound to the board is what snowboarding is about. Find a section of the hill where you would like to make your first connected turns. When both of your feet are bound to the board it is much easier to maneuver. If this is your first time doing this, it will probably be a wonderful new sensation. Sometimes getting from one turn to the next is difficult. This is because you must point the board straight down the hill before switching edges. You already know that if you catch the downhill edge, you will fall. To turn in both directions effectively then, you will need to use both edges. In order to change edges without engaging the golden rule, the board must point downhill. This way you do not have a downhill edge, only a left and right edge. Whenever the board points straight down the hill, you will accelerate quickly. This can be a scary process but don't let it get to you. Just relax and commit to each new turn. It will soon come to you. Once you are doing this, you are snowboarding. This is the tough part, it only gets better from here.

Start by pointing your board across the hill and standing up. Relax and focus on what you are about to do first. When ready, look in the direction you want to travel down the hill. Shift your weight toward the tip of the board and gradually let go of the edge. By the time the board goes flat to the snow, it should be pointing down the hill and you should begin to accelerate very quickly. This is the time to start the new turn. Keeping your weight tipward, look into the new direction of travel. Turn your body and commit to the new direction. As the board turns beneath you, use your edge to control your speed. It may take a few tries, but keep at it. The more you can commit to shifting your weight tipward and gradually letting go of the edges, the quicker the board will point down the hill. The more quickly you can get the board to point down the hill, the less you will accelerate in between exchanges. Once the board points down the hill, the new edge can be engaged. The new turn will then control your descent.

Your first turns are going to be made with lower edge angles. This will be easier to control, skid around, and transfer into the next turn. Easier slopes do not require high edge angles to resist the forces of gravity. Start out on the easy stuff and when you get to the steeper slopes you can then work on high edge angles in the turns.

QUARTER TURNS

If you are having difficulty getting the board to point down the hill, that's all right. I've got a little trick here to help you out. We are going to "cheat" into our turns by applying an exercise I call quarter turns.

Start by standing on the board and pointing it across the hill. Remember the 180 turns we learned earlier? We are going to use a 90 jump turn for this exercise. Wind up and compress your body. Then extend and unwind. You want to turn and point the tip of the board down the hill. As soon as you touch mother earth, the board will start to accelerate down the hill. When you are ready, look into the desired direction of travel and turn. Keep on turning until the board is pointing across the hill. Try to come to a complete stop without falling or sitting down. Now that you have done that, do another quarter turn to point the board down the hill and turn in the other direction. Keep alternating turns, left and right all the way down the hill. When the board points straight down the hill, you have the option of turning in either direction. This drill allows you to get the board to point straight down the hill without accumulating too much speed, and makes your turns easier to initiate.

Some people cheat even more by rotating more than 90. In effect they are turning into the new direction as soon as they touch down The more and more you do this drill, the less and less you will find yourself jumping to get the board pointing down the hill. If you keep on this course eventually you will not need to jump at all. This is your desired outcome. The rush of pointing your board straight down the hill, accelerating, and going from one edge to the next is scary for some people at first. That's all right; eventually you will become used to it and consider it fun.

CROSS-OVER TURNS

The basic turn that everyone starts to ride with is called a cross-over turn. It is called that because your body rises and crosses over into each new turn made. You probably know by now that heelside turns can be more difficult than toeside turns. This is especially true if you ride with low binding angles. The reasons for this are simple. Your knees are designed to bend in one direction only. The way to overcome this difficulty is easy. Look where you want to go first. Trust yourself and bend your legs anyway. Think of it as sitting down in a chair as you move into your turns. You can see to your heelside without looking over your shoulder. This takes some confidence to do, but if you keep at it and let your body work the way it is meant to, it will eventually click.

RIDING THE LIFT/TOW
CHAIR LIFTS

Chair lifts are supposed to make our lives easier, so easy that people pay to use them rather than hike up a hill for free. So, let's talk about making our journey on the chair as safe and pleasant as possible.

Getting on a chair lift is very easy. Skate to the loading area and wait your turn. Then skate to the pickup area. Look over your shoulder to anticipate the chair. Turn toward the hanging support bar. As the chair reaches you, reach for the chair with your hands and guide your body into the seat. As you're taking off, lift the board off the ground. This is important. By doing this, you will prevent the hanging board from catching anything underneath the chair. Make yourself comfy, and if there is one, draw the safety bar down in front of you. Riding the chair up is even easier. Just hang out or talk with your traveling partners. Think of that perfect run you have been dreaming of all season or whatever strikes you at the moment. You might want to rest the board on your trailing foot, or on the foot rest of the safety bar to take pressure off of your leading foot. Unbuckling your hard boots or loosening the clips on the straps on your soft bindings might also make your journey more comfortable.

Getting off the chairlift can be the hard part. Often the offramp is the steepest part of the run on easier terrain. Many people fall off on this part of the hill. I used to fall off of the offramp all the time, and then have no trouble for the rest of my run. This was very frustrating for me. Here is how I solved my problem of falling off lifts.

Make sure that your binding does not have any parts trailing in the snow. Near the top of the lift, buckle up your boots & leading binding for a bit more control when getting off the chair. Anticipating the ride off the lift, sit on the trailing half of your bum. This helps to point the board tipward down the offramp, making sure to look in the direction you want to go. Don't look at your toes unless you want to join them on the ground. Put your trailing foot on the stomp pad or even up by the leading foot. As

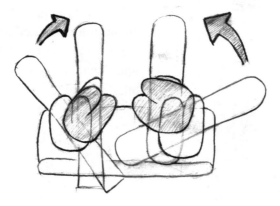

the board touches ground, push your body up from the seat using your hands and stand upright. It is hard to get your weight forward when sitting down over the tail of the board. As you start to descend the off ramp, flex your legs and try leaning down into the hill a bit. This gets your weight forward, and over the board. Hold your hands out over the front of the board to get your weight tipward. I tell my little students to think of the way Frankenstien walks around. Try not to turn on the steep part of the ramp — go straight first and run off some speed, then turn when you are comfortable. When you come to a stop, look around to make sure that you are out of the flow of traffic. Then find a comfortable spot to buckle in and ride off.

Riding on and getting off the lift really is an easy thing to do. Just make it a point to stand up out of the chair before you attempt to ride away. Sometimes I wonder why it took me so long to figure it out.

167

POMA/T-BAR & J-BAR LIFTS

Riding Poma/T-Bar & J-Bar lifts may look difficult but don't worry, looks can be deceiving. Get ready by placing the board in the tracks of the lift, pointing up the hill. Put your trailing toe into the snow to keep yourself from sliding down the hill. Wait for the lift attendant to give you the Poma/T-bar. If you are riding a Poma you will need to place the Poma disk in between your legs behind the leading leg. If you are riding a J/T-Bar, place the bar under your bum and put your other foot on the board. Grab the pole with your hands and use your arms as shock absorbers. Also, use your legs to push the board uphill and keep it underneath you. Hold on until you are ready to let the lift pull you up the hill. Do not allow yourself to sit down on the Poma, T/J-Bar. Try and maintain an upright body position as you ride up the hill. When you get to the top just let go and skate away.

ROPE TOW

Stand next to the rope tow & point the board up the hill. Put your other foot on the board & look for the rope or the bar. If you start to slide backward, put the toe of your trailing foot into the snow, keeping your heel on the board. This should keep you still. Look over your shoulder for the rope/bar if you have to. As the bar approaches, reach out and grab on to it. Use the muscles in your legs to keep the board underneath you. This will keep you from "falling over" the tip of the board. Try not to pull your arms in toward your body. If you do that you will accelerate until your upper body reaches your hands and then your upper body will stop moving up the hill as your board keeps going. Try to let your arms straighten out in front of you and stand upright as you ride up the hill. Getting off is simple, just let go and skate away.

Here are a few things to help you ride up the hill safely. If you get pulled or thrown off balance, hold on to the bar/rope tow and scootch the board beneath you. Don't allow yourself to be pulled from your position over the board. If the board starts to travel off the trail, point the nose up the hill. Use a little bit of an edge to correct yourself if you have to. Once the board gets back on the track you should be fine. Lastly, if the trail is rutted or bumped out, just use your legs to absorb the terrain as you would when you ride down the hill.

If you do fall down, let go of the lift. Don't try to pull yourself back up onto the Poma/T-bar — you are just going to get dragged up the hill if you do. It is funny to watch, embarrassing and sometimes painful to experience. I call it "Trolling for patrollers".

BOARD CONTROL

UP & DOWN PRESSURE MOVEMENTS

Now that you can turn in both directions and use the lifts, I am going to introduce you to up and down pressure movements to control the board. As you start to turn, use the muscles in your lower body, bending your ankles in particular, to pressure the board. Drive into the turn with your knees and hips. I like to think of this movement as "sinking " into the turn. This will transmit a great amount of pressure upon the board and into the snow. If you have pressured the board correctly, you will be able to feel the board bend underneath. Snowboards are designed to flex, what is technically known as de-cambering.

When you flex the board it helps you do three things. One, it helps you to place more pressure through the board into the snow to attain some serious edge bite. Two, it decreases the radius of the sidecut which will make you turn more quickly than before. Three, there is more effective edge contact with the snow meaning you have a longer platform to work over the snow. All of these things help you to control the board more effectively. Try it, when you do you will find yourself making quicker turns and moving more efficiently. You can experiment with this by flexing your legs at different points during the turn to see how you might add a greater degree of riding control.

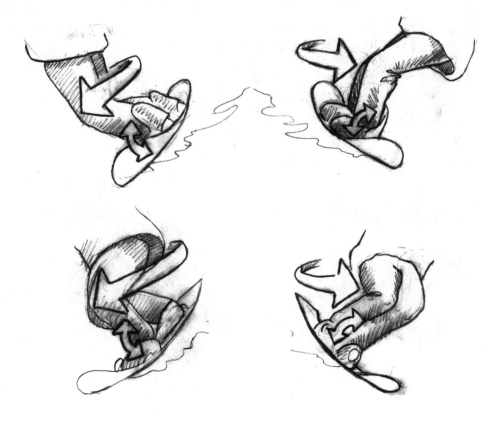

This pressuring also causes energy to be built up inside the board. You can often feel the energy being released when the board returns to its original shape. This recambering can even spring or kick you out of a turn. Use this energy to rise out from your turn and project yourself into the next one. As you finish your turns, you want to gradually extend your legs (not all the way, you still want a little bit of bending in your legs) and shift your weight tipward. The more extended the lower body is, the easier it is to have less edge contact from the board to the snow. This partially has to do with a narrower cone of balance over the board. To stay balanced over the board during this part of the turn, you have to be almost directly above it. When you do this your edge releases and you can transfer your weight across the board to get onto the new edge.

170

FLEXION & EXTENSION

From rising and crossing over to the new turn, you start your next turn. Flex your legs during your turns to flex your board. Extend out of one turn and flex into the next one. And so on, and so on, all the way down the hill. As an imaginary visual, I tell my younger students about the lions and the fraidy cats. Lions with big claws represent the leg extension phase, fraidy cats with tiny paws represent the flexion phase.

UPPER BODY INITIATION

The rainbow drill incorporates the initial turning of the upper body into the turn as well as flexion and extension movements. Start by pointing your leading hand out over the tip of the board. If you're riding with high binding angles and facing forward, try pointing with both hands.

172

Start down the hill. Shift your weight tipward and look down the fall line. Rise and point your hand(s) down the hill over the downhill edge. As you move your hand(s) over the side of the board, gradually drive your hand(s) toward the snow. Use your legs to really get down there and flex the board.

When your board points across the hill, gently start to rise and point your hand(s) over the tip of the board again. Link turns by pointing your hand(s) and sinking to the other side of your board. Repeat back and forth, all the way down the hill. As the terrain you ride gets steeper, focus on turning your board across the hill first and then sink your edges into the snow for optimal speed control.

BREATHING PATTERNS

You may notice when you feel stressed that sometimes you hold your breath when you ride. Breathe. You can't get very far down the hill if you don't breathe. Stifling your breath affects your whole body. Breathing properly will help you to relax and get your body working. This will help to divert your focus from any stress and direct it toward your body's movements. It will add rhythm and consistency to your turns. Try forcefully exhaling when you pressure your board. Force out as much air as possible from your lungs. As you release the pressure from your board relax your chest and let the fresh oxygen flow back into your lungs. This will happen naturally as the forceful exhalation creates a vacuum in your lungs. I like to think of a song in my head, or just sing out loud as I ride to add rhythm and consistency to my turns. Keep on turning, keep on riding. The more you ride the better you will get. When you feel you are ready, try taking steeper, more challenging terrain.

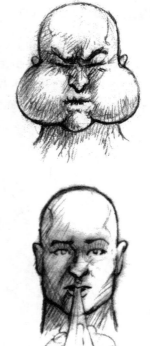

Q & A

for the
NOVICE RIDER

173

Q *Why do people bend over only at the waist when they ride?*

A *These riders are trying to do a couple of things. They are trying to get lower when they ride, and (heelside turns in particular) get their board up on its edge. However, they are bending at the wrong joint to accomplish this goal. By bending over at the waist they can get their board on edge and establish lower position, but when they do so in this manner they end up throwing their weight far over to one side of the board. It is very difficult to ride a board with straight legs, much less absorb the terrain beneath. This can be very tough on the knees. Some riders have the tendency to reach out and touch the snow on their toeside turns — fight that urge. Try to keep your upper body upright. Relax, bend those ankles and knees, and bend a little at the hips so you can get lower to the ground while remaining over the board. This will lead to safer and more stable riding.*

Q *I feel like the board is not under me when I skate. Why is it always slipping out from underneath me?*

A *It's easier to stay over the board if you get low, so bend a lot at your leading ankle and your leading knee. Use your leading leg as a shock absorber to help keep your body over the board. Maintain an upright body position over the leading foot. If your bum isn't over the board, you are probably pushing it away from you with each step that you take.*

Q *When I skate, I find myself drifting to the side, and the board spins around a lot as I skate around. Also, my edges tend to catch which often spins me around and causes me to fall. What's the problem?*

A *If you let your board go flat, there is little friction between the snow and the base of your board. Gravity takes over. If your ride is spinning around* **backward,** *your* weight is over the tail. The way to counter this is to shift your weight tipward and use your edges. The idea is to stabilize yourself with the metal edge and still have as much P-tex contacting the snow as possible for maximum speed on the flats. If you are drifting or being bounced about from edge to edge, pick an edge, get on it, and stay on it using as little edge angle as possible.

Q Why do I want to scootch the board underneath me rather than lean side to side, leaning seems to be much simpler?

A Leaning may be simpler, but learning to use your legs to manipulate the board is a much more effective method. Try to lean from tip to tail, back and forth as quickly as you can. Then try scootching back and forth as quickly as you can. Which is faster, more forceful, and more stable? The scootch is the winner in this contest.

Q What is a safe riding speed?

A Traveling at a safe speed requires two considerations. First, what can you anticipate? If you can see all the way down the hill, no one is in front of you, and your horizon is clear, chances are it is safe to blaze away. If the visibility is poor, lots of people are in front of you, and the trail takes a blind left-hand turn, your horizon is limited, so adjust your speed to account for the surrounding environment and your inability to read it well. Second, how quickly can you stop if you need to? The faster you move, the longer it will take you to stop. Travel at a speed that you can control as dictated by your environment. If you feel like you are going too fast, turn the board across (or even back up) the hill, slow down, and take a breather. When you are ready again, go for it. You will often find yourself making these adjustments as you ride along. Sometimes you won't think of them until...uh, oh. Make it a habit to plan ahead by looking ahead, before you get to...uh, oh.

Q I have difficulty controlling my board, why won't it turn where I want it to?

A First, look into the desired direction of travel, then turn your body and board. Stick to the program. Commit to your turn and use the strong muscles in your legs to stay over your board. Be patient, you will eventually turn around.

Q I catch a whole lot of speed as I point the board down the hill. Then my board keeps on spinning around, especially at the end of a turn. What can I do to keep this from happening?

A This is a progressive fall that takes place as you accelerate down the hill. A big part of this is fear taking control of your mind. To overcome this, just get your weight tipward over the board and concentrate on keeping it there, especially when you want the board to point down the hill. Remember, whichever end of the board has the most weight over it goes down the hill first.

Q *I start a turn and then the board takes off from underneath me. I end up railing my turns and spinning out. How can I stop doing this?*

A *This often starts when you sit way back on the board and really dig in (usually your toeside). Don't let this happen — keep true to your stance. This particular problem has a downward spiral effect. Once it starts, it gets more and more difficult to defeat. So keep your weight tipward and don't let this start to happen to you.*

Q *I'm sliding out of all of my turns. Every single turn is a struggle. I hate this sport! What is my problem?*

A *There's a couple of things you can do here. First, take a break. If you're that angry, snowboarding is only going to be a bad experience for you. Step back and start up again when you feel better. Second, check your stance. Are you riding over the board? Where are you bending? Use both your legs and bend at the ankles and knees or over at the waist? Remember, you can't ride the board if you aren't over it.*

Q *I'm having trouble keeping my trailing hand forward. Every time I start down a hill, both my hands fall behind me. Then it doesn't take long for me to fall down. Any suggestions?*

A *Grab your leading shoulder with your trailing hand; or with both hands, lock your fingers together and point your hands into the desired direction of travel.*

175

Q *My board is pointed straight across the hill and I still have little or no change in either speed or direction. What can I do to change this?*

A *You need to add some edge bite into your turn. Use your feet to get those edges started into the snow. Lean a little bit more into your turn to get the board (like a lever) up on its edge. It is difficult to get your board on edge if you do not get your weight inside the turn. This is more easily accomplished on the toeside edge, so try that way first.*

Q *Something is right in front of me, and I have got to stop NOW!!! What Is the best way to do this?*

A *Turn the board across the hill on the heelside edge. The heelside edge should give you more leverage than the toeside edge (unless you aren't wearing highbacks). Pressure the board to bite into the snow by sitting down. Get down in this position to maximize your ability to pressure the board.*

Q *I'm consistently falling onto the snow during my toeside turns. Why is this?*

A *There are two things that are common contributors to this problem. First, many people tend to look into their toeside turns so far that they end up looking down at the snow. Then they meet the snow shortly after. Try to look in the direction where you* want to go. Try looking over your shoulder into the next turn if you have to. Second, many people lean straight out over the snow into the turn. As the turn progresses, they decelerate. They do not have the same amount of force placed against them. The forces that have held them into the turn are now gone, and they fall over onto the snow. Think of using the muscles in your legs, and your torso to keep your upper body over the board, rather than over the snow during your toeside turns.

Q I'm having difficulty transferring from one edge to the other. I find myself getting "stuck" in a turn and I can't start my next one. All I can do is get to the side of the trail, fall down, turn over, and start again. What can I do to stop this from happening?

A Relax. Tension is the biggest obstacle for this kind of trouble. If you can convince yourself that you can do it, then you can. Focus on where you want to go. Most often the problem you speak of happens by the side of the trail. Getting the board to point down the hill is difficult if you are focused on the trees to the side of the trail. What if you can't seem to stop traveling in the direction of a turn once it is initiated? For the most part, this happens when you focus on an object across the hill, or you're just plain scared. Allow yourself to see where you want to go by looking down the hill. This can also help to release the grip of fear. If you're stuck in a long toeside turn, simply look over your shoulder and start your next turn. If you're stuck in a long heelside turn, look down the hill and you will start a new heelside turn. Go to a wide gentle slope and look down the hill into the desired direction of travel. Your body will follow your mind's lead, relax and let it happen.

9

INTERMEDIATE
TECHNIQUES

When you are comfortable with riding down easier trails, and hopefully a few blue trails, you have all the basic skills to ride a snowboard. Now you need to emphasize and improve upon those skills that you have already learned. You'll start with taking your skidded turns and turning them into carved ones. As the chapter progresses you will start to get into some tricks, jumps, wheelies, and spinning maneuvers. Take these ideas and play around with them, they will lead you to steeper trails, the sensation of airs, greater challenges and rewards.

IMPROVING TO THE NEXT LEVEL

TRANSFER DURING CROSS-OVER TURNS

You transfer between turns by rising and leaning back and forth from one edge to the other. You pressure the board by flexing and you transfer your weight by rising from one turn into the next. At this point your COG travels further away from the board meaning you are most unstable during this transfer between turns. This can be scary, especially on steeper terrain and many people have difficulty at this point. What you need to do is try and make transfers as smooth and quick as possible. Start by looking down the hill as far as you can and let your peripheral vision help you with the rest. You will find it easier to relax if you know where you're going and you'll be able to travel faster, too.

KERRI HANNON-MARSH

Skidded turns come before carved turns. These turns are accomplished by using both legs to steer the board around. By guiding the board around and across the fall line, you can control your progress down the hill. These turns change both your speed and direction gradually. Skidded turns use lower edge angles which only hold a small amount of force into the snow. They sound like you are scraping the snow. If more pressure is applied than the edge can hold, the board will lose its grip, or "wash out". When you are consistently making strong skidded turns, you are ready to try your hand at carved turns.

Skidded turn

Carved turn

179

CARVING

Carved turns are simply a more pro-nounced version of skidded turns and they use employ the same abilities and skills. Carved turns do not guide the board around as much with both feet, but use higher edge angles and the shape and flex pattern of the board to define the shape and speed of the turns. By placing the board high on its edge you can utilize its design features more effectively, and make the board do most of the work.

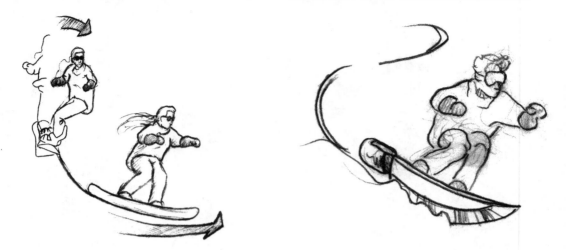

When your board is turned using very high edge angles, it can support more weight and turn more effectively. This makes washing out of a turn less likely. Carved turns sound like a knife cutting through the snow. The change in your direction is immediate — you really feel the board bend underneath and rebound you into the next turn.

To get the board up on its edge your knees must be close to the ground. The closer your knees are to the ground, the higher the edge angle of contact the board will have to the snow. Think of an "L". The tip of this "L" represents the knee. The perpendicular angle and the short bar of the "L" represent the ankle point and your feet on the board as it would appear looking at it from straight on.

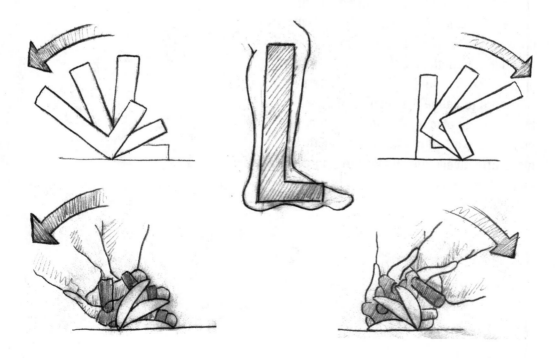

When you pressure the board you decamber it, building energy inside your ride. When you transfer into the next turn, you release this energy. Some people relate it to getting "kicked" from one turn into the next. This is the best time to change edges because you have minimal or no contact with the snow, there is little resistance to your movements. You can switch edges quickly with a small amount of effort. This may feel unnerving at first, but when you learn to control it, it's great. As you get better you can use this kick to loft yourself over an obstacle that is in your way.

Start down the hill and start a turn. Set your snowboard high on its edge and let it carve. Start out at medium speed with big round turns. Try not to pressure the board, just get it on edge and run its course. If you pick up too much speed, skid out your turn. Or even better, stick with the carved turn and continue the turn back up the hill if necessary.

Understand that you cannot carve turns on all types of terrain. You want to adapt the turns to the terrain. Controlled skidded turns can get you just about anywhere. It is nearly impossible to carve turns on steep icy moguls, death cookies, crust — all the really hairy stuff. I am not saying don't try to carve on such difficult conditions. I am saying try some skidding and some carving. Life is full of variety. Cutting up the corduroy is only part of the game.

THE FREAKER

A good way to increase your edge awareness and find the center of your board's edges is the falling leaf exercise. We're going to do this again. However, this time you are going to use sensory deprivation to accentuate your ability to "feel" what is happening through and under your body. When you close your eyes, make sure you have someone spotting you (an instructor or someone you trust). You want to make sure you don't run into trouble and trouble doesn't run into you.

Now that you're ready to try "flying blind", find a gentle green trail to work with, relax, and start down the hill on either side. I call this drill the "freaker" because it is very scary at first. You will feel like you are traveling a million miles an hour down the hill, but you open your eyes to find that you've only moved about 10 feet. This always makes me laugh, it makes me realize how dependent I am on visual connections to the environment. Take your time with this drill. Give yourself some time to adjust to this voluntary loss of the visual sense. Let go of your fear, stay relaxed, and feel the world around you. (No peeking! Stick with the program and feel the board and the snow beneath you.)

As you shift your weight back and forth you should start to feel the ends and the center of the sidecut. When you feel like you are traveling straight down the hill, you are over the center of the board's sidecut. Open your eyes and try to see the point over which you were centered. This may take some getting used to. If you start with the falling leaf drill, before too long you will be able to feel your body over the center of the board. The more you do this drill the more aware you will become of the slight shifts your body makes and what a significant difference they make. You will find that it really doesn't take much movement over the board to change your direction. Play around with this and experiment for yourself. When you are satisfied with your progress, switch to the other edge. When you feel like it, take a few turns down the hill using this newly acquired "feel for the board". Now go out and ride, think about how your body and board interact. When you turn, try to place your body directly over that same center of the board's edge that you have just felt beneath your feet.

If you are riding new equipment for the first time, this is an excellent way to acquaint yourself with the performance properties of your new ride. Feel the flex, the edges, and the sensitivity of the board to your movements.

The infinity symbol

Here are some ideas to help you better understand and apply your riding skills. Imagine an infinity symbol in the middle of your board. When you ride, your center of gravity will stay over the center of the board. However, during the turn itself, there is deviation from the perfect center. Your COG also shifts along the length of the board. At the start of the turn, your COG will be closer to the tip of the board to initiate the turn; as the turn progresses, your COG will shift down past the middle of the board through the turn then toward the tail to finish. This is represented by the rounded ends of the infinity symbol. As the next turn is initiated, the COG shifts both across the board and forward, toward the tip of the board. This is the diagonal or the "x" of the infinity symbol. These movements are subtle and not easily recognized at first. They have a profound effect on your riding, however, especially at higher speeds.

185

Shifting along the sides of this infinity is best done with your legs. Use your leg abductors and adductors to do the job. When you do this, your legs do most of the work. If you are having difficulty staying over the board, try pulling the board underneath you. Remember the scootch? Which is heavier...your board or your body? Your body is relatively huge and heavy compared to a snowboard. Many people try to move their body over the board when they ride. Move the lesser of the two masses, it should make your riding easier. This way the muscles of the torso can be devoted to stabilizing the body and your head as you ride.

If you are turning down the hill and you are too far tipward or tailward from the center of the board, you will often feel the board skip or "sketch" underneath you. This happens when you have so much weight on one end of the board that it cannot handle the forces being applied to it. Consequently, the board twists torsionally in an effort to release this energy. If you keep shifting toward that end of the board, chances are the board will wash out from underneath you. If you transfer your weight toward the opposite end of the board either by leaning or scootching the board, then you should be able to attain better control over your ride.

Different conditions require different body positions to achieve balance over the board. Harder conditions give you very little surface area with which to contact the snow. This requires a more tipward and precise balance over the board. As the turn ends, the body is very far tailward. Also, the harder the surface ridden, the higher the edge angle needed to hold the turn. Softer powder conditions call for a more tailward balance over the board. This is especially true starting out in the deep stuff where you have to keep the nose of the board from diving down into the snow. The softer the snow, the lower the edge angle necessary to hold your turn.

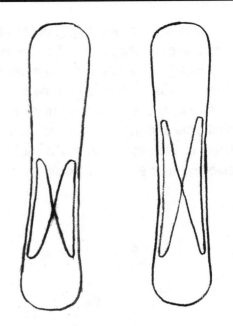

Now that you are getting faster, you will need to look ahead farther and anticipate more of the hill. Remember, the mind leads and the body follows. You must be sure that the mind stays ahead of the body's pace. Before, you focused on looking one or two turns down the hill. Now that you move faster, look at least four or five turns down the hill. This means that your head is constantly turning on top of your upper body to look down the hill. If you find yourself looking at the sides of the trail (especially at the end of your toeside turns), you're not doing it. Look all the way down the hill if you can.

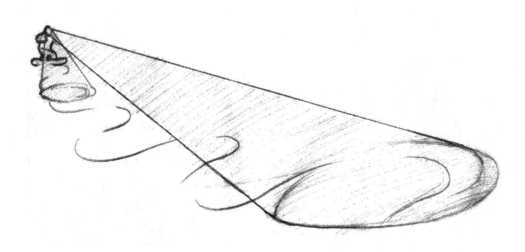

You want to direct your upper body into the turn first. You can use the body spring to guide the board as you travel down the hill. The upper body's direction will anticipate the board's direction down the hill. As technique improves, you will need less and less rotation to turn the board — rotational movements become more and more subtle. As you learn to use the board to work, your upper body rotation is almost negligible and other forces are much more prominent when turning. Learn to ride heavy on the edge pressure and angulation. At high speeds your turns need maximum stability, there should be almost no upper body rotation in these turns.

188

Skidded turns

Carved turns

THE LAYDOWN TURN

Getting used to riding in a position lower to the snow is not an easy thing for some people. Once again fear is usually the culprit. You can face that fear, literally. Getting used to being close to the snow starts with the laydown turn, known as the Bauercarve or Eurocarve, an extremely low leaning turn. This kind of turn is best performed on groomed or powdery conditions. This drill is simply initiating a leaning turn, and getting lower as the turn progresses. Go to your favorite gentle slope, pick up some speed, and start to make a turn. When you are ready, lean toward the snow. Don't be shy, get down there. If the conditions are nice enough, and your edges are sharp, you will hold the turn. As you progress into the turn, continue getting lower. Take your time with this, it may take a while to get used to. Keep practicing the turning, keep getting lower. You'll find that as you get lower on the turn, the edge angle of your board increases. This can make for a surprisingly sharp turn, one that will turn you across and sometimes even back up the hill.

You will also slow down as you get lower. If you do hit the ground, impact will be minimal. The funny thing is that when you're low to the ground and you fall, you obviously don't actually fall that far. In fact, you will probably slide for a bit, lose some speed, and then slip back into the turn. You may be surprised at how low you can get before the edge lets go of the snow. There's only one way to find your limits, and that's to push them. When you finally do fall/slide on the ground, get up and try turning into the other direction.

This leaning kind of turn is flashy and can give you quite a rush. On harder conditions and higher speeds, the turn will not hold. It's like a peacock, it looks beautiful, but it doesn't fly very well. Leaning over one side of the board will bring the board up on its edge. However, the more you lean away from being over the board, the less stable you become. This kind of a turn is a good way to learn to how to get low and carve. But, learning to angulate the upper body movements from the lower body movements leads to more effective and efficient riding.

ANGULATION

Angulation uses your body in a manner that keeps the board on edge and keeps you balanced over the board. Grip not slip. With good angulation you can add stability to the high edge angle of the laydown turn. Allowing your legs to project out toward the sides drives the hips and knees down toward the ground and into the turn which lets you raise your board up on its edge very easily and guide it through the turn.

192

For the subject of angulation, the upper body is defined from the hips up and the lower body from the hips down. Your body's COG is close to the bellybutton. With the laydown turn, the COG projects far out over the snow giving you a very narrow cone of balance. That is why the laydown carve is so unstable. The closer the COG is over the board, the more stable the body is going to be. Angulation brings the COG over the board. This greatly expands your cone of balance and ability to hold turns.

Another idea behind strong angulation is to let the hard structures of the body (your skeleton) hold the entire body inside of a turn. This is very efficient and much less strenuous when done effectively. Bones don't tire like muscles do. It takes much less energy to support yourself with the hard structures (bones) of your body than to support yourself with the soft structures (muscles) of your body. Strong angulation helps you to support yourself as efficiently as possible and still be able to act/react easily to the world around you. Generally speaking, the faster you go, the more you will want rely on your skeleton for support. In this way you can go faster, hold an edge better, and ride without tiring as easily as before.

The joints closest to the COG that have a large range of motion are the waist and the hips. Bending with your waist is accomplished with the lumbar vertebrae. Each one of these 7 joints has a small range of motion. This is because your waist is designed to protect your spinal column. This area is also the most muscularly complex part of your body. Bending with your waist is extremely energy intensive.

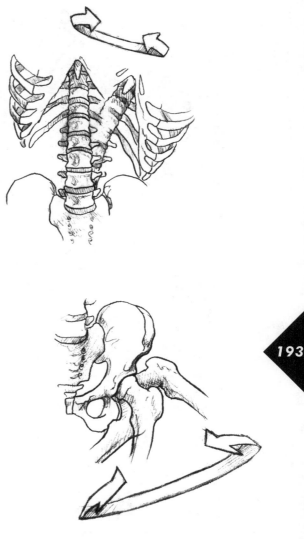

Your hip joints on the other hand are ball and socket joints designed to move easily in just about any direction. Your hips mark the junction between your upper and lower body. Bend with your hips. Strong angulation in a turn means bending at the hips as much as possible, and a little at the waist (esp. side to side) to raise the upper body upright and over your board. It involves keeping the body, from the hips up, as quiet as possible. The closer the COG is over the board, the more stable the whole body is going to be. This greatly expands the cone of balance and the ability to hold turns. You can take this even further with the spinal column. The spine intersects the shoulder line at a perpendicular visually making a "T" head on, from the shoulders to the hips. ideally this "T" stays upright over the board as you ride.

193

A low position close to the board keeps the cone of balance as wide as possible. The main thing that keeps us upright and rigid is fear. It is our natural reaction. Eventually you will gain the experience and the knowledge that riding lower is riding "safer". Then you will have the ability to ride with maximum stability and without fear.

With strong angulation, your legs project out toward the sides and do the work. This drives the hips and knees down toward the ground and into the turn. It allows you to raise your board up on its edge very easily, and guide it through the turn.

194

THREE PART SEPARATION: EXPANDED

We looked at three part separation earlier in the first day/novice chapter. Now we are going to expand and add angulation to this idea. The first part is your head, which is now always looking down the hill. Your mind is leading your body. The second part is the upper body. Imagine a line between the shoulders and parallel to the ground. The spine intersects perpendicular to this imaginary line forming a "T" from the shoulders through the spinal column to the hips. The upper body and head are drawn over the board through angulation and as quiet and stable as possible. Your body's motions are emanating from your center. The third part is your lower body. The hip joint is where the most angulation takes place. The knees will be driven to the ground more easily with the hips over the board. From this body position you want to drive your knees into the turn. Think of the upper leg as an arrow, the arrowhead is at the knees and the feathers by the hips. Point with this arrow into the turn. Now your lower body is doing almost all the work. Your knees are low to the ground driving into the turns. Your legs are constantly flexing to absorb the forces of the hill and keep you over the board. You can this idea even further by applying information from the advanced section (See Chapter 10).

PRACTICE DRILLS

Body awareness drills

Here's a body awareness drill for you to have some fun with. Run back and forth in the manner you shift across your board. Run back and forth if you use low binding angles; side to side if you face forward; diagonally if you ride an asymmetric. When you change your direction, notice how your body works. You should bend at the hips to keep upright, and the forces of the transition are absorbed by bending your legs. Your legs then shoot you off into the next direction just like they would on the snow.

Put your hands on your hips and keep the line between your hands parallel to the snow, just like you did with your shoulders. By doing this you limit your ability to balance and counter-balance using your arms. This means you will be forced to rely on your ability to angulate to stay over the board. Another way to try this is to ride with your hands behind your head or back.

195

Do not confuse a quiet upper body with a rigid, tense upper body. The real idea behind a "quiet" upper body is that most of your body mass is stable and balanced over your snowboard by many different muscle groups. All of these muscle groups work together to keep your head and upper body steady while the rest of your body is moving.

Bend with your hips as much as possible. You will probably need to bend at the waist anyway to keep your upper body upright. If you are bending with your hips and still having trouble getting your upper body upright, try this — pinch your ribs to your hips. This uses your waist to keep your upper body over the snowboard. But it will give you a stronger body position to work with compared to a leaning turn. Try to keep your arms relaxed, you will need to use them to extend your cone of balance. By keeping your arms over the sides of the board you will be able to balance yourself better and ride more efficiently and gracefully. Now when you ride you can use your entire body to obtain balance over the board rather than rely on flapping your arms about like a bird.

Using high binding angles, some riders use a tipward facing body position to help them angulate. Because their body is already facing far forward, it does not take them much energy to hold this position. Riding with low binding angles on the other hand requires a very different body position for angulation. This results from the basic fact that your knees bend only in one direction. Therefore heelside angulation is relatively easy with low binding angles. Just sit down with bent legs and make sure to drive your knees into the turn.

On toeside turns, the task is a little more challenging. You can try to project your hips toward the ground, but this leads to a turn where your back is highly arched. This draws your COG out over the snow instead of over the board. Resist the temptation to reach for the snow with your trailing hand. Try a more crouched/kneeling body position to drive your knees into the turn, close to the ground while keeping your body over your ride. By bending at the knees, you can raise your body over the board. This makes it much easier to raise your body upright and gives you a stable movement pattern without twisting your body position around. Arching the back to stay over the board is very difficult, and sometimes uncomfortable. Use your whole body to ride over your board.

You will find that there is a point where being low to the snow is too much of a good thing. A balance must be struck between good edging with body position over the board and centrifugal forces pulling you outside of the turn. If your weight is over the snow when your board loses its grip, you will fall down onto the snow. If you are over the board when this happens you have a good chance of bouncing right off the snow and back over the board again. Balancing on this tightrope is a big part of what snowboarding is all about. Practicing good angulation technique and riding with proper body position makes snowboarding a lot easier.

197

Randy Price

People with low binding angle setups tend to settle into their turns by bending or breaking at the waist. Here's a quick drill I call the hand settle drill which helps develop the use of proper body angles while riding with an upright stance.

During toeside turns press the palm of your leading hand down toward the snow at the same rate that your leading knee settles toward the toe edge. Your ankle and knee flex should be equal to your hip/waist flexion.

During heelside turns press the palm of your trailing hand toward your trailing foot. Take care not to let your trailing hand pass over the toeside edge. You don't want to twist around, you want to settle down into your turn. As with the toeside turn, the heelside hand should settle toward the ground as the ankles and knees flex.

DRY LAND DRILLS

198

Here's a couple of dry land drills you can practice. Sit down by a wall and put your upper body upright against the wall. Try doing this with your snowboard on, do this with both the toe and heelside turns. Close your eyes and feel how your body angulates from the hips up.

Standing in a doorway push yourself from side to side. Put your snowboard on if you want. Let your weight cross-over the board to the other side and get the board up onto the other edge. Start out with the arms far out to each side to allow you to take "small falls" from side to side. Make your falls as smooth and as relaxed as possible. As you become comfortable with this sensation let yourself go further over to each side — find a bigger doorway if necessary. When you have difficulty pushing yourself up and over your board, try pushing yourself straight across the snowboard.

You can also practice the motions of shifting back and forth along the board as you would in turns. Think about shifting your weight toward the tip of the board to initiate your turns. As the turn progresses, shift your weight toward the tail. At the end of the turn shift forward again and transfer your weight and edges into the new turn. Close your eyes and feel this happening. Feel the infinity symbol beneath you.

Another variation of this exercise is to stand on your board on and see how far you can get on edge without teetering over. Get as close to the edge of your cone of balance as possible and try to hold it.

JUMPING

Jumping is one of the most enjoyable parts of snowboarding. Start out by merely jumping up and down as you travel down a gentle slope. You want to learn how to leave the ground over the board. If you leave the ground and you are not over the board, you may not land with your body over the board and this kind of landing can be immediate, embarrassing, and painful. Everybody falls; we just want to do so as little as possible.

A solid piece of advice — start small. Get skilled at executing the smaller jumps to begin with. When you are either really comfortable or starting to get bored, then move on to bigger jumps. This progression will save you great deal of frustration and pain. Know that the more energy (speed and extension) you put into the jump, the higher/farther you will travel. The final point to remember is that smooth movements allow for smooth liftoffs with more predictable landings. Try to be as strong as possible without using jerky, unstable movements.

Scouting jumps

Always scout out your prospective takeoff and landing, making sure that it is safe for you and everyone else around. Be wary of kicker jumps that shoot you straight up into the air. Look for jumps with a smooth takeoff and a downsloping angle. Flat landings or upsloped landings can be very tough on your body, especially the knees.

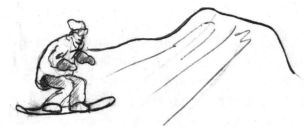

Jumping blind is just plain stupid. If you can't see where you're going to land, you can expect the excitement of the un- known. You can also expect the possibility of injury to others, smiling lawyers, seri- ous pain, high medical bills, and lots of time off the snow to reconsider how you might have prevented your "accident." Please, I beg you, scout out jumps before you take them. It is very difficult to adjust your in- flight path to avoid the stump that you didn't see under the lip you took.

200

BUILDING JUMPS

When you build a jump, take your time. Build it bigger than you want the final form to be. Your jump will compacted and worn down with use. The transition of the jump should be as smooth and predictable as possible. The trajectory should shoot you outwards more than upwards. Make sure to scout out the landing, preferably it should be on a smooth downsloping surface with nothing to get in your way.

JOHN CAMP

What is the most important thing to do right after takeoff? Stay really low to the board when you catch air — think compressed, not extended. Always remember to stay low to the board until you are ready to land.

201

There are actually two ways to jump off the snow. The first, using active air, is when you jump up into the air by using compression and powerful extension to loft yourself. Passive air is accomplished by the absorption of the legs into the upper body. This can be demonstrated by standing upright and bringing your legs up off the ground so quickly that you are momentarily "suspended" in the air and then you fall. This is a necessary skill for absorbing rough terrain, developing effective bump riding and implementing the "cross-under" turn (which we will later on).

PROTIP

STEVE ALTERS

Get yourself the proper equipment and learn how to ride before you start huckin' yourself around and go for tricks. Spot your jumps, and get up very early if you want to get first tracks. Larger jumps are similar to smaller ones except that you spend much more time in the air. When you spend lots of time in the air you want to be compact and stable. Bring your legs up underneath you. A simple grab is often the best way to go. Focus on your landing, extend your legs, and prepare to absorb the impact of the landing.

INFLIGHT TACTICS

Scooch your board underneath your body while in flight. Prepare for touchdown by angling your board with individual leg action, shifting parallel to your landing zone. If you get scared in the air, you may scarecrow or starfish. This is what happens when you freak and fully extend your arms and legs. Rolling down the windows or flapping like a bird is also a good indication that you are off balance as you flew through the air. This is not good. If anything, scarecrowing will make your airtime more difficult to control. If you feel fear taking over and your limbs start to extend, get a grip on your nerves and your board. Sometimes you can recover from situations like this. Then your friends will want to know how you pulled off a crazy move when it looked like you were going to bail.

LANDING JUMPS

Landing your jump is important and far less painful than the alternative — not landing your jumps. Your flight path will be determined by the manner in which you approach the jump as well as by your inflight movements. When you prepare to touch down, extend your legs. Try to land with both legs at the same time. If the snow is very soft or very deep, or if you are not sure of the landing itself...shift your weight tailward just to be safe. Upon contact, use your strong legs to absorb the shock. Get your board back under you and ride away. If you are going really fast, try to turn as soon as possible to break speed.

Find a small jump and try jumping. Relax on your approach, and think in terms of being smooth. Quirky movements on a jump can easily throw you off the board. As you get close to the lip of the jump, extend your legs. You want to have almost full extension as you hit the lip. You want to leave the jump with your body over the board so that you can land over the board. Look for your landing, absorb the impact with your legs, and ride away. If you are concerned with speed control after landing, make a big turn across the hill as soon as you recover control.

203

JANET ANTRAM

Going big — it's fun to fly. The more you fly, the more fun you have. Working your way up is definitely the safe way to go — start small and go big as you get better. When you are comfortable in the air, go bigger...when you are comfortable with that level, push yourself and go bigger again...and so on. When you're in the air, grabbing your board makes flying a lot easier and more stable. It also helps to have friends that go big. Ride with them, learn from them.

OLLIES & NOLLIES

An ollie is basically a wheelie that you jump off of like a springboard to gain extra "POW" when you jump. Ollies can help you to harness the power inside of the board. However, learning to ollie well can be difficult. I recommend starting to work on this skill off of your board altogether. An ollie can be accomplished in a single smooth movement. The best way to describe the motion is to call it a sideways hop. This hop is more of an upwards than a tipward movement. Imagine yourself riding your board. In one smooth motion you want to lift and drive your leading leg forward which loads up the tail of the board. Follow this by using the same motion with your trailing leg then try to leap as high as you can with this movement.

Ollies present a way in which to significantly increase takeoff height. Ollies also give you a greater amount of control over your flight path. Just jumping off of a hit, your trajectory is determined by your speed and the angle of the jump. By adding the ollie to your jump you give yourself a much greater degree of how high, and how far you go. The power of the ollie also drives the force of the jump from your center, instead of underneath your feet, adding to in-flight stability.

When ready to try an ollie on the board, do it on the flats and then on a gentle slope at slower speeds. Notice how the board decambers and recambers. By using the energy you have built up in the tail, you can use your ride as a springboard to shoot you forward and upward and gain even greater loft into the air. Try to get yourself completely off the flat ground. Try hitting a jump with this technique, and see how much higher you can get than by just jumping straight up.

A nollie is an ollie that springs off the nose of your board. You can practice this one by hopping sideways also. This time you want to start by lifting and driving your trailing leg tipward. This loads up the nose of your board. Follow with your leading leg to release the energy you have just built up. You will spring forward and upwards off the tip of your board.

GETTING FANCY: GRABS & TRICKS

Creativity is always a good way to go. There are a few things to think about though. First, the more speed you are carrying when you hit the jump, the more air-time you will have. Second, the more airtime, the more time to play. Third, the faster you go, the harder you fall, especially from up above. So give yourself the time and practice you need before dropping that 30+ foot 900 Tai Pan maneuver.

GRABS

Why grab the board? There are two reasons for doing grabs. The first reason is that with your board closer to your body in the air, you become more compact and stable in flight. The second (and most important) reason is that grabs can help you look really cool. Grabs are both functional and styley, so why not do them? There are many different ways to grab your board. Grab with one or two hands. Grab at the tip or the tail. Grab between or around your legs. I have yet to see someone do it with their teeth. But if you can imagine it, try it.

Some simple grabs to start with are: the Method, grab the heelside edge between the heels with your leading hand; the Indy, grab between the toes with your trailing hand; the Mute, grab between the toes with the leading hand; the Slob, similar to the mute but grab closer to the tip of the board; the Tailgrab, simply grab the tail of the board with your trailing hand and go to work — always in style.

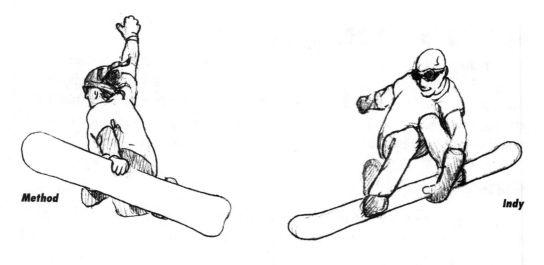

Method

Indy

Mute

Slob

Tailgrab

Some of the more difficult grabs are: the Croil, grab the toeside edge of the board near the tip with your trailing hand; Nuclear air, reaching to the other side of the tip; Walt air, grabbing the heelside edge by the tail with the leading hand (tougher than it sounds); Seatbelt, reaching to the toeside edge by the tail or to the tail (when you pull one of these it feels like you are putting on a seatbelt in your car).

Croil

Nuclear air

207

Walt air

Seatbelt

Grabs that go through the legs were all the rage in the day-glo late eighties/early nineties. These grabs are technically difficult to execute and have very silly names with secret meanings known only to their creators. The Tai-pan grab goes through the legs with the leading hand to the toeside edge. If the hand goes the other way through to the tailside edge it's called a Stalemasky. The Roast Beef grab uses the trailing hand through the legs to the heelside edge. Boning out your leading leg with this grab makes it a Chicken Salad (don't ask me why, because I don't know why). Through the legs to the toeside edge with the trailing hand makes Canadian Bacon.

Tai-pan

Stalemasky

Roast beef

Canadian bacon

BASIC TRICKS

Shifties and pokes are airborne scootches. These tricks are very easy to do. A poke is a quick scootch, and a shifty is held for as long as you want to hold it. These tricks and their variations make for easy flowing styled airs. I highly recommend them.

Wheelies (nose or tail) are accomplished by traveling straight down the hill and scootching away from the end of the board that you want to lift from the ground. Make this easy on yourself — find a gentle run to start. Keep on scootching until the desired end of the board starts to leave the ground. This will be tricky at first, but if you keep with it, you'll figure it out. I recommend figuring out tail wheelies first, then going for the more difficult nose wheelie. Riding your tips is a basic part of freestyle riding. When combined with riding sideways (for a blunt) or spinning, a great number of tricks can be accomplished.

SPINNING

Spinning is also a very basic part of freestyle riding that's easy to do. The toughest part is convincing yourself that you can do it. Start with ground spins, this is an excellent way to get an introduction to spinning while minimizing the risk of injury. There are two ways to spin — Frontside/Open and Backside/Blind. Frontside/Open spinning means that you can see into the direction you are spinning into when you start the spin. With a Backside/Blind spin, you cannot see where you are spinning when you start the rotation.

Start by looking in the direction that you want to spin and stay centered over the board. As you slide down the hill, the board should start to rotate. When the board points up or down the hill, that is the time to change from one edge to the next. Look over your shoulder and keep looking there until you want to stop spinning. Try spinning in the other direction. Try combining spins with wheelies to complete nose spins, tail spins, blunts, and other tricks. Be creative. That is what freestyle is all about.

GROUND SPINS

Ground spins are a great way to get used to the sensation of rotation. Spinning around on the ground or in the air uses the same body mechanics. If you want to prepare for spinning in the air, do lots of ground spins. There are a few things to remember when spinning. The first is the theory of the snake. Lead with your head and the rest of your body will follow. Remember the golden rule — try to stay on your uphill edge or with the board flat pointing either straight up or down the hill. This will help to make your landings easier. Do ground spins with compressed legs to make it easier for you to manipulate the board.

At freestyle/pipe contests people say "spin to win". If you want to spin around like a human gyroscope, here are a few ideas to help out on your roundabout journey. Just like anything else, start with the easy stuff (ground spins on gentle terrain) and then go for tougher tricks when you feel ready.

Spinning with your arms spread out adds to your swing weight and will make you spin slowly. When your body is compact your swing weight is lessened and you will spin much more quickly as a result. I like the image of a figure skater. When skaters spin they rotate slowly at the start of the spin and as their arms are pulled into their bodies, the rpm greatly increases. By bringing the arms into the body, total swing weight is greatly reduced. Try this out the next time you want to take a hit and add another 180 or two to your flight pattern.

211

Janet Antram

A good way to practice spinning is to stand and jump off the ground without your board on and spin 180, then 360, even 540. Try it with your board on, to really feel what you need to do. This will help you to know when to stop as well.

Another good way to get used to the sensation of spinning while reducing the risk of injury is to sit down in a swivel chair. Imagine yourself riding and mentally visualize yourself jumping. Then spin in the chair and feel what it's like to spin 180, 360, 540 and so on. Close your eyes and really feel what is happening. Then get out there and apply that feel to in-air rotation.

SPINNING JUMPS

Spinning jumps require you to generate two forces — one for the jump, another for the spin. As you forcefully extend your legs against the ground, you can create enough energy to leave the ground altogether. In order to spin, the twisting forces inside your body must be placed against the board's edge. Otherwise you will simply slide out of your spinning movements. Generally speaking, blind spins are easier to launch from the toeside edge, open spins from the heelside edge. This has to do with the forces already built up in your board and body from the turn. Toeside spins are easier to create with the muscles of the legs doing the work instead of the leverage of your highbacks for heelside turns. That is not to say that that you can't spin blind from your heelside edge, it's just that different jumps require different jumping setups and body movements. You'll figure more of this out as you get on the snow and play.

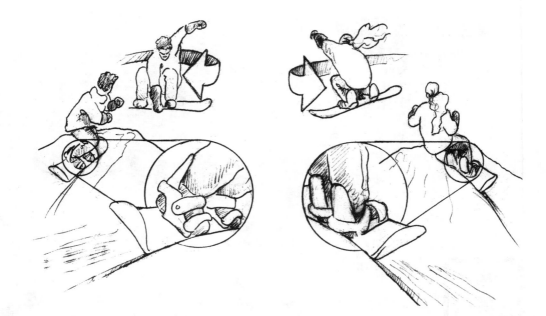

CORKSCREW SPINS

Corkscrew spins are spins that operate on more than one axis, and make it appear that the person is spinning through the air sideways. Sometimes people "accidentally" spin like this. If you want to experiment and push your spinning to insane convolutions, you can start learning to do this by taking a hit spinning blind and tucking your head toward your trailing foot. This will add another dimension to your spinning pleasure.

ROB CANDELARIA

If you know you are going to roll in the air, stall the rotation as long as possible before you actually spin around. This way you can spot your landing rather than end up flying blind before impact.

CHALLENGING YOURSELF

Here are a couple of basic ideas to help improve your overall riding. Think of the forces you create with your muscles. Rate the forces on a scale of one to five, five being the maximum muscular effort, and one being the minimum. Take a run at five, then take a run at four, and so on until you take a run at one (your muscles barely resisting the forces placed against it). You will notice a couple of things happening as you progress with each run. First, each consecutive run will get faster. Second, each consecutive run will tire you less than the previous run. The reasons are simple. You are not fighting the board on the hill. You are flowing and accepting the hill as you travel. With each run you relax more.

213

RIDING FASTER

Find someone who is faster than you are. Follow them and keep your eyes on them at all times. Ride with skiers if you have to. Look all the way down the hill and focus on an object in the distance. Keep your eyes on that object, using your peripheral vision to see everything else around you. Another way to work on your focus is by having people (preferably friends) throw things at you (preferably soft things) as you travel down the hill.

SPEED & STEEPER TERRAIN

High speeds can sometimes be a disguise for weak technique. Once in a while you will see a rider start out on a steep slope and do fine for about three turns, then lose it. By the end of the run they are rocketing down the hill at mach speeds, unable to control themselves. If you see someone like this, stay away from them, they can be potentially dangerous. If you feel like this riding steeper terrain, go back to easier terrain and work on traveling at a consistent speed over variable terrain. Steeper slopes require more board and edge control; flatter slopes require less control over the board to maintain consistent speed. A good snowboarder can control speed by turning (carved or skidded) all the way down the mountain.

214

REFINING TECHNIQUE FOR TOUGHER CONDITIONS

On steeper terrain you will have to exaggerate your turning technique. When you turn the board you will have to point it further across the hill than you normally would. Your edge angle will have to be very high. You will also have to pressure the board more to effectively control speed. Don't let yourself be intimidated by the terrain. If anything, get psyched. Being aggressive and confident is extremely important when riding steeper terrain. If you find yourself absolutely scared by the terrain in front of you, find another trail to ride on. Save the scary one for later.

Riding can be difficult when weather conditions offer low visibility or the light is flat. You now have the option — you can either pack it in for the day, or use the crazy weather to your advantage. Conditions like these are an opportunity to work on your ability to feel the terrain beneath you as you ride. Accept ridges, bumps, or whatever you encounter. Just ride over it. Try to find some visible land reference to help you navigate down the hill. Ride by the side of the trail or even in the trees with your friends. Bumps are usually visible in light like this, so go ride them.

Riding blind can be dangerous. especially if you are not in a familiar environment. If you become unsure of what to do, stop and think, then make your decision.

Night riding requires that you prepare for the cold with warm clothing, goggles (a clear lens helps in low light situations), and the ability to adjust to a foreign environment. Snow conditions are usually a little bit harder, but the slopes are also a lot less crowded than in the daytime. Riding at night is a great way to increase your sensitivity to the snow underneath you as you ride.

RIDING FAKIE

Riding the other way round is called fakie or switchstance. I really don't think there is a difference; you're just learning to ride backward. So for now, I'll refer to riding backward as fakie. Riding fakie opens up a lot of doors for riding creatively. When you ride fakie, the leading side of your body becomes the trailing side, and vice versa. Your weight will shift from toward the tip to toward the tail of the board. Riding fakie is very much like riding in your usual way. All the principles are the same, you just direct them toward the other end of the board. Learning how to ride fakie will take you back to your first days on the board. Just like before, stick with it and it will get easier. Before you know it, you will start to enjoy it, too. You'll have twice as many ways to ride, twice as many options, twice as many tricks, twice as much fun.

The closer your feet are to 0 degrees or ducked out across the board, the easier it will be to switch your body around into the new direction. Some people even ride in a duck stance. This kind of stance is specifically designed for bi-directional travel and works well at lower speeds and when switching/spinning around. At higher speeds, however, it can put a great deal of stress on the insides of your knees. If you ride with a stance like this and feel pain when riding, change your stance to one that is comfortable.

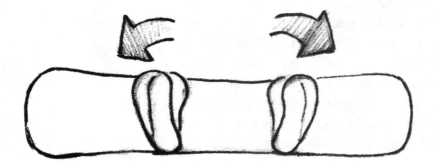

216

Yes, you can ride fakie with 45-degree-plus binding angles on your snowboard, but you can also expect to be traveling down the hill butt first and blind at times. This is not recommended. If you cannot see where you are going you might hit something or someone. Another thing to remember is that alpine or race boards have no kick on the tail. If you dig the corner of the board into the snow you may be in for a jolting experience. This can be particularly dangerous for your knees if you are wearing hard boots.

Riding fakie with high binding angles can be very difficult. It can lead to a "butt-first" stance. Most boards that accommodate high angles do not have much of a tail on them either. But if you do want to ride fakie on an alpine/race board, it can be done. Just expect to ride with a large blind spot. If your angles are high enough, you may have to look from one shoulder to the other between turns. If this is the case you will have a different blind spot for toeside and heelside turns. Ride with this in mind. High angles on snowboards are designed to accommodate travel in one direction only. Riding fakie in this manner is going to be difficult.

217

Here are some ideas that can help you ride fakie. Find a gentle trail and try the falling leaf drill. When the board is weighted over the tail and starts to point down the hill, go with it. Put all your weight on the tail, look in the new direction of travel, and try to become comfortable moving the other way down the hill. Try a toeside turn fakie. When the turn points the board across the hill, shift your weight toward the tip of the board. Now you should be pointing the tip down the hill again. Next time try a heelside turn fakie. You can also try ground spins to fakie or put a toeside and a heelside turn together. Keep on trying, keep on pushing. The more you do it, the better it gets.

You can also work with ground spins. Spinning to fakie is another easy way to transfer your direction of travel. Spinning is easiest when your weight is over the center of the board. When the tail of the board points down the hill, shift your weight over the tail. Look into the new direction and ride away fakie.

A 180 jump is the quickest and most efficient transition you can make. Remember the discus thrower. Move from your center, but keep your mind ahead of the board. Keep looking into your spin until you spot your landing. The toughest part is convincing yourself that you can do this. Practice spinning on the flats and gentle slopes first. Learn how to land with a tiny bit of uphill edge. That way, if you don't make it all the way around, you will know how to spin out the last part of the 180.

When you're ready, try riding and do an open 180 (remember the discus thrower?) at low speed. Generally speaking, open spins are easier to execute than blind ones. Now that you have gotten the board around, you should be riding fakie. Spin back to your regular riding stance or play around riding fakie. You have the freedom to do whatever you want — it's all up to you.

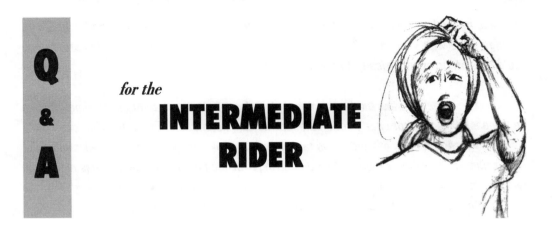

Q & A

for the INTERMEDIATE RIDER

Q I find myself starting out fine early in the day. Then I gradually start to ride a little worse as the day wears on. Before too long I am riding awfully bad. What is happening to me?

A It sounds like you are trying too hard to make things work. You are putting so much effort into your turns that you are becoming more tense as the day progresses and that excess of effort eventually makes it for you to "unflex" your muscles during turns. Each turn becomes more difficult than the last, so consequently, even greater effort is put into the next turn. Before long your body is one big spastic knot and it's difficult for a spastic knot to ride a snowboard. Relax, and breathe rhythmically. Try to accentuate your exhalation as you pressure the board.

Q I feel like I am falling from one turn to the next all the way down the hill. It's lots of fun, but when I go over a bump I sometimes get tossed off the board. What can I do to establish more stable transitions in my turns?

A It sounds like you are standing almost straight up as you go from one turn to the next. If you do this, you are narrowing your cone of balance. This may be why you feel unstable between turns. Try absorbing some of the pressures that are felt when you finish your turn. By "sucking up" your board with your legs at the end of a turn, you can remain closer to the board during your transfer. Your board will also be easier to guide with flexed legs. Look into the cross-over turn (See Chapter 8).

Q I ride with low binding angles. When I'm riding my toeside turns feel fine, but I find myself with all my weight on my trailing leg at the end of my heelside turns. I also feel like I'm wound up. Sometimes the tip of the board leaves the ground and I just can't hold these heelside turns.

A Ride bending both of your legs. If you find yourself riding with a straight leg all the time...try to ride in a more aggressive centered stance by turning just your head into the direction of travel. If you are doing that...get lower by bending more with both legs. See if riding in a more sideways stance and sitting down into heelside turns makes a difference. If your leading leg is straight, bend it at the ankles, knees, and hips. Think of lifting the board up on edge more with your toes. If you ride an asym, try a symmetrically shaped board — you could be shifting symmetrically on top of an asym design.

Q I ride with low binding angles and my leading leg is straight all the time. It's fine on the easier slopes, but once I get on steeper terrain, I can't hold my turns. What can I do?

A Adopt more of a sideways facing stance. Look over your shoulder, twist with your neck rather than your whole body. Try transferring over the board by leaning across more than twisting into the heelside turns. If you are riding an asym board, try "sitting back" into the heelside turns. You should be bending your legs a lot more when you ride.

Q I keep on falling over onto the snow when I try to make a toeside turn. What's going on here?

A If you feel like you always want to touch the snow with your trailing hand, don't. This will extend you further over the snow, narrowing your cone of balance as you ride. Keep the line between your shoulders in line with the snow beneath you. Bend your ankles and knees to keep your upper body upright. If you ride with low binding angles, think about crouching down into your turns. If you ride with high binding angles, pinch your hips and ribs together to keep the upper body over the board instead of over the snow. And, as always, drive your knees into your turns.

Q When I place pressure on my board, I end up fully extending my legs. When I do this my board keeps on blowing out from underneath me. What can I do?

A Your legs may be too straight to begin with. You may be bent over at the waist instead of...ankles, knees and hips. Because your knees bend in only one direction, think of "sitting down" on the snow during heelside turns (especially if you ride with low binding angles). Don't be afraid, get your butt down there. If you feel your leading leg straightening out, ride sideways and look over your shoulder. This will keep you in a more natural riding stance. If you fully straighten out your legs when you ride, you can actually push the board out from underneath you.

Think of pressuring and guiding your board with the lower body. Try to keep your lower body flexing at all times and driving into turns with the knees. Use your legs to work the board. This will help you to stay over the board and in control. Lastly, ride with your torso upright and your shoulders parallel to the snow.

Q The board washes out and spins at the end of my heelside turn? Why?

A You may be rotating too long into your turns. Rotating into turns works great, but if you find your having trouble looking over your shoulder at the end of the turn, it might be too much. Try looking back down the hill as the board starts to cross the fall line. This will help you return to your ready position. From here it should be easier to balance yourself over the board.

Q I'm riding with my shoulders parallel to the ground, but I'm sliding out of my turns anyway, especially my toeside turns. Why?

A It sounds like you are trying to angulate but only getting the job half done. You need to use your hips more. Go back to the image of the upperbody "T" from the head on. The descending line represents the spinal column and from what you are telling me, your riding does not have this. Instead it is more of a leaning turn with arms only parallel to the snow.

If your spine is really upright to the snow your hips will feel like they really are moving to keep your upperbody stable. Also, when you really get into your turns you will feel a locking sensation in your trailing hip joint. This sensation means that you are angulating and you are more upright than you were before.

Q One end of my board shakes and I wash out my turn. What can I do?

A Get lower and closer to your board by bending more at your ankles and knees. This will expand your cone of balance. If this doesn't work, your weight may be too far over one end of the board. When the board starts to sketch, shift your weight toward the other end of the board to place yourself over the carving portion of the board's edge. Look at your bindings — do they look like they are much closer to one end than the other? If this is the case, try shifting one or both bindings around on the board. Most boards are designed to have their bindings placed toward one end or the other. If you need to drill the board to do this, check with your shop first before poking it with a drill bit. Then ride and see if that alleviates your difficulty.

221

Q On normal or harder conditions I'm fine, but in soft snow the board keeps on blowing out from underneath me, and I end up falling over the tip of the board. What is the problem?

A Ride with a more tailward stance to keep the tip of your board over the snow. Softer, powdery conditions do not require the precision that harder snow requires. Relax, let the board run underneath you. Don't try to force the edges into the snow, they will cut too deep. Try to think of riding with the base, rather than the edges. They call it hero snow for a reason, you can get away with a lot that you wouldn't normally be able to on normal conditions. So don't force it, just let it happen.

Q Why do I have to angulate?

A You don't have to angulate. However, if you want to ride at higher speeds, angulation helps you to deal with the forces being placed against your body. Angulation uses the hard structures of your body to support yourself and consequently leverage your board when you ride. Trying to support yourself with your muscles when you ride at higher speeds will tire you out very quickly. Angulation raises your COG over the board. This widens your cone of control, making it easier for you to ride your board. Angulation allows for more powerful riding that uses less energy.

Q *Why does it feel like my weight has to be further back over the tail when I go faster?*

A *As you have gotten better, you have started to ride differently. You use your body and manipulate your snowboard much more dynamically than you did before, taking advantage of the forces you create. You also have much better edge control. You use your whole edge in the snow to turn effectively. You start your turns closer to the center and finish using the tail of your board to spring you from one turn into the next.*

The faster you travel, the more you gain momentum. This inertial energy keeps you moving in the direction you are currently traveling. Through experience you have learned to use the energy and the forces during the turn. Using your edges and these forces around you, you can hold yourself in the turn and carry yourself into the next turn. You don't need to transfer your edges when the board points straight down the hill. You can transfer your edges when your board points slightly or even all the way across the hill.

Q *When doing a spin, how do I know when to stop? What should I be looking at as I spin? My board, the side of the trail, or what?*

A *You should always be looking into your spin. When you are about to touch down, then focus on your landing.*

Q *Is it dangerous to jump a snowboard? What should I watch out for?*

A *It's dangerous to drive a car, walk down the street, or eat a burger from a fast food place. Anything you do can be dangerous. If you are concerned about safety, it comes down to one thing: use your head. Remember the ten-second rule. If you don't think you can do it, don't do it. When you're out on the hill, especially when you are catching air, be responsible and keep an eye open for any traffic.*

Q *Is it legal to get air at all ski areas? I saw some kids get their lift tickets taken away once for jumping.*

A *It's not legal at all resorts — liability is the big problem resorts face. Check with your local snowboard resort. Most do not tolerate inverted airs or jumping into out of bounds terrain. And some resorts are much more friendly toward snowboarders than others. In some cases it may come down to an individual with a bad case of "Authorititus Faux Giganticus". In this situation it is better (and much more fun) to humor the poor deluded soul. If the person is honestly nasty...take their name. Then call or write to the resort in question. The last thing resort management wants to do is keep you from spending your hard-earned cash at their resort because of surly employees.*

10

ADVANCED
TECHNIQUES

Here we'll focus on advanced skills, techniques and strategies for taking your riding to the limits of your imagination. It is assumed that by this time you are riding black trails with increasing frequency and you are looking for new and exciting challenges. It should now require less work to achieve successful turns. At this point you should have figured out that there is a place for skidded and carved turns in any snow condition, and by now you are using your technique and equipment to do most of the work of riding for you. Still, many of the following ideas and progressions are merely specialization and refinement of the information and techniques that you have read about earlier in this book.

THE INTERMEDIATE RUT

Here you will find less talk about specific techniques and more about tactics. You will also get insights into what different types of techniques apply to different types of terrain. Powder, bumps, trees, steeps, chutes and backcountry riding need specific considerations to be ridden safely and effectively.

If you feel like you are trapped inside of the dreaded "intermediate rut", I have a few suggestions. First take a lesson. Find the best instructor you can and tell that person exactly what you want to do and what you expect from them. Second, spend as many consecutive days riding as you can. Riding for a week straight will make a much better rider out of you than riding three or four consecutive weekends. Becoming an expert rider takes dedication and commitment. But you must master the skills yourself. Third, don't forget to play. You can refine your riding technique too much and you'll know that this has happened when you start referring to riding your snowboard as "work".

Advanced riding requires that you learn from your experiences and push your limits. Try that one trail that has been scaring you all season. Take a road trip and go to a different resort. Plan a trip to ride the backcountry. If you ride hard plates exclusively, try a soft binding setup. Head into the pipe. If you are concerned about looking like a beginner, relax. Even the most experienced pros were once floundering novices. Letting your ego prevent you from new experiences is an awful way to restrict yourself from having fun. Expand your horizons, don't fall into the "comfort zone". Push yourself to be a better rider. I have found myself on the quest for the perfect turn, the perfect run, a state of grace that I know I may never find. In the meantime, however, I'm going to try my hardest to find it. And looking for it will probably make my life much more enjoyable in the process.

HONING YOUR RIDING SKILLS

Riding a snowboard well requires the use of all your riding abilities. You need to know how use your body to manipulate the board. Advanced technique applies only what you need. Think of music. Great music is just noise with well placed silences. Great snowboarders know when and when not to use their body and board.

EFFICIENT ROTATION

Advanced technique relies on the upper body for stability while the lower body guides the board and does most of the work. This means there is little or no upper body rotation to turn the board around. Instead it is the primary responsibility of your lower body to guide and manipulate the board. By using high edge angles and pressure against the board, you can use it the way it was designed to be used and maintain maximum stability.

The faster you go, the less you want to rotate your body into and during your turns. The reason for this — the more you twist your body at speed the more unstable the upper body becomes. At higher speeds, things become more delicate. In effect, the same forces of the bodyspring that helped you to guide your board around at lower speeds are now amplified and working against you. This can lead to instability and forced movements. Twisting your body and board around at high speeds can throw you off balance, and maybe off the board altogether. This is not to say that the upper body does not use rotational forces at all. Rather, after a certain point it is speed, leverage, and the forces of the turn itself that will turn the board. Pressuring movements coupled with the leverage of angulation at speed will be more than enough to make your board arc.

226

CROSS-UNDER TURNS

All right, now that you are making beautiful turns down the hill by crossing over the board, it is time to step up even further by learning to use cross-under turns. This type of turn guides the board to cross-under the body as your COG travels down the hill. The body dictates the direction of the board. This is a much more forceful turn than the cross-over turn and requires a good sense of balance and a great deal of practice to execute.

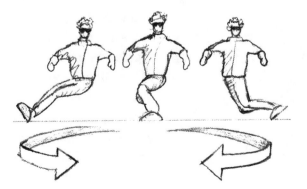

227

The cross-under has certain advantages over the cross-over technique. Cross-under turns are lower and more stable. Your COG doesn't need to rise as much from the snow — the closer and lower the COG, the greater the stability. Cross-under turns turn your board underneath and around your center. This is accomplished by pushing your legs out to the side as soon as your edge engages the snow which in turn loads up energy inside the board. When this energy releases, you can use your legs to absorb it and the board will shoot you into the next turn. This way you can harness the board's energy and accelerate out of each turn. By using your legs to build and absorb the board's energy, your COG does not rise as far from the snow.

By pushing out to the sides rather than down against the board, you are creating a higher edge angle between the board and the snow. You can flex the board more effectively by utilizing both the forces being applied against you and your own muscular forces. This is not to say that cross-under turns are the only kind of turns that you should make. Most advanced riders use a combination of cross-over and cross-under turns to accommodate different conditions on the snow.

High speed traveling requires you to widen your cone of balance for bodily stability and control. This means you will have to ride lower and closer to the board at all times. Try to keep your eye level at a constant altitude over the snow. Your upper and lower body movements will be very different.

The upper body, from the hips up, should look like the "T" that we discussed in the last chapter. The cross on top represents the shoulders and the descending bar represents the spine. The primary function of the upper body is to provide for balance and maximum stability. By keeping the upper body as free of movement as possible, your body's energy goes directly into the board rather than in all directions at once. It is also easier to angulate effectively.

The lower body, from the hips down, is extremely active in guiding, angulating, and pressuring the board into the desired direction. You can ride much more efficiently and much more forcefully if you use your legs to make the board do the work. By adding a "reversed" powerful extension and compression movements to your technique, you will project the board out to the side to flex the board. The more you pressure the board, the more your board will react to the energy created. To control this energy, you will absorb it with your legs. The more work you can do with your legs, the less work your upperbody has to do to maintain stability over the board. As I've explained before, imagine your legs as the shocks and the engine of your snowboarding machine.

229

DAVE LEWIS

An extremely simple way to get your body over the board, improve balance and angulate effectively is to grab the edge of the board that is out of the snow during turns.

HIGH SPEED TURNS (DOWN-DOMINANT)

Going really fast on a snowboard requires you to be as stable as possible when riding. For this you will need to utilize down-dominant types of turns. Cross-under turns can get out of control when you're trying to turn as quickly as possible, and the last thing you want at 40+mph are the speed shakes.

A combination of slight angulation and fore/aft movements is necessary. You want to use smooth, gradual movements into and out of each turn to build rhythm and consistency. Concentrate on driving your knees tipward, scooching your board beneath you as each turn progresses in order to shift your weight from the knees up tailward. This really helps you to feel and use your infinity symbol with your turns. Try to sensitize yourself to the tip/tail dimension of your riding. This is more stable and energy efficient than trying to hoist your entire body back and forth over the board. Push and pull the board around using your legs. Feel your legs doing the work to help keep your upper body stable and over your board.

Essentially what you want is a slow and deliberate cross-over turn that also employs a cross-under flexion/extension pressuring movements. Even though you are using cross-over turns, you must still press hard against the board at the start of the turn to define and maintain your line because of the increased power of the forces that are upon you.

Learning to turn like this is a great addition to your inventory of riding skills. By getting the board do as much work as possible, you will ride more efficiently. Remember, lower is more stable. But if you want to go faster, quicker, bigger, better... and maintain maximum stability at near warp speeds, this type of turn will probably help you achieve desired results.

JUMP TURNS

Jump turns are made for extremely steep terrain where speed control is of great concern. This kind of turn allows you to spin your board around in the air from one edge to the next without (hopefully) gaining a great deal of speed. Prepare for your turn by looking in the direction you want to go. Compress your legs and turn the upper body into the new turn. When you jump, try to get the whole board to leave the ground at once. Try not to touch the ground until you have turned your board around as much as necessary. Catching part of your board in the snow can unbalance you and even make you fall. Absorb the landing with your legs and stick the turn. Then just continue down the hill. Practice this turn on not-so-steep terrain to get the feel of extreme extension and rotation.

231

THE WIGGLY

Learning to use a cross-under turn takes time and practice. I was first introduced to this technique by a snowboarder named Will Garrow. Although this progression is not exactly what he taught me, I have to credit him with many of the ideas I am about to present to you. He's a superb instructor and one of the fastest riders that I have had the pleasure of trying to keep up with.

To make the process of learning cross-under turns as easy as possible, find some gentle terrain and do the Wiggly. The Wiggly is a simple little drill designed to work on quick edge-to-edge transfer. It is not for the steeper slopes, just the not-so-killer bunny trails. First, point the board straight down the hill. Then bring the board up on edge so that you can just barely feel it catch the snow. As soon as you feel it, go to the other edge, back and forth (toe-heel, toe-heel, and so on) as quickly as you can. This is what you want your edge transfer to feel like. More leg movement and less upper body movement is what you're after here. Challenge yourself, try to change edges faster and faster each time.

Now do the wiggly but add a bit of a push as the board starts to catch its edge into the snow. Push your board out to either side. What you will find is that by doing this, you will flex the board and build energy inside. The board will release this energy and rebound. It will snap back like a diving board, which will shoot you accelerating into the opposite direction. Start out with little pushes and as you get better, push harder. This may be hard to get used to. Sometimes you build so much energy in the board during the cross-under turn that you kick yourself right off the snow.

Rather than standing up and crossing over into your new turns, retract your legs and the board up into your upper body when the board rebounds out of one turn and into another. You need to use extreme lower-body flexion and extension to maintain a low body position throughout the turn. By doing this you can harness the energy you build in the board and make it do the work for you. Imagine a glass ceiling that your head never rises above. This sounds strange and it feels even stranger at first, but it is a good image to represent the idea.

MARK FAWCETT

This is an idea that my coach Jerry Masterpool gave me. He said to think of trampolines at the sides of your turns as the board points down the hill. You want to pressure the board during the middle of the turns. The board will act like a tramp, bouncing you down and across the hill. This idea can help you to train at working the board as it enters the fall line.

When you use cross-under turns you alter the flexion and extension phases of the turn. With the cross-over you rise out of the end of one turn and sink into another. Then, during the turn, you sink down and add pressure to the board. With cross-under turns you flex your legs and the board toward your body as you finish the turn. From a low, stable body position you transfer onto the new edge. As soon as you set the edge, you want to quickly extend your legs out to the side. If you are low throughout the turn, you are able to apply pressure upon the board as soon as a turn is initiated. Your body will not rise or fall significantly as you extend your legs laterally. By pushing out rather than down against the board you are able to create higher edge angles between the board and the snow. This will also help you to flex the board more effectively using the forces you ride with and your muscular forces. With cross-over turns you flex your legs to create pressure inside the board. By using cross-under turns you can extend your legs and use those strong quadriceps instead. The more you pressure the board by pushing it out to the side, the more the board flexes and the shorter radius of the turn.

Whenever energy is built up inside the board it will want to release that energy and return to its previous shape. When you feel the board starting to pressure against you, this is the point where you would normally let your body rise and cross over the board into the next turn. Rather than standing up, try to suck your knees up into your chest. The board will now snap back or "recamber". Your body will not rise a lot at the end of the turn, and you will feel the energy in the board release. The board will turn itself around for you.

235

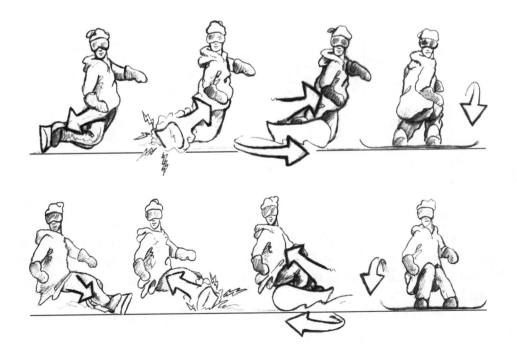

If you do not absorb the energy with your legs, the board will do one of two things. If the edges are not biting into the snow, it will skid out from underneath you; if your edges are digging into the snow, the board will lift you off the ground, see ya! When you feel the board starting to recamber, don't fight it. Retract your legs up toward your chest. This will feel strange but the board is working the way it's supposed to. You will find that your body remains low when you transfer to the next edge as well.

Here's the tricky part. As the board passes under you sideways, you want to commit to the next turn and transfer edges. You will have to transfer your upper body over the board. This may mean your upper body will actually be further down the hill than the board. Once the board is on the new edge, you need to raise it high on edge and extend your legs as soon as the transfer over the board takes place. There you go, you have just learned your cross-under turns.

Start by going back and forth edge to edge. Now, as soon as you transfer to the next edge, push the board away from you and out to the side. Because you are lower throughout the turn you are more stable at all times. It is much easier to apply pressure upon the board as soon as a turn is initiated.

PRACTICE DRILLS

There are many effective snowboarding drills that can work wonders for your riding. Some originate from the practice methods of snowboarding professionals; others are merely ideas that everyday riders have used along the road effort toward self-improvement. Ask an instructor or fellow rider if they know of any special on-the-snow exercises. Pick up one of the many snowboarding publications and apply what you read.

The pole drill is one such example of an effective drill designed to accentuate your feel for the board and the snow beneath you:

DAVE DOWD

The pole drill is one that I used a great deal while training with Rob Roy. It is a drill that emphasizes upper body stability and overall body angulation. Find a race gate, bamboo stick, or ski pole. Lay it across your shoulders behind your head and as you start down the hill try to keep the pole parallel to the ground. As you turn you will find that your body has to compress and form angles to keep the pole level. When you do this, you will create stronger angles with your body and pressure the edge more effectively.

237

If you do this correctly, you will feel the muscles between your ribs and hips getting pinched. This is a good indicator that your upper body is being raised over the board instead of over the snow. If the pole drags in the snow inside your turn, you need to angulate more. Try to keep the pole off the snow and make your movements as smooth and consistent as possible. This drill will make your body feel awkward at first, but it will allow you to feel the board working beneath you. I can work wonders for your riding.

Another way to make this drill work for you is to exaggerate the whole movement. Work on tuning your fore/aft balancing skills. See if you can touch the end of the pole to the edge that is out of the snow. You can also try holding the pole out in front of you, over the tip of the board. Then with your hands about a foot or two apart, try to keep the pole level to the ground.

ADVANCED TRICKS

SWITCHSTANCE

A switchstance trick is when you do a trick backward, just as you would do it riding forward. To do switchstance tricks you need to be comfortable riding fakie. Practice turning and hitting jumps fakie. The best way to become comfortable with switchstance is to just do it backward until it becomes natural. Before too long you won't even think about it. You'll just do anything you want to, both ways. Switchstance can make for some confusion as to the names of tricks. Is it a full open cab? Or is it a switchstance 360? I'll let you figure that one out for yourself.

SLIDES

Slides are fairly easy to do and surprisingly addictive. There are a few things you need to do when looking for a slide. Look for a smooth surface. Kinks, stems, knots and other strange surfaces can lead to a quick end to your perfect slide. Eliminate them or find another slide to work with. Look for lots of space around the slide. Falls happen, so try to find a slide that isn't surrounded by trees, rocks or other unmoving and unfeeling masses. If you are not comfortable with a certain slide, go somewhere else, or make your own in an area where you are comfortable. The idea is to ride on the slide, just as you would ride on the snow. Relax, and approach at a comfortable speed. As you start to ride the slide, try to stay low and centered. Let the board be as flat as possible. Metal edges and solid objects don't mix well. Riding forward, P-tex only is a good way to go. If you do travel sideways, try to use just a bit of uphill (upslide) edge. The golden rule still applies here, so try to stay off the downhill (downslide) edge if at all possible. Ride the slide.

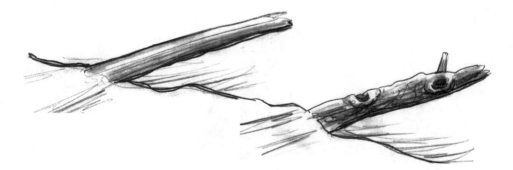

INVERTS

Inverts are very dangerous maneuvers. To do them you need to be very comfortable with spinning through the air. If you really want to do them, prepare yourself. Go to a supervised gym and learn how to do flips on a trampoline or a gym mat first. Do them without your board and work up to doing them with the board on your feet. You want to be comfortable and aware of where you are in flight and rotation. Landing on your head can have severe and sometimes permanent consequences. I enjoy pulling inverts myself, but only in certain places (resorts will kick you out for attempting such tricks) and over softer conditions.

TRAMPS

Trampolines are lots of fun, and a great way to try out tricks before you get onto the snow. There are a couple of things that you want to do before you take your ride onto one of these contraptions. First, get permission and supervision. Trampolines can be dangerous. Don't leave yourself to chance in this matter. Second, tape up your edges. A double layer of duct tape should do the trick. Those metal edges on your board are sharp. Uncovered they can easily cut through the skin of the tramp and leave you with a hefty bill.

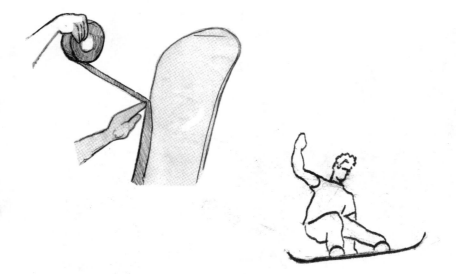

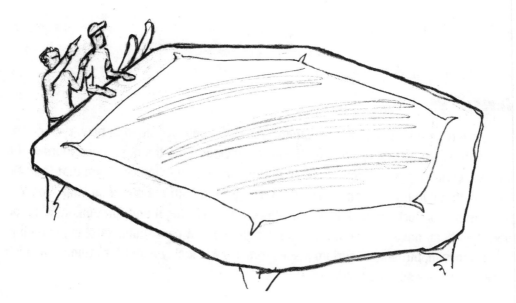

ADVANCED TERRAIN TACTICS

POWDER

Riding powder is one of the most wonderful sensations you can ever experience. Floating down the hill on a cloud of light snow cannot be put into words, it has to be experienced. Fortunately, riding powder is very easy to do. There are a few things that can help you out, though. Try to find an area that is not too deep to put on your bindings. Snow will get in your bindings and freeze into ice, so try not to let it in. Also be careful of steep open powder fields. I know it is so tempting, but understand that it is prime avalanche terrain. Take all possible precautions before you take the leap into the hands of mother nature. We're going to go into further depth about avalanche danger in a few pages.

Remember that in powder speed is your friend. Powder is a slow snow condition to ride in. With both feet strapped into your board, you are a slave to gravity. Look out for flats, sinks, run outs or other areas that you can get stuck in. If you have a choice between two safe paths, take the one that travels down the fall line to maintain your speed. Adding rhythm to your turns is important as it will keep you consistent and flowing. Think of a song that you really like, and set your body to that beat or even sing out loud. Hey, it works.

243

Turning in powder is easy to do. Relax, and let the board turn itself for you. Think of just floating down the hill, letting your board run underneath you. Before too long you will find yourself flowing with long arcing turns. If you push the board around too much, you can actually push the soft snow and the board out from underneath you. Angulation is not as necessary in powder as it is on the harder conditions. Soften your technique for the softer snow. Riding in powder means that you are riding on the whole base of the board, not just the edges. If you try to ride with edge heavy technique, you will get tossed over the tip on the board. It's fun to do that actually, but riding fresh powder and staying dry is even better.

MICHELLE TAGGART

When riding in powder, get a longer board and set your stance tailward to allow more nose length over the snow. Shifting your weight a bit toward the tail will help you to get the board floating over the snow. As you pick up speed, shift your weight closer toward the center. Riding deeper snow will require a slightly more aftward stance. If you find yourself riding with a straight leading leg all the time in powder, change your board's stance. To adjust your stance for powder riding, simply place your bindings closer to the tail.

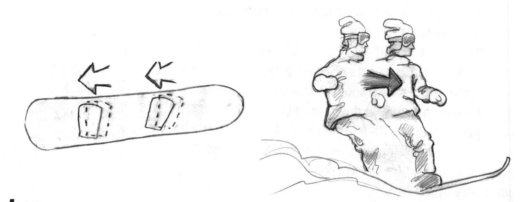

ICE

Despite what most people will tell you, ice is not very difficult to ride over. It's just a lot scarier. Ice is hard, so it will make your riding a bit more of a tightrope act. Your cone of control relies on the board's edge surface area which you use to work against the hill. With this in mind your movements need to be smooth. Slashing away at the hill with your board will not work. If you try to do this the hard surface of the mountain will simply reject your efforts and bounce you off the ground. Imagine your edges as knives and guide them. Strong technique and strong movements will prevail.

It takes a great deal of commitment and concentration to block out all negative influences (fear) that can distract you from riding ice. Ice has the tendency to freak people out. As you already know, fear tends to bring out the worst in anyone's riding technique. The most obvious signs are rigidity, leaning into the hill, and straightened legs. This is probably the worst thing you can do riding ice. This reaction will raise your COG and make your task even more difficult than before. If anything, you want to be in the opposite state of being. Relaxed, ready, smooth and over your board is definitely the way to go. When I get the speed freakies on ice, I do this myself. When I feel this happening, I relax, commit, and I'm (usually) back in the saddle again.

There are a few things that will help you ride over harder conditions. A tight boot/binding interface and sharp edges will make your task easier. Ice riding technique itself is very aggressive. You need to be further forward than usual to ride the ice. If you start to shift aftward over the board, you could be on your duff in no time. Stay aggressive and tipward over your board at the start of your turns and work your infinity symbol to be over the carving portion of your edge throughout and at the end of your turns. Turns on ice should be emphasized with strong pressuring movements to really stick your turns and control your speed. The other thing you will need to emphasize is your edge angle. It has to be high. Otherwise you will not be able to cut your edge into the hard surface. If you are skidding, angulate more, and work those edges.

If you feel like you are losing control when you are riding ice there are two effective ways to deal with the situation. The first is to try to relax and go with the momentum of the turn with a skidding turn. Some control over your ride is better than none. The second choice is to increase your edge angle and let your board bite into the ice.

Riding ice does have certain benefits, the first being that not many other people will ride it. When it gets icy on the hill, you can have the whole place to yourself. The other thing that ice can do for you is really fine tune your technique. After riding a full day on the hard stuff, all the softer conditions out there will be a cakewalk. Finally, ice is fast. If you can stick your turns on harder conditions at speed, the rush is amazing.

CRUD

If you are having difficulty in the "crud" or uneven snow conditions, relax. If you see a pile of snow in front of you that you want to get over, shift your weight tailward. This will keep you from being thrown over the tip of the board. As you contact the snow, use your legs and let the board plow through the mess. If you are moving fast enough, you should be able to let your momentum carry you over/through the choppy conditions. Down dominant turns work well in this snow condition. Still, there are some days that the crud is too deep, chunky and difficult to ride through. This kind of snow can also be tamed by using jump turns. This way you can get the board up out of the crud and in the air where it is much easier to maneuver. Think of popping out of each turn using leg extension.

DAVE LEWIS

To work your ability to absorb terrain, try to find a gentle ungroomed slope. Go straight down it and try to absorb everything that you encounter with your legs. Think of having a wire that your head runs along. Your legs and body act/react to everything that the board runs over, but your upper body and head stay as still as they possibly can.

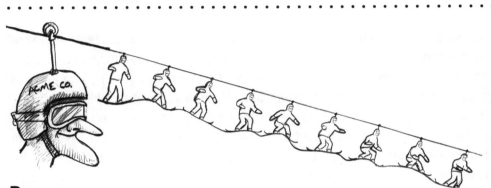

BUMPS

Bump riding is intimidating for many people. Why can't the trail be flat? Flat trails are easier to ride than bumpy ones. The good thing about this predicament is that the riding skills you use on the flats are the same skills you will use in the bumps. It is the terrain that you ride that is different. The "secret" is to keep your board on the terrain underneath you. To accommodate this bumpy terrain, you will need to specialize certain portions of your riding, leg movements in particular, to maintain control.

Start out with easier terrain and move on to something more difficult when you are ready to accept the challenge. A good way to get used to riding bumps/uneven terrain is to find a gentle slope with little bumps and ridges. Usually these terrain irregularities can be found along the side of trails — use them to get yourself accustomed to movements that will be needed on the larger bumps on the steeper trails.

Start out with a small solitary bump and traverse right over it. The idea is to use your legs to do the work and keep your upper body stable as it passes over the bump. Look for more little bumps and ridges on easier trails. Try riding over these obstacles keeping your upper body as free from movement as possible. These movements are the ones you'll need to use in the mogul fields — leading side first, trailing side following. Relax your legs as the board meets each bump. Let the bump push your board, feet and legs up and over the bump. As you ride over the bump, push your legs down back to your normal riding position — leading side first, trailing side following. You want to keep your entire board on the snow to maintain control.

If this does not work well enough for you, try pulling your leading, then your trailing foot and leg up as you encounter the bump. If you feel your upper legs and abs tighten up as you do this, you've got it. Push your leading, then your trailing foot and leg down over the other side of the bump, and return to your normal riding position.

Start by making quick turns on gentle, then steeper flat terrain. Make the quickest complete turns you can possibly try to make. Guide the board across the hill from one side to the next making even turns on both your toe and heelside edges. The best way to accomplish this is to look straight down the hill and use your lower body to turn the board. Turn so that your body travels down the hill in a straight line, with your legs pushing out to the sides to turn your board. Try to develop a solid rhythm in your turning. This is very important as you progress. When you are in the bumps, you want to ride with rhythm. Focus on your breathing to start your inner rhythm going. This will help to get your legs moving and keep them moving.

MIKE KILDEVALD

When riding the bumps, "Don't fight, flow." Look for a line through the bumps. I like to think of water flowing down the trail. Water (like a snowboarder) is a slave to gravity — it will take the path of least resistance to get where it wants to go. Flow like water in relation to the fall line making sure to keep your upper body and head traveling in the same direction. The fall line may dart back and forth a bit, but it should travel in a fairly direct path down the hill. Indentify this path and follow the most direct line that you are comfortable with. When you have found your line, go for it. Guide the tip of your board through along this line.

Bumps are difficult to ride but well worth the effort and an excellent way to hone your riding skills. If you feel like a fool in the moguls then make yourself better the old fashioned way — go out and work at it. If you are honestly interested in improving your bump riding, this book can help but you must still put in your time and take your lumps in the bumps.

One really good thing about being on a snowboard in bumps is that you don't have to worry about crossing your tips or catching a pole. If you are riding in stiff hard boots try loosening up or even unlatching (but not opening) your boots to allow for added flexibility in this difficult terrain.

Soon you will want to focus on improving your skidded cross-under turns. Bump riding rarely utilizes carved turns. It mostly uses skidded turns. Add lots of flexion and extension to these tight cross-under turns. This will project your board out from side to side and bump to bump. This will keep your upper body stable while traveling almost straight down the hill. Some really good bump riders rarely ever use their edges. They end up traveling down the hill mostly on the base of their board, accelerating from one turn to the next.

250

When you are ready, find some bumps on intermediate terrain first. Stop at the top of the trail, and take a good look down the trail. Think of the fall line. Can you see one forming between the bumps? If you dropped a large bowling ball down the hill, do you think it would travel erratically and without rhythm, or would it travel downward bouncing quickly with rhythm? Look for places to help you to turn. Can you see a continuous line between the bumps? Can you see one elsewhere on the trail? Mogul racers call this valley between the bumps "the zipper". This line is the most direct path down the hill. Riding in the troughs and around the sides of the bumps, your board can make even round turns. You will also have less variation in terrain height compared to riding over the tops of the bumps.

Once you feel like you can accept the bumps you have gone over, try traversing across the hill. As you go across the hill you will go across all the bumps on the hill. Absorb them as you did earlier on the easier trails. Go across the hill both ways and work legs, toe, and heelside. Before too long you will start to develop rhythm and feel how your body works riding over the bumps.

When you feel comfortable with these movements it's time to start using those bumps to turn. Start out by turning every third bump. This way you can ride the bumps and still easily maintain speed control. When you are comfortable with every three bumps, try every two bumps. Then make the big leap by turning every bump. This may be intermittent with two- or three-bump riding, but the important thing is that you are doing it. Now, just keep on doing it until you get better. At first that may seem to be quite the task, but if you keep at it will only get better.

Starting down your line, point the board down the hill, as you approach a bump, you want to extend your legs and guide the board across the hill. When you encounter a bump, you can feel yourself deflect off the bump into a new direction. Absorbing this energy with your legs into the new direction is the best means of stabilizing and controlling your speed. Learning to absorb the bumps with your legs diverts the energy from your center and allows you to travel easily. Try not to counter the bumps with your whole body, just your legs. You will find that your hips will flex and extend a lot more than normal to compensate for the crazy terrain. This works your lower body more, but will keep your center from being tossed around. This part of your mogul turn is the absorption phase, and is your speed control in the bumps.

In the ruts between the bumps, focus on extending your legs to keep your board in contact with the snow for maximum control. As you pass the mogul, push your board down the other side of the bump with your leading, then trailing leg/foot, guide the board into the other direction and extend your legs to make the next turn. Guide and absorb all the way down the hill. As you can imagine, this can be quite the workout.

Make your legs do as much of the work as possible. Upper/lower body separation is the key to consistent, controllable bump riding. If you feel like you are being tossed or thrown around as you travel over the bump, use your legs even more.

Keep your upper body as stable as possible. When you come in contact with a bump, you will have to accept and absorb the bump with your legs. Think of this motion as a controlled reaction, and think of your legs as shocks. Don't let yourself be bounced around like a pinball. As you pass over the bump, guide the board into the new turn and push it back down the hill and onto the snow.

Imagine there is a glass ceiling over the trail again. If you rise too high, you bump your head. Rather than rising with your whole body to transfer from one edge to the next, absorb with your legs to bring the board underneath your body, just like a cross-under turn. Extend your legs out to the side into the next turn. This will help you to quiet your upper body and stabilize your bump riding (or just about any other type of riding for that matter).

Try to keep your turns as consistent as possible. If you start to get lazy, you might catch too much speed. Concentrate on even toe and heelside turns. Guide your turns across the hill with your legs. As the terrain varies in "altitude" down the hill you will need to absorb the terrain and then extend your legs to keep your board in contact with the snow. You have great range of movement in your legs and lower body, use as much of it as possible. Doing this will also help to keep your upper body stable and quiet. This is important — you must give your head a steady platform from which to perceive the world. It is difficult to control your body from a chaotic perspective.

If you are having a great deal of difficulty in the bumps, look down the hill when you ride. If you are only looking at one or two bumps ahead of you, you are not anticipating the hill. Force yourself to look down the hill and the zipper line, instead of the bumps directly in front of you. This will help you to mentally anticipate and project down the hill. The mind leads...As before, if you cannot see both hands in your field of vision, this is a good indicator that your weight is tailward. Take your hands and drive them tipward into your sight. If you can see both hands, even just your fingertips, your weight is probably over the board.

253

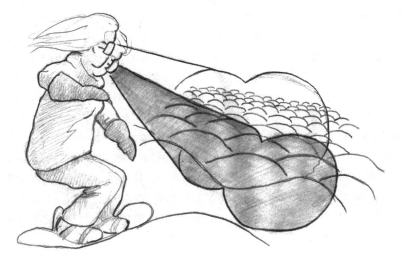

ALEX BIRCH

The trailing hand needs to be forward when you ride the bumps. If your hands starts to trail behind your body, chances are that your weight is shifting back toward the tail. Think of your trailing hand as a sign of your body's position over the board. If you can see your trailing hand, you are probably driving your weight forward as you go down the hill. If you cannot see your trailing hand, you are probably letting your weight slip further over the tail than it should be. This will quickly lead to loss of speed and directional control. So, if you cannot see that hand behind you, get it forward. Get in control.

If the terrain suddenly becomes too aggressive for your abilities, you can still get down the hill without having to point your board straight down the hill very often. Start out with a slower means of travel. Long traverses straight across bump fields are a great way to get used to the terrain. However traveling like this takes a great deal of time and energy. You will become very tired if you choose to ride like this all the time. Try turning on every third bump then every other bump (or however many bumps it takes) that you encounter. This manner of travel may be awkward, but it works. Now you can still ride the bumps and not have to concentrate on turning at every single mogul.

Before too long you will be turning every bump right down the zipper line. Moving like this teaches you to accept and use the bumps consistently without putting you into the "rush-and-catchup" snowboarding mode. Once you've got it with a single bump, look for two bumps, then three bumps in succession. Once you feel like you're ready, go for it. Feel your legs working to keep your upper body as quiet and as stable as possible. Ride 'em cowboy!

RANDY PRICE

When most people ride the bumps they align their shoulders with the flat top of the bump. When this happens the rider's weight tilts toward the tail of the board as they drop over the edge of the bump. To change this, align the shoulders and hips to the steep backside of the bump. This will give you a more "aggressive" stance in the bumps. If you ride in a sideways facing stance, try to keep your leading hand higher than your trailing hand. This will keep the line between your shoulders aligned to the backside of the bumps and your body will be in a more "aggressive" stance in the bumps. Stay relaxed and flexed. Aggressive is not just a stance, it's an attitude.

255

There is more than one way to ride the bumps. For instance, you may use such terrain to help turn your board about. You can try riding the tops of bumps and take advantage when neither the tip or tail of the board have direct contact with the ground. You can turn on the ridges in between bumps. Many times when you find yourself far over the tail of the board, you can even jump and scooch your board beneath your body, right where you want it before you land. You can really turn anywhere in the bumps.

You can also use the bumps to catch air. Bumps scare people and sometimes cause them to forget how to ride their snowboard properly. If you feel scared, relax, commit and let yourself take control of your descent in the bumps.

Learning to control yourself in the bumps takes time. Being out of control in the bumps is scary. I relate this feeling to becoming a rag doll. First, I feel like I will be tossed over the tip of the board. Then I feel like I am falling straight down toward the next bump. If you have trouble controlling your speed and direction in the moguls, just think of it as any other turn. Turn your board across the hill (mogul) and use the edges of your board in the snow.

Big jump technique is almost the same as smaller jump technique, you just have to be more refined with the jumping technique. Takeoff has to be perfectly balanced and smooth. In-flight form is best compressed for maximum stability. Your landing will need the full strength of the muscles in your legs to absorb the impact and keep yourself over the board. If you're trying to clear objects when you jump, make sure you have enough speed to clear the object(s). This is an imperative. If you don't clear the objects, you risk injury. If you honestly don't believe you can clear the object, don't do it. It's that simple. If your friends mock you out because you are "chicken", let them. Better a live chicken than a broken fool.

THE BACK COUNTRY

If you really want to know what the origins of snowboarding were...try hiking for your turns. Think of it as a trip back in time, back to the roots. This is how the snurfer/early snowboarders made their runs, before resorts realized they could make money selling lift tickets to snowboarders. For many people, battling the back country offers a reward in itself. Although you don't need to be a mountaineering guru to enjoy the it, you do need to be realistic about matching your own skills against the desired task. I recommend hiking small hills first, then conquering the big ones. In the back country, there is no one to tell you what to do or get in your way. The snow is usually untouched to set the stage for a pure riding experience. And if that's not enough, I'd be willing to bet that earning your turns will make you appreciate them all the more.

257

TRIP TIPS

If you are going on a serious trip, there are a couple of things you should know before you place yourself in nature's hands. If you really want to get into riding the back country I recommend that you educate yourself by reading books and taking courses specifically about these subjects. When you ride in this environment, go with people who know what they're doing (there is no substitute for experience). Get a transceiver with fresh batteries and learn how to use it. Learn about outdoor survival, first aid and rescue techniques. Learn the necessary skills you need to know, before the life or death trial by snow. Be a good scout and be prepared. Riding in the backcountry takes special precautions. Go with a guide, know your snow, and if there is a doubt of what you are going to do, don't do it.

A good precaution is to notify someone who's not going with you, where you'll be and what time you expect to return. This way if something goes wrong, hopefully you won't have to spend a freezing evening in an already bad situation.

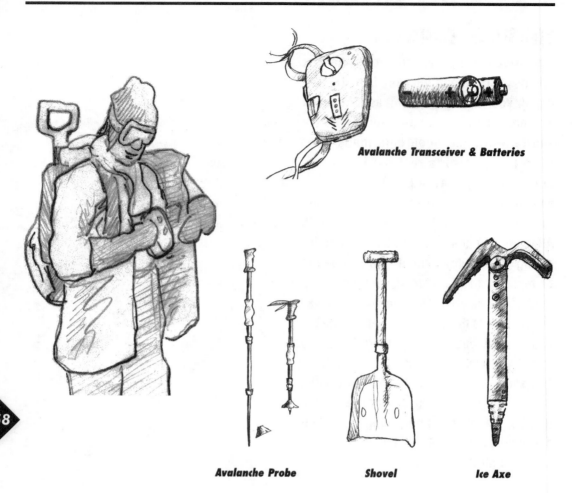

Avalanche Transceiver & Batteries

Avalanche Probe   **Shovel**   **Ice Axe**

258

The mandatory back-country safety equipment for everyone in the party includes an avalanche transceiver with fresh batteries placed inside your clothes next to your body, an avalanche probe, and a shovel. Learn to use them before you place yourself in nature's hands. Everyone in the group should have a shovel, to asses the stability of the snow. Shovels come in very handy for back-country jumps. Also it is hard for you to dig your buddies out if you don't have one.

If you're going to ride the super steep stuff (45 degree+ slope angles), learn how to make the best of skidded turns that turn your board across the hill quickly and then really sink your edges into the hill. Jump turns are good for this. Ride with self-arrest poles or an ice axe. Take a mountaineering safety class and learn to control yourself in case of a fall. If you feel a roll coming on, try to avoid it. You do not want to tumble uncontrollably down the hill. If you are facing down the hill, try to use your ax to dig into the snow. Pivot around it if you can. Then put your weight over it and dig it in. Be careful with your board in this situation. You can catch your edges and be thrown over the board, down the hill.

If you are planning to go out on a serious excursion, take mountaineering, first aid, rescue and survival courses. Learn how to dig and read a snowpit. Learn how to asses the possibility of avalanche danger with shear and pressure tests before you put yourself in avalanche country. Weather and temperature changes are the biggest contributors to avalanche risk. Check with your local forecasters and other organizations associated with the tracking of snow conditions or snow stability.

When you go on an excursion like this, bring a lot of food and water. All that hiking makes you very hungry and thirsty. If you have a lengthy hike out, be sure to leave early enough to get out before the sun goes down. The temperature drops drastically as the sun disappears and you'll find yourself freezing after sweating just minutes before.

Plan on packing everything that you take in, back out with you. You can usually do this with a small kitchen bag. If you have got to go, you've go to go, here are a few thing to keep in mind. Find a spot at least 500 feet from the nearest water source and cover up your deposit with some snow. Also toilet paper has an amazingly long life. Burn it or take it back with you. Better yet, use the snow around you, You'll appreciate the amenities of civilization all the more when you get home.

RIDING TREES

Riding trees is a great way to find fresh snow, days (in some cases even weeks) after a snowstorm. It does, however, require the rider to consider additional hazards. Many people are afraid to try this type of riding because of the potential dangers, namely avoiding one obstacle after another. But if you know you can make quick, controlled turns, chances are you are capable of riding this environment. You should also find your bump riding skills to be easily adapted into tree riding technique.

What special considerations should you concern yourself with before entering the trees? First you will want to remind yourself of one thing — hitting a tree hurts. If the tree is thicker than your forearm it can put you in the hospital. The really big ones don't even move when you smack them. Aside from the trees you must look out for other dangers such as stumps, limbs and other buried objects that you can't see under the snow. These obstacles are politely known as "snowsnakes."

During your descent you will need to focus on the line to be taken through the tree-laden environment. Look at the white snow spaces between the trees — DO NOT look at the brown and green of the trees. Your mind will lead your body in the direction it is looking. Since you will gravitate toward the object of your focus, make sure that focus is on the spaces in between the trees rather than the trees themselves.

In the event that you snowboard into unforeseeable danger (a cliff or cornice drop, an avalanche, etc.) be aware that it may be a tree that you find yourself hugging to prevent a tragedy. To ride in this type of environment, you must learn how to effectively avoid the trees or use them as a last resort should a threatening situation arise.

260

When riding in the trees, never ever under any circumstances ride alone. Always ride with friends. When you do so, be sure to keep in visual/audio contact with your partners. If you or someone you ride with gets hurt or stuck, a helping hand may save a life.

For general safety reasons you should always wear proper eye protection. We already know that it is important to block out the powerful UV rays reflected off the snow. But in the trees protective eyewear has a whole new meaning. It is this protection that can save your eyesight from the damage dealt by branches and pine needles.

261

RIDING CHUTES/CORNICES/CLIFFS

Riding the chutes can be a major rush to even the most experienced rider. Steep narrow passages are one of the ultimate tests of a rider's skills. Before you attempt such dangerous terrain you should be able to turn quickly anywhere at anytime on any condition. This may sound like a hefty prerequisite, but a fall in a steep rocky chute can be scary, painful and possibly fatal. Before you drop into your narrow path, make sure to check snow conditions and plan your route down as much as you can before you drop in.

Another extreme temptation are cornices. Cornices are large snow lips that hang over large drops onto steep terrain. These jumps can combine the best of takeoffs, stable flight lines and steep landings under the right conditions. But, cornices are often major avalanches waiting to happen.

With good snow conditions, wind-packed cornice lips are the best. These jumps shoot you straight out over the snow. Because you are not being kicked upward off the lip, you usually catch an extremely stable flight path. Landings are almost always steep and stable. There are a few things you need to check out before you attempt such a jump. What were the recent weather conditions like? Are avalanches predicted for this area? Check the stability of the cornice itself. Is the overhang very large or soft? The last thing you want to think about after a big drop and a high speed landing is "Avalanche?" Once you have established the necessary strength of the cornice, take a few steps back, check your flight path and surrender to the void.

In snowboarding videos you often you see 5-15 seconds of riders taking sick leaps over cliffs. What you don't see is the weather info studied even before the day is started, and the scouting of the prospective terrain and the snowpits dug out of the snow to check for stability, and the hours or more of effort placed into the shot before the attempt is made. Often in the movies you will see riders taking cornices and flying like they had wings. Again, what you don't see are the safety checks, time and effort put into these feats before the cameras start rolling.

Cliff jumps are similar in scale and steepness to cornices with one big exception — rocks. Most of the time the big wind lips that make up cornices are heavily covered with snow. Cliffs are not always that soft. Make sure you check your landing, before you leap over a cliff. There may be solid rock just inches under what looks like a baby smooth landing. Start out with the 5-foot. leaps first and then go for bigger game. You can test for trajectory by using a snowball toss. If the snowball lands in the snow, you should be able to clear the rocks; if it does not, you will want to choose another spot from which to jump. As always, use your mental movies to program yourself for the perfect jump. Relax, focus, commit, and if you honestly don't believe that you can clear the rocks...don't take the jump.

ANTICIPATING BACKCOUNTRY DANGERS

Learn to recognize avalanche danger areas: Steep bowls (30+ degree slope), chutes, downward paths through trees, steep narrow valleys, and large, soft overhanging cornices or snowdrifts. Look for signs of avalanche activity such as recent slides, stands of saplings next to wooded areas. Can you see trees with no uphill branches, or overturned trees with their tips pointing downslope?

If you're walking along and you see evidence of recent slides, gauge your surroundings. Does the snow you're walking on sound or feel hollow? Can you hear the "whoomph" sound as you walk along? Does the snow send out cracks in all directions, or do slabs of snow fall out from under feet? These are all indicators that an avalanche is about to occur. Backtrack and find another route.

Go out to enjoy, not to prove something, and go with someone who is experienced, preferably a local who is familiar with the terrain and who you trust. Even then, snow conditions can change quickly over 50-100 feet. As soon as you enter the back country you enter an uncontrolled environment. There is no safety net, if you mess up, or get hurt, you can die. Never underestimate mother nature, even when things seem to be their best. Never ever let your guard down.

When going into steep terrain areas (avalanche areas) be extremely cautious. If you don't know much about avalanches, don't chance it. Anybody who's ever been buried alive will tell you that it's the last place you will ever want to be. Stick to terrain you can trust. Big open powder fields are the most tempting, but also the most dangerous. Just know your snow, or go with someone who does.

If you are in an avalanche's path, usually the first thing you will hear is a "whoomph" sound of the snow compressing. This in turn leads to the slide, the feel of the snow moving underneath your feet. If you are in the path of an avalanche, do not try to outrun it. Ride to one side to get out of the avalanche's path. If you are on top of the avalanche, try to ride out of it. Don't just accept the fact that you've been caught by an avalanche. This is your own life in your own hands. Ride for your life. If you are caught in an avalanche try to hold onto a tree or another solid object. If you become swept away in the avalanche, try to stay over the surface of the snow. Swim, kick, pull, do whatever it takes to get on top of the snow. And if you can, make your way over to one side of the avalanche where the snow is not moving as quickly.

Snow settles once it stops travelling. It may not be possible to move once the snow stops moving. If you are buried, make a pocket of air around your mouth with your hands, so you can breathe. If the snow moves, dig yourself out. Orienting yourself upward in a situation like this may be difficult. Let gravity tell you which way is down. Spit and feel which way it goes. That is downward. Hopefully you will never have to experience or be with a party that experiences an avalanche accident. Learn all you can before you place yourself in mother nature's hands.

THE HALF-PIPE

At this point I am assuming that you can ride pretty well and that you may be looking for new challenges. This may naturally lead you to the half-pipe. Before you start you will want to know this: the pipe is not easy to ride. However, the rewards are worth the effort. Here are a couple of things that will help make your introduction to the pipe as easy as possible.

NECESSARY SKILLS

Jumping into the pipe before you can ride well is not a good idea. You will first want to be comfortable traveling both regular and fakie. Having confidence in your ability to pull 180's helps as well. Knowing how to jump smoothly will be a big aid with the transitions between the flats and the walls of the pipe. You should expect to fall. Leave your pride home for a while, maybe even for a couple of years. I felt like a beginner again when I first dropped into the pipe, sometimes I still do. With this in mind, try to pick a first day when the snow is not too hard. When you start out, try starting a bit further down the pipe. This should make your run a bit less trying. As you progress, go further up the pipe to take your runs.

RIDING TIPS

A good way to introduce yourself to the pipe is to ride from side to side facing up or down the pipe. Ride all the way down, both ways. This will get you used to the sensation of riding up and down the pipe walls on both edges. Next try riding down the pipe using 180's (open is easiest first) to face your direction of travel.

When you are ready and you start riding the pipe (and warming up in it as you get better) just take some relaxed runs in it first, then progress. When you feel like you can ride the pipe in control, then go for it.

As you approach the wall, set yourself up to ride straight up the transition and invert. This will feel weird at first, but it is what you need to do to ride the pipe well. It will help you to go bigger and project yourself straight up and out of the pipe. The goal is to drop straight back into the pipe rather than onto the flats or at the bottom of the pipe (ouch!). You must also control your speed. Projecting yourself down the pipe toward the base will point you further toward the fall line and therefore propel you faster. It's not that doing this is a bad thing, but you just might want to save this for a later time when your pipe riding skills have advanced and speed becomes necessary in your quest to be a pipe ruler. As you get better you will find yourself getting braver and pulling bigger, more technical tricks.

A great trick is an "old school" maneuver called the handplant, basically a handstand on the side of the wall of the halfpipe, quarterpipe or a natural hit with a nice transition. Approach the wall with moderate speed in a compressed body position. Pump the trainee and spot your hand plant(s). Let the momentum of the pump take your board above you, and place your hand(s) on the hit. If you do this just right you'll simply have to put your arm(s) out straight without having to do much work to support yourself. Grab your board and stall for style points (the judges are all watching now). Spot your landing and push off the wall with your hands to spin yourself rightside up, back on top of your board, and ride away. Try practicing some cartwheels on the flats without, then with your board on to get the feeling of momentum involved with this trick.

If you want more flexibility in your boot binding setup to twist and pull tricks on your board, you can. Keep your boots as tight as you normally would. Just loosen up your bindings if you want to roll your feet and still have strong boot support.

To be a responsible pipe rider, common sense and awareness of your fellow pipe riders is all you need. If you fall, or you know someone else is heading right toward you, get out of the way. Cutting up the sides of the wall to climb out destroys the half pipe you are riding in. If you do cut up the walls of the pipe, take a shovel to it later and repair the damage. Half pipe riding is a very individual thing. All of the riding skills and tricks you have learned can now be applied to the pipe. If you want to be come really good at riding the pipe you need to know yourself, start out with the easy stuff and practice, practice, practice.

JOHN CAMP

What is the most important thing to do just before landing in the pipe? Try to land as high on the wall as possible. Then stay low all the way into the flat at the bottom This will make it easier to set up for the next wall through the transition.

268

COMPETITIVE RIDING

Contests are an excellent way to improve your riding skills. Training and practice for competitions will certainly make you a better rider. If you are interested in the possibility of sponsorship, visibility through competition is a tough but proven route. A good way to get into competitions is to check out your local scene, shops, resorts and publications. Larger publications will also have regional contacts for contests and the organizations that put them together. There is a list of competitive organizations that run these events in the appendix of this book.

Q & A *for the* **ADVANCED RIDER**

Q The snow is hard and I keep losing it on my toe side turns. This is really starting to get to me. What's the problem?

A It sounds as though our COG may be too far out over the snow. Try using an increased edge angle. Angulate to stay inside your cone of balance and maintain control. Staying lower and over your board does gives you a larger cone of balance and more stable turns. Get the knees and hips down to the snow and get your upper body upright. Keep your shoulders parallel to the snow for maximum control on toe side turns.

On a general note, relax. You are doing yourself no good by getting angry. If this is a long-standing plateau for you, try a new perspective. Take a lesson with an instructor that you like. Have someone film you riding down the slope. This is not a showcase, so go to an area that you know will give you trouble and bring out your bad habits. Then break down your technique, and hit the snow with the knowledge of what you need to do.

Q I keep on blowing out of my heelside turns on harder conditions. Why?

A You may be completely straightening out your legs. You may be bent over too far at the waist. Bend with your ankles and drive your knees into the turn using your knees. You've got to angulate to stay inside your cone of balance and maintain control. Try to keep your upper body upright and your shoulders parallel to the snow. If you are riding with lower binding angles, try sitting down into your turns.

Q I'm trying to carve in the powder, and I get tossed every time I go for it. What's wrong here?

A You're missing the point of powder riding. You're trying way too hard. Ease into a less angulated leaning turn rather than a deep digging carve. Think of riding the base of your board rather than your edge. Let your weight shift tailward for softer snow conditions. If you find yourself leaning way back over the tail of your board just to stay afloat, you may need to set your stance tailward to make your riding easier.

Q *I can't get moving in the powder, even when I'm on steeper terrain. Help, I'm stuck in this hip deep snow. Why am I stuck?*

A *It sounds like your board needs wax. Even a once-over with a rub-on wax will make your board accelerate like a rocket.*

If you are riding in powder, look as far down the hill as you can. If you see a flat section or a rise in the terrain, bomb the hill to carry your speed, you can always turn after the flats to slow yourself down. If you get stuck, you may have to take off your board and walk your way to an area you can ride from.

Q *How do I get my weight over the board consistently in the bumps?*

A *If you are having trouble in the bumps, project your trailing hand forward into your field of vision (Alex's pointing hand). If you cannot see both of your hands, chances are your weight is starting to shift or is already too far tailward for you to be in control of your snowboard. Another big help is to use the strong muscles in your legs to pull your board behind you. Rather than pulling your body over the board, move the lesser and lighter of the two — pull your board under your body.*

Q *As I'm riding I see a patch of ice right in front of me. There is nothing of danger around me, but I'm afraid I'm going to fall when I hit the frozen ice. What do I do?*

A *Relax. Being rigid will not help your cause out in the least. Commit. Look past the patch of ice and focus upon where you want to go. I see people ride beautifully, and then they hear that grating sound beneath them. A look of fright takes over their face, they freeze up, and down they go. Don't let fear get the best of you on the ice. Skidded turns may sound ugly, but they work. One last thing, take a relatively straight line over the ice — the less you turn over the ice, the less trouble it will give you. Take a little bit of speed and turn after you get back onto the softer snow.*

Q *What can I do if the trail I'm on falls away to one side?*

A *If you are on uneven terrain with one side being higher than the other, you can even out your line by shifting your route toward the lower bumps. Try to ride higher on the lower bumps, ride lower on the higher bumps. This will help you to even out your turns, and make your travel downhill as fluid as possible.*

Q *I can't carve my turns in the bumps or on very steep terrain. I'm trying as hard as I can, but I can't always do it. What am I doing wrong?*

A *Relax, nobody can carve on all terrain at all times. You can try, but sometimes it is better to acknowledge that you are human. Try to use smooth skidded turns that you can control when the terrain does not allow you to carve.*

CARING FOR
YOUR RIDE

This is a short guide to tuning, maintaining, and caring for your board. Snowboard bases and edges are constructed almost identically to ski bases and edges. Eventually you will learn to tune your board for your own personal style of riding. For instance, racers keep their edges sharp along the whole contact length, only detuning (dulling) the board at the tip to prevent the edges from "hooking" into the snow. Spinny pipe/park riders will detune nearly all the edge except for maybe the portion just beneath the feet. If you are really interested in learning how to tune a snowboard like a professional, try picking up a ski tuning book, or ask your local ski /snowboard pro for advice. If they won't talk to you about this subject, find another shop and take your business there.

BOARD MAINTENANCE

TOOLS TO USE

To take cake of your board, you need the proper tools for the job. Most of the tools can be bought at a hardware store (designated with an 'H') which can keep your tuning kit costs to a minimum. The necessary tools are:

File

Edge tools: A long flat file ('H') for the bottom of the edges. An edge tool will sharpen the sides, and bevel the edge angles. Deburring stone or soft/diamond stone, should be used for fine tuning, polishing, and dulling an edge. Think of a rose with thorns. By detuning/deburring the edge you can remove the thorns from the edges. With fine sandpaper, 200 grit or finer, you can detune/de-sharpen portions of the edges.

Edge tool

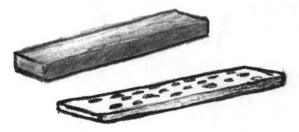

*Deburring stone /
Soft diamond stone*

Sandpaper

Base tools: Iron ('H') to melt your hot waxes. A biodegradable citrus cleaner ('H') will create a clean bind between the base and repairs/wax. P-tex candles to fill in the holes and scratches in the board's base. Waxes, paraffin, and other base coats are used to reduce drag between your board and the snow. There are many different types of wax that may be used to make a board go faster. Spray waxes last for a couple of runs down the hill. Rub waxes work for a day or two of riding. Hot waxes last the longest and work the best. These waxes are melted then left to soak into the P-tex. Unless you are racing and need the performance of a temperature specific wax, try an all-purpose wax for all but the warmest/coldest conditions. Plastic or metal scrapers ('H') will remove excess wax from your base. Nylon or brass brushes ('H') will clear the texture grooves in the base of your board after a layer of wax has been applied. Riller bars are also great for this purpose. Consider a Scotchbrite pad or cork ('H') for buffing the wax job.

Iron

P-tex candles

273

Wax / paraffin / base coat

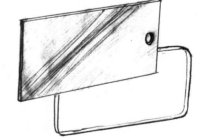

Plastic / metal scraper

Nylon / brass brushes

Scotchbrite pad / cork

SHARPENING EDGES

When you file, scrape, brush, or sharpen the edges of your board, use smooth, even pressured strokes in one direction, preferably from tip to tail. Filing in more than one direction can remove more edge than necessary. Working in a consistent manner like this will also help to ensure optimum performance from the board.

Sharpening edges is simple. First take your long base file and draw it down the board. As long as you use smooth even strokes and you don't sharpen in both directions, you'll do fine. Keep on doing this until you feel no resistance to your efforts. Then using your edge tool, do the same to the sides of the edges. When you feel no resistance, you can make the edges even sharper by using your deburring stone to add an exceptional edge to your ride. Your brass brush can then be used to clean out the steel fillings that the board has left in your files.

274

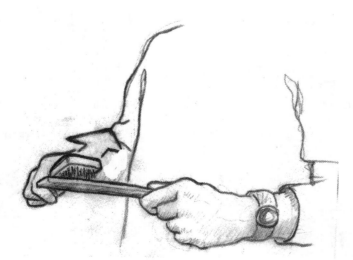

Use a 90 degree for an edge that will hold well on just about any surface. A side beveled edge can add extra bite to a racers edges. A base beveled edge does not provide as quick of a contacting edge. This is good for spinning and allows for a "forgiving" landing. Freestyle/pipe riders often use a beveled edge at the tip and tail. Make it flatter under the feet (closer to 90 degree) for trannie control. There are other variations on edge angles, usually race style specific. If this is what you're after, I recommend looking into a ski tuning book for racing.

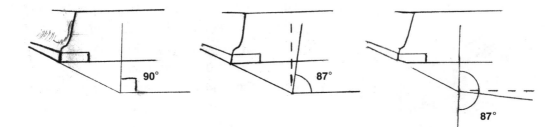

You can check for sharpness with your fingernail. If you draw your fingernail down on the edge and you peel shavings from your nail, the edge is sharp. Be careful, sharp edges can cut through the rest of your finger as well.

DETUNING EDGES

Detuning your edge is easy to do. Simply take your detuning medium (high grit sandpaper or deburring stone) to customize the tune job to your riding style. Run them at an angle to the portion of the edges that you want to detune. You only need to pass a few times over the edge to achieve the desired effect. This should be done gently and carefully, you want to detune your edges, not remove them from the board.

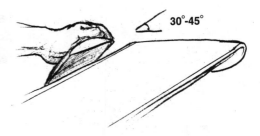

DO-IT-YOURSELF REPAIRS

If your base has been damaged, start the base repair using a base cleaner. It is best to use a biodegradable citrus form of cleaner with a paper towel/clean rag to scrub out the gouge.

If you do your own repairs, the important thing to remember is that a patch job should be clean. Carbon forms on/in P-tex when it burns and contacts oxygen. Examine your P-tex candle before you light it. If you see any black matter (carbon) on the P-tex candle, cut it off. A dirty patch job polluted with carbon in the base will cause the board to react slower over the snow and make the patch job less likely to stay in the board. This is not to mention the fact that the repair will be quite unsightly. When the candle is burning keep it as close to the base as possible to minimize the chance for an unwanted chemical reaction. P-tex will burn more uniformly and more cleanly if it is close to the board. Keep in mind that the flame from the stick should be blue. If it is yellow or again if held far from the board, black carbon flakes will form and drop into the patch. Filling the damage works best with the candle less than an inch from the base. You can literally flow the P-tex from the tip of the candle into the repair. Keeping a scraper under the lit candle as it burns is a good way to cut down on the resulting mess.

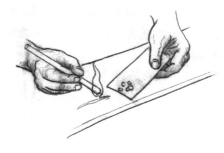

Once the damage is filled with new P-tex, let it cool and shave the base flat with a scraper. If base damage to the board goes all the way to the core, I recommend taking your ride to your favorite shop for repair.

To understand how wax affects drag between board and snow, you first need to understand the properties of the snow you ride over. Friction between two surfaces causes drag. Drag reduces speed. And since wax and water do not mix, waxing your board essentially serves to repel the frozen water from the board, thus reducing drag.

If your base looks and feels like a dry chalkboard, you need to wax the board. If you put the board on the ground then pick it up and snow sticks to the base, you need wax. If you just put wax on your board and it still sticks, you may have applied too soft of a wax or simply applied too much wax without scraping off enough excess. Scrape off the excess wax or warm up the base and apply harder, cold-temperature wax to the base. It is hard to travel down the hill when your board sticks to the spot where you're standing. Keep in mind that wax also provides a protective layer against the snow and other objects you ride over.

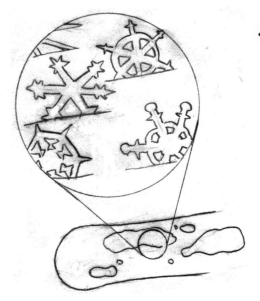

To keep this barrier in place in different temperatures, different types of wax can be used. In cold snow and harder surfaces, snow crystals have very prominent arms on their bodies. Harder, cold-temperature waxes form a strong wax-to-snow barrier. As a result, a barrier is created that keeps the hard edges on the snow crystals from digging into the wax. The surfaces of the snowboard base and snow repel each other, which reduces drag and gives you the type of board-to-snow contact you're after.

With warm snow and softer/wet conditions, the snow crystals have become rounded from the higher temperatures thawing and refreezing the terrain. Wetter conditions create air pockets underneath the board. This can create a vacuum underneath your board that "sucks" you to the snow. To combat this, softer waxes can be used to repel the softer/wet snow conditions.

Try not to use soft waxes on harder conditions. The hard arms of the snow will actually stick into the wax build up and cause drag. Harder waxes on soft, wet conditions can make for large pockets of suction that can actually toss you off your board.

A little wax goes a long way. The less you put on now the less you will have to scrape off later. If you want to use more than one wax at a time, simply melt both onto the board simultaneously.

Take an iron (the old ones that have no holes in the bottom are the best) and heat it just hot enough to melt the wax, but not burn it. If you see smoke coming from the iron, you are burning wax. Point the tip of the iron downwards, melt the wax and let it drip from tip to tail, back and forth until there is enough wax to spread over the entire base. After you drip the wax, spread it out with the iron until the board is covered with a thin layer of wax. Leave the base until it is cool to the touch (15-20 minutes). Take a base scraper and scrape tip to tail until no more wax curls up from the P-tex. Rub-on waxes or Teflon coatings are easy to rub on and make for great on-the-hill quick fixes.

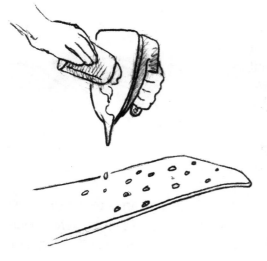

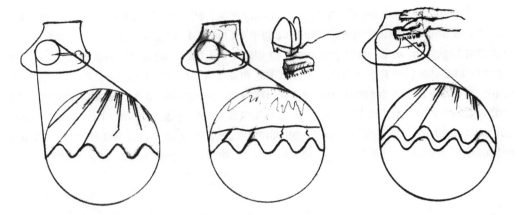

OK, this is for the techheads who want to know exactly what base structure really is. Base structure is the series of little lengthwise grooves in the base of your board. The grooves increase the surface area for the wax to bind with. Base structure will make your board go faster on almost any type of snow. Most of the time a very tight vertical line crosshatch pattern is used. In wet conditions a wider crosshatch pattern that looks like diamonds, is used to break the suction created underneath the base. Base patterns can be changed with the help of your local shop and a grinder. After waxing you have covered up your structure. By using a brush (thick plastic for wet conditions, fine brass bristles for harder conditions) you can raise the excess wax out of the structure's grooves.

279

The final step is to lightly brush the base to remove any leftover excess wax. Buff from tip to tail with a Scotchbrite pad or cork until it feels smooth and polished.

If the base of your board is extremely convex (base high), or concave (edge high), I recommend getting your board to a shop that has a base grinder. A couple of passes on this machine will set your base and edges to an even plane and restore your board to its original operating condition.

Minor topskin/sidewall damage is easily repaired with 1) epoxy binders that you can get at any hardware store. Chemically it's close to the same stuff that the board was put together with. First you want to clean out the damaged area with 2) citrus cleaner and then let it dry. Next, 3) mix the epoxy as per instructions. When you are ready, 4) apply to the desired area and let it dry for a day or two. 5) Minor delamination problems can be fixed in this manner with the help of a vise/clamp or two. 6) Finally, cut and sand off the excess, and you should be ready to go. If the damage is too extensive for you to deal with, go to your local shop and see if they can help.

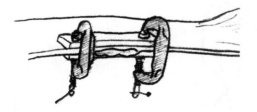

1)

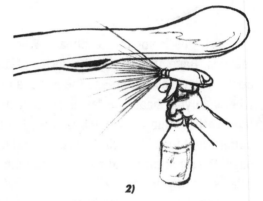

2)

3)

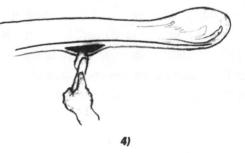

4)

5)

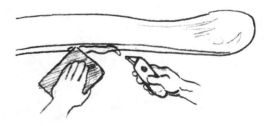

6)

EQUIPMENT INSPECTION

Every day, before you go out into the great white winter world, you should make a daily equipment/board inspection. I examine my board and boots before and after riding. Assuring that your snowboard equipment and especially your board are in good shape should become habit. Look for cracked, broken and distorted parts. Check for frayed leashes and a tight fit between the boot and binding (especially with hard plates). Make sure that mounting screws are nice and tight but be sure to tighten by hand only.

DAILY BOOT CARE

As for daily boot care, nothing can ruin a potentially great day of riding like wet/frozen boots. After riding all day, I recommend taking the liners out of your boots and placing them next to (not over) a ventilation/heating vent overnight. Nothing warmer. You want to dry out your boots, not crack the leather and melt the plastic or rubber. With hard boots, keep them buckled so they don't lose their shape. There are special air blowers specifically designed to dry out boots. Don't stuff a hair dryer into them, this can overheat and burn out the coils in the hairdryer, not to mention present a significant fire hazard. As a rule, I check my boots daily for wear and tear damage. For leather soft boots, I treat them once a year with a waterproofing finish.

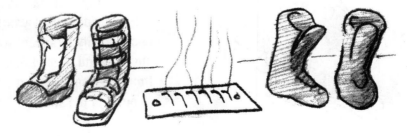

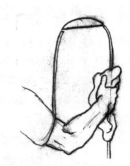

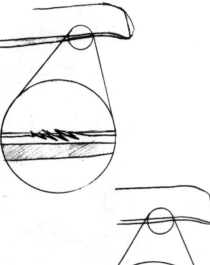

DAILY BOARD CARE

After a good day of riding, take a look at your board's base, examine it for scratches and decide whether new layer of wax is necessary. Dry off edges with a rag so they don't rust. Run your fingers along the edge to check for burrs and sharpness. Polishing stones can help you maintain sharpness of your edge. As you put your board away for the day, simply run the stone from tip to tail on the base and the sides. If you encounter a rough spot, go over it until it is smooth again. Those little rough spots are burrs. When you run over something hard enough to roughen up your edges, the edges burr out. Over time the tips of these edges curl upon themselves and can permanently hinder the performance of a board. When you use a stone after a day of riding, you can repair these burrs without having to grind off a significant portion of the edge. I keep one of these stones in my pocket for the end of the day, or for immediate on-the-hill first aid.

UV rays can damage P-tex. The result will be evident in slower speeds and a reduced ability to accept wax. If you are going to spend a good amount of time away from the board, lean it against something or put it in the shade.

TRAVEL PREPARATION

Preparing your board for a trip need not be a difficult chore. If you are driving, try to pack the board in a way so that it's not exposed to the elements. Keep it inside your vehicle if possible. If the board must be on a rack, put it in a snowboard bag or cover it with a garbage bag to protect it when driving between destinations. Road rocks and salt can mess a board up even before you've reached the hill. If you are mailing your board or flying with it, take the extra half hour to protect your board from the Samsonite gorilla tossing luggage at the airport. Start out by getting a box that your board will fit in. Most local dealers keep a few extra boxes around for their own shipping needs. Start out by filling the bottom of the box with packing material. Crumpled up old newspapers work well and are more ecologically safer than Styrofoam peanuts. As you slide your board into the box stuff paper around the board on all sides. Use a broomstick to pack the stuff in. When the board box is sufficiently "stuffed", close it up with the toughest duct tape you can find. Then to make sure the board box doesn't spill its guts, wrap up all the edges and reinforce the openings with a little more duct tape. This should prevent damage to your precious cargo.

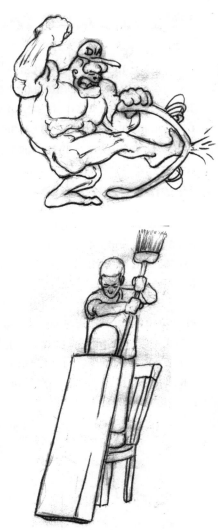

283

STORAGE

When the snow has left the ground and the season has ended, follow a routine of recommended care for your board before you store it. Apply a generous amount of base wax over the entire base and edges without scraping it off. Store the board in a bag and keep it a cool, dry place. Extended exposure to heat will warp, distort and wreak general havoc on your board, and any moisture will rust the edges and inserts.

PERSONALIZING YOUR BOARD/THEFT PREVENTION

It's a good idea is to carve, write, or burnish your name, social security number, blood type, whatever, into a board to identify it as yours. Permanent marker identification in the P-tex base on the tip and/or tail works well. Most snowboards have a production number on the top of them. Record it and put it somewhere safe. Register your board with the local shop, resort, and even the police.

PAINTING YOUR BOARD

I love to paint the top of my snowboards. I find it satisfying when someone looks at my ride and says, "What kind of board is that?" Just another avenue of personal expression that makes snowboarding all that much more enjoyable. It would be selfish to keep it to myself so...

Plan your design as carefully as possible before starting the process of personalizing your board. Break out the sketch book and draw out your idea. Make sure you leave room for bindings. You don't want to cover up the best parts of your work with your feet. If you have a stomp pad, understand that rubber foam does not hold paint very well. When you're sure that you want to do this and you have a design that is right for you, go for it.

Understand that once you start to paint a board, there's no turning back. Painting your snowboard is done with the knowledge that some manufacturers may void their warranty if the original surface is painted over. Make sure to call the manufacturer first so you know what to expect. All the manufacturers I have dealt with maintain that their warranty would remain valid but it doesn't hurt to be sure. There are a couple of options besides painting, I have seen a number of "wallpapered" snowboards that looked really nice. I never thought paisley would look cool on a snowboard, but you never know until you've seen one that does.

Begin by roughing up the surface with fine sandpaper. Remove your bindings and use a 200 grit (or finer) wet/dry sandpaper on a flexible sanding block. The wet/dry sandpaper will reduce unwanted scratches and keep the paper from filling up with unwanted residue. The flexible block will help to ensure even sanding over the board's surface. Start sanding with water on the board. Use smooth and even strokes and gentle pressure. You don't want to tear up your board, just put some teeth into it so that the base paint will have something to adhere to. Keep in mind that oils or greases from your hands can keep artwork from staying on your board. Try not to touch the painting surface if at all possible. When you are done sanding, clean the board with a citrus cleaner. This will remove any leftover agents from the board's production that might repel paint. When the board is in condition to accept the paint, cover the edges with duct tape. This protects the rest of the board from the paint. Covering sidewalls makes for a crisp and professional look Cover up your base as well. Cut off the excess tape with a knife. P-tex "accepts" paint and absorbs foreign materials that can get inside the board's base and slow you down on the snow.

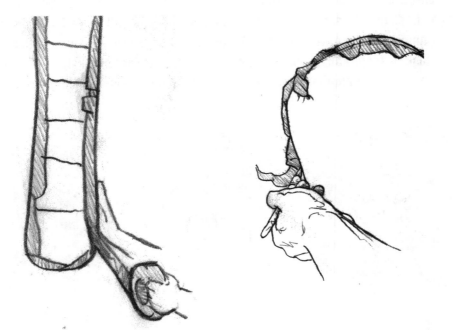

286

When everything you don't want painted is "masked" and covered, your board is ready for the new paint job. Room temperature (60-75°F) is usually the best temperature to paint in. Warmer temperatures take longer to dry. Colder temperatures can cause your work to freeze and crack before it dries. I like to use a matte (non reflective) black or white paint for the base coat, depending on the subject of the image I want to create. When I'm ready I usually take my materials and go to a well-ventilated place where I know I can get messy without upsetting anyone. Make it a point to work in a well-lit, well-ventilated environment. It is extremely important to work in an area that has fresh air. The same binders that stick to the board will also stick to the insides of your lungs. Even in a well-ventilated area, it is wise to protect your health by wearing a mask or respirator. If you can smell the paint, it's getting inside you. Blue and orange boogers are another good indicator of what materials are going inside of you.

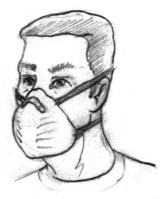

Airbrush, spraycan or wash painting techniques are best suited for this type of work. Acrylic or other chemically inactive paints are ideal. You don't want your artwork to chemically interact with the board so stay away from oil paints and other alkyd-based paints. I recommend either an automotive primer/ paint with a flex agent. When I'm short on cash I use a spray can of polyurethane or epoxy to do the job. When you are all set up, begin painting in steady strokes that pass the end of the board during each stroke. When I paint I try to spray the board up and down no more than three times before I stop and take a break. The thinner the layers of paint, the less likely your paint job is to crack, split or fall off. By waiting 10-15 minutes you can come back again and put some more paint to cover it more completely. The liquid paint will be less likely to build up and run if you follow these guidelines. Try practicing first on a test object first if you are unsure this will work. Be patient, especially around the tip and the tail — the trick is knowing when not to paint. If you put too much paint on the board at once the paint won't dry clearly and will probably run or streak. These types of mistakes are not easy to correct. Just relax and let the work come to you. I suggest painting the base coat until you can no longer see the topskin.

287

When the base coat is in place, your board is ready to become a masterpiece. Go wild. I like to paint with a white base coat and place transparent colors on top. This gives a layering effect which allows light to pass through the transparent layers, reflect off of the white base coat, then pass through the paint again. The result — your image will have visual depth. After many layers and a bit of time, the final result is well worth the effort.

To protect the masterpiece that you have just completed, wait for the paint to thoroughly dry. When dry, use a clear topcoat to cover your work. A good clear coat will further add to the depth of your work and add protection from scratches, dings and whatever might confront your board on the mountain. Clear polyurethane with a flex agent works great. Polyurethane or epoxy from a can does the job as well. Be sure to apply the same technique used with the basecoat to cover the board. You don't want any messes now, so relax, and don't rush the topcoat. Take the time to enjoy a little pride in your worksmanship. Your snowboard is now a "one of a kind".

Caring for your painted board is pretty simple. A well-protected snowboard can take a lot of damage. There is one cosmetic change, however, that will probably take place over time. Prolonged exposure to the sun's UV rays can cause the paint/clearcoat to yellow over time. Again, remember to store your board in the shade. This is often all it takes to protect your personalized board from premature aging.

THE HISTORY OF SNOWBOARDING

The history of snowboarding is a very short one. The actual "birth" of the sport is debatable. The "snurfer" was invented by Sherman Poppen in 1963, and is considered to be the predecessor of the modern snowboard. The snurfer was a wooden board designed so that a person could stand on it with the aid of a rope (attached to the nose of the device). During that same year, Tom Sims created what he called a snowboard in his junior high shop class. However, numerous claims as to who actually built the first snowboard date back to 1929. Some attest to the claim that the snowboard originated from bored skiers at Cottonwood Canyon in the fifties. Here is a general timeline for snowboarding, how we got to where we are today.

BS - BEFORE (THE BIRTH OF) SNOWBOARDING: "THE DARK AGES"

◆ **A gazillion BC:** Bang, A really big one!
◆ **A billion BC:** Life begins on our planet.
◆ **Five hundred million BC:** Dinosaurs rule the earth.
◆ **Two hundred million BC:** The first Ice Age hits. Dinosaurs die out and little warm-blooded Ice Age creatures take over the planet.

◆ **Twenty million BC:** Modern man walks the earth...China creates paper.
◆ **2500 BC:** A 3 1/2-foot long, 6-in. wide wooden ski takes final rest in a peat bog in Sweden. (In the twentieth century the ski is discovered at an archaeological dig site in Sweden and estimated to be 4500 years old — proof that humans learned to ski and truly started to evolve.)

◆ **2400 BC:** Pyramids under construction in Egypt.

◆ **300 BC:** The great wall of China is built.

◆ **45 BC:** Julius Caesar conquers the western world.

◆ **1492:** Christopher Columbus "discovers" the new world.

◆ **1776:** Captain Cook arrives in Hawaii and finds the local population happily surfing naked offshore. Surfing was called "He' enalu" and their surfboards were called "Olo". Boards were solid and measured up to 18 feet long, weighing up to 150 pounds. Often bets were placed on the competitions that ensued offshore. Hawaiian history is passed on verbally, so it is difficult to trace the exact date that marks the origin of surfing. A rough guesstimate places the date between 400-1500 AD on the Polynesian and Hawaiian islands. Surfing and nakedness were considered heathen by the white settlers, and its practice was nearly extinct by the turn of the 20th century. (What were they thinking?)

◆ **1904:** Scooters appear, devices built by nailing a pair of strap-on roller-skates to the bottom of a 2x4. Placed on top is a crate with handles out to each side. Scooters like these were the predecessors of the scooters and skateboards of today.

◆ **1907:** George Freeth takes surfing from Hawaii to California for the first time.

◆ **1912:** Duke Kahanamoku visits the US and Australia. Surfing starts to spread around the world...the Wright brothers fly in North Carolina.

◆ **Early forties:** Bob Simmons creates a fiberglass/foam surfboard. This development greatly reduces the weight of the average surfboard. The production principles will not be used by the larger board makers until the early fifties.

◆ **1945:** Man harnesses the power of the atom and enters the Atomic Age.

◆ **1957:** Bob Lange makes the first plastic ski boots. Bob also produces hula hoops.

◆ **1958:** The Logan Bros. created the first modern mass-produced skateboard using a simple deck and roller-skates that were cut in half. The retail cost was $8.

AS- AFTER (THE BIRTH OF) SNOWBOARDING: "THE RENAISSANCE"

◆ **1963:** Sherman Poppen invents the Snurfer by taking two skis and binding them together as a toy for his children...Tom Sims creates a monster in his junior high shop class and calls it a "Snowboard".

Tom Sims

◆ **1969:** Man walks on the moon. A strange contraption called a monoski is invented, it never really catches on.

◆ **1968-79:** The Blockhouse race is held in Muskegon, MI. Contestants hike roughly a mile up to get to the course. Once there, racers would stand on their snurfers and attempt to get down the hill as fast as possible. Speeds of 60+ mph are recorded. Snurfers have no metal edges, no bindings, and do not use special boots. Generally, about half the contestants who enter a race finish. Top money for the champ — $500.

The "Snurfer"

294

◆ **1970-72:** Dimitrije Milovich starts to develop and patent snowboards. Feeding off of surfing and ski design theories, he produces snowboards with foam cores, fiberglass wraps and metal edges. He starts Winterstick Snowboard Co. in Utah.

◆ **1977:** Another shop class wizard, Mike Olson, builds his own snowboard. He eventually starts Lib Tech/Gnu Snowboards.

◆ **1978:** Chuck Barfoot creates a fiberglass snowboard.

◆ **1979:** Jake Burton Carpenter shows up at the Blockhouse with one of his creations. A new "open" category is created to accommodate his new fangled contraption.

◆ **1981:** The first modern snowboard competition takes place at Ski Cooper in Leadville, CO.

Jake Burton Carpenter

Paul Graves   **Jeff Grell**

295

◆ **1982:** Paul Graves organizes the National Snowboarding Championships at Suicide Six in Vermont. This event attracts national competition. There is a slalom and a downhill event. Speeds of 65+ mph are recorded.

◆ **1983:** Jeff Grell invents the highback binding. With this contraption snowboarders can leverage heelside turns effectively on hard conditions. Jeff never sees any money from this great invention. So, if you see him, give him your money and say "Thank You"...Burton holds the National Snowboarding Championships at Snow Valley, UT. Sims creates The World Snowboarding Championships at Soda Springs. The particular event marks the world's first half-pipe competition.

◆ **1984:** After taking repeated diggers on the hardpack, Mike Olson constructs the first "modern" snowboard. This creation has a deep sidecut, metal edges, a variable flex pattern, stepped sidewalls, camber, an ABS topskin and a P-tex base. This board carves and in many ways acts like a ski...Ski technology is also introduced by Burton via the Elite Snowboard model. This board distinguishes itself with a urethane core — definitely ahead of its time.

◆ **1985:** The first Mt. Baker legendary banked slalom is held.

◆ **1986:** Stratton offers lessons for those who want to learn the sport. The first modern soft boot with a lace-up bladder is introduced by Burton.

Chuck Barfoot

◆ **1987:** Chuck Barfoot invents the totally symmetrical twintip design snowboard.

◆ **1987/88 Season:** The first World cup snowboarding competition takes place. Events are held on both sides of the Atlantic.

◆ **1989:** Carl Miller invents the releasable snowboard binding. It finds a limited market in the Speed Record crowd.

◆ **1991:** Vail creates the first snowboard park.

◆ **1998:** Nagano, Japan features snowboarding as an official Olympic sport.

◆ **2010-2020:** The world snowboarding population surpasses the skiing population.

◆ **2025:** Shaun Palmer buys Taos. After years of financial losses and physical disrepair, millions are invested and slopes are opened to snowboarders. In one fell swoop Taos immediately reclaims its former glory and marks the death of the bigoted resort.

◆ **2078:** Skiing makes a comeback, but it never really catches on.

◆ **2134:** Man snowboards on Mars.

◆ **2346:** We all live in a perfect world, there is no need for money, or lift tickets. Satellite weather control systems keep the mountain resorts snowing, even in the summer. Everyone gets at least one new snowboard every Christmas. Life is perfect.

13

PERSONAL CODE
OF RIDING

Your development as a snowboarder should be thought of as a progressive learning experience. Regardless your individual level of expertise, there are always technical skills that can be improved upon and new on-snow challenges waiting to be attempted. With the steady growth of the sport opening more and more slopes to snowboarding enthusiasts, your skills can be practiced and perfected at a greater variety of resorts. There is one thing, however, that should remain constant throughout your development -- your attitude on the snow. I refer to this as your "personal code of riding." Understand that the following ideas are opinions expressed and held by the author and should not be thought to represent the opinion(s) of the professionals nor any of the organizations who have contributed to this work. Understand that by making these suggestions it is not my intention to tell anyone how to act. I merely wish to express what I have learned, how I act when I ride — my code. These ideas work for me, they might work for you, too.

DEVELOP A RIDING CODE

I assume responsibility for my own actions. This means that if I help to destroy a jump, I rebuild it. If there is an accident (whether I am involved or not), I try to make sure that the people involved are OK, and if they are not, I go for help. In an activity as inherently dangerous as snowboarding, I can expect to get hurt on occasion. I've been hurt before, and it will likely happen again.

I make it a point to know the resort responsibility code. This code is made of standardized rules that resorts use as safety guidelines. These codes are simply common sense for the resort environment, rules of the road to keep the resort a safe place to ride. I memorize them. This is especially useful in the case of an accident where I am involved. Unfortunately, some people still automatically assume that if a snowboarder is involved in an accident, the snowboarder is the guilty party. In this case "knowing the code" can be your greatest asset.

Keep in mind that if you disregard these simple rules of conduct and fail to conduct yourself responsibly, it is only a matter of time before you will be dealt with by the resort ski patrol.

Some snowboarders view the patrol as baby sitters on skis. This misconception of their purpose is one of the gross injustices in the resort community. The ski patrol members are deserving of your respect. After all, these people are charged with your safety, it is their duty to promote safe and responsible behavior on the mountain. To become a patroller requires years of training and classes. Most patrollers really don't want to be the policemen of the mountain. It's just that the insurance companies and the legal system we live with require them to so. These are the people who will take care of you when misfortune comes your way or anyone else's way for that matter. If you see the patrol at the scene of an accident, ask if they need any help. Although the answer will usually be "No", be willing to help out (even in the smallest way) if the assistance is needed.

RESORT REPONSIBILITY CODE

◆ **"Always ride in control and be able to stop or avoid other objects or people."** Running into other people or objects can really hurt. Minimize the risk to yourself and others around you by riding in a way that you know is controlled. Most importantly, think before you act.

◆ **"People ahead of you have the right of way. It is your responsibility to avoid them."** If you bomb down the hill and hit someone, it is your fault. If someone is in front of you, don't look at them. Look at the beautiful white snowfilled spaces between you and them. Try to keep your eyes focused on where you are going — down the hill. The only time you really need to look back up the hill is when you have stopped and are looking to start back down again — when you merge to continue your descent, anticipate other people coming down the hill toward you.

◆ **"Do not stop in the path of traffic, or where you cannot be seen from above."** If the trail is packed, you make yourself a target by occupying any space where others will likely be going. Taking a rest under a jump is not the smartest thing to do, for instance. I like to stop at the side of the trail by a tree. That way if someone is heading right for me, I can stand behind the tree protected from an incoming human missile.

◆ **"Whenever starting downhill or merging into a trail, look uphill and yield to oncoming traffic."** This way you can enter the trail knowing that you aren't going to get clobbered by the mad bomber who just happens to be heading right towards you. Taking blind jumps, or jumps that exit onto a trail is a source of danger both for yourself and those around you. Look for jumps that aren't going to throw you into the flow of traffic.

◆ **"Always use retention devices to help prevent runaway equipment."** A leash will help keep your board from becoming a high-speed mountain projectile. It will also keep your board from disintegrating upon impact with a tree, a rock or the lodge. If you are concerned about your leash being attached to one of your bindings, you can directly attach the leash to your board with a t-nut and a metal loop through the topskin of your board.

◆ **"Observe all posted signs and warnings. Keep out of all closed or roped off areas."** Resort signs are intended to make the mountain as safe as possible for all users. That means safer for you, too. Riding out of bounds is dangerous. If you get hurt out of bounds, the chance exists that you may not be found until spring thaw.

◆ **"Before using any lift, you must know how to safely get on, ride, and get off the lift."** When you are 50 feet off the ground, it's safe to say that this is not the best place to learn the hard way. Ask questions if you have to. Resort lift operators know how to use these machines properly (some of them are snowboarders too). They can take you off to the side and explain how get on, ride, and get off the chairlift before you get on.

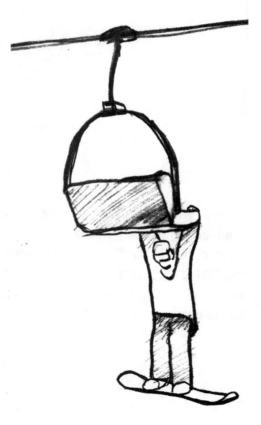

302

RESPONSIBLE SNOWBOARDING

By riding safely with concern for myself and others, I am acting as a snowboard ambassador to the rest of the alpine community. The better I ride, the better the example that is set for others. The goal is for each rider to adopt a code of on-the-hill etiquette. Upholding the standard is positive representation and the best means for encouraging change. When I go out and DO good deeds, people notice. They may not pat me on the back and tell me what a wonderful person I am, but they will remember how I acted and what I did. Seeing results requires a lot of patience, but if I can help to promote good will, I'll do it. As much as I don't like to admit it, there are a lot of snowboarders out there with an anti-skier attitude. The bigotry goes both ways. I may not like the way that some people treat me just because I ride a snowboard, but that is not a reason to reciprocate the sentiment. The last thing I or anybody for that matter should want to do is fall into the us vs. them trap. Everyone on the hill is sliding in the same direction — down —some people do it with two edges, some with four, some sideways, some forwards, some using a sled, so what's the big deal? Try not to bring each other down.

I make sure to give the timid riders some space. They may not say it, but they will appreciate it. Buzzing Aunt Gussie and her flock at supersonic speeds will not impress her, it will scare her. People who are sincerely fearful of you will tend to lash out in one form or another. Sometimes they give you (and other people who ride snowboards) the hairy eye, other times they will actually voice their sentiments. It may not be you but their friends, the patrol or area management who wind up on the

receiving end of a lashing. Even if they keep it to themselves, their image of you is not a good one. Sometimes a friendly "hello" to someone like this is all that is necessary to change or at least start to change a negative opinion.

Unfortunately, for every hundred good deeds done on the hill, the single bad one will most likely be remembered and talked about. Personally if I see someone being a jerk to someone else, whether they are on a snowboard, skis, a toboggan, whatever, I do something about it. It might be offering them a few words or notifying the patrol of their actions. The point is that their actions can hinder or revoke your right to ride wherever you want to. I refuse to let someone else's disregard for others bring snowboarding or any other part of the mountain community down.

For some people, snowboarding is about image. Some people like and identify with the image of "the outcast." Other people also correlate this image with "the jerk." If I act like a jerk to someone, they will probably react like a jerk back to me. However, for some people snowboarding projects an immediate negative image. For these people there is an assumed association (i.e., snowboard + person = jerk). I have had people scream at me for no reason other than the fact that I was riding a snowboard. "Get away from me with that THING! Go somewhere else, we don't want you here!" Some people feel as though it is their right to tell others what to do and what to ride. People like this make me laugh, but they also make me angry — that is why I am writing this opinion.

I try to be friendly — even toward those people who harbor a negative predisposition toward snowboarders. After all, someone who is a jerk is a jerk regardless of how they choose to travel down the mountain. The problem lies largely in the fact that snowboarding is viewed by many as a radical sport. When you say radical, some people think, "Wow, That's great! Dude, it's sooooo rad!" For others the perception of the word radical is taken in a different light — radical is different, radical represents change, and for some "change is bad". This type of negative connotation is often held like an umbrella over all snowboarders. That is simply the way some people think whether they know a single "snowboarder" personally or not. And yet I can't tell you how many times I have stopped to help someone out at the resort and wind up hearing a comment like "I never knew you snowboarders were so nice," or "I wish more snowboarders were like you." My response to the last remark is: "Anyone can be a snowboarder." When someone asks me "Is it fun, is it easy?" I can say "Yes!" And the next question will often be... "So how can I get into it?" If I can influence someone's attitude, change their perception from "there goes a snowboarder" to "I know a snowboarder", I can help to change a stereotype into a familiar association with a name, a face, and an individual who just happens to ride a snowboard. This is how eyes and minds are opened. This is how snowboarding grows.

CHECKLIST OF THINGS TO BRING:

Destination — resort:

Board, boots, bindings and leash
Hand held screwdriver, polishing stone
Clothing to suit weather conditions
Gloves and hat
Goggles / eyeglasses
Sunscreen and lip balm
Food and drink (resort cafeterias can be extremely expensive)
Money

Destination — backcountry:

The above list and:
Shovels
Transceivers
Collapsible search poles
Ice axe
First aid kit
Maps of the riding area
Compass
Flashlight
Matches
Snowshoes
Backpack
Food and water

INSTRUCTIONAL ORGANIZATIONS:

Association of American Snowboard Instructors (AASI)

national-hq: 303.987.9390
east: 518.452.6095
west: 916.587.7642
northwest: 206.244.8541
central: 414.476.2400
intermountain: 801.942.2066
(north) intermountain: 208.678.8347
rocky mountain: 970.879.8335
(north) rocky mountain: 406.837.3663
alaska: 907.586.1946

SNOWBOARD CAMPS:

Delaney Adult Snowboarding Camps
PO Box 4488, Boulder, CO 80306
303.443.6868

High Cascade Snowboard Camp
PO Box 6622, Bend, OR 97708
Wild Women Snowboarding Camp
PO Box 290, Teton Village, WY 83025
307.733.2292

Tim Windell's Snowboard Camp
800.765.7669

SNOWBOARD CLUBS:

Snowboard clubs are a great way to get involved in the sport. Most snowboard clubs can be reached through local shops, resorts, schools and publications. Here's one that covers the CA, AZ, NV, UT, & CO states and will be expanding with each season. They also do a lot of learn to ride programs and trips to resorts.

United Riders Association
CT: Doug Sumi
5318 E. 2nd St. #108
Long Beach, CA 90803
888.935.8887
email: info@unitedriders.com

COMPETITIVE ORGANIZATIONS / SANCTIONING BODIES:

Professional
International Snowboarding Federation (ISF) US, Asia, Europe
PO box 477
Vail, CO 81658
970.949.5743

US pro tour/Jeff Grell
16555 Gulf St.
Van Nuys, CA 91406
818.782.8920 / fax-818.782.1401

International Ski Federation (FIS)
check with USSA (below) first then:
FIS International Office /
Blochstrasse 2 CH_3653
Oberhofen-Tnurnersee, Switzerland
011.41.33.44.6161

Amateur
United States Amateur Snowboarding Association (USASA) US
PO Box 4400
Frisco, CO 80443
970.668.3350

United States Ski/Snowboard Association (USSA) US
National office
PO Box 100
Park City, UT 84060
801.649.9090 / fax- 801.649.3613

PHILANTHROPIC / CHARITY ORGANIZATIONS:

Snowboard Outreach Society (SOS)
CT: Arn Menconi
Box 2020
Avon, CO 81620
970.845.7040
email: SOS@vail.net
Website: http://vail.net/sos

Boarding for Breast Cancer
CT: Dennis Healy
431 Pine St. 2nd floor
Burlington, VT 05401
802.864.7123 / fax-802.864.2595
fuse@together.net

Board Aid can be reached through Transworld Snowboarding magazine
board aid hotline: 760.722.7777 x192

BACKCOUNTRY ORGANIZATIONS — AVALANCHE SCHOOLS:

Cyberspace Snow & Avalanche Center
www.csac.org

National Avalanche School/
National Avalanche Foundation
133 S. Van Gordon St.
Lakewood, CO 82258
303.988.1111

National Avalanche Center
CT: Doug Abromeit
Ketchum Ranger District
Box 2356
Ketchum, ID 83340
208.622. 5371 / 622.3912 (fax)

American Avalanche Institute, Inc.
Box 308
Wilson, WY 83014
307.733.3315

American Association of
Avalanche Professionals
Box 34004
Truckee, CA 96160
916.587.3653

Alaska Avalanche School
Alaska Mtn. Safety Center, Inc.
9140 Brewsters Dr.
Anchorage, AK 99516
907.345.7736

BIBLIOGRAPHY / RECOMMENDED READING

The Avalanche Handbook McClung and Schaefer, The Mountaineers, Seattle, WA 1994

Hypothermia, Frostbite and Other Cold Injuries Walkerson, Bangs and Hayward 1989

The Ultimate Skateboard Book Cassorla, Running Press 1976

The History of Surfing Young, The Body Press 1987

Hypothermia, the Facts Collins, Oxford Medical Publications 1987

Inner Skiing Gallaway and Kriegel, Random House 1978

Ski Woman's Way Slanger, Summit Books 1979

The Centered Skier McCluggage, Bantam Books 1983

The Handbook of Skiing Gamma, Alfred A Knopf Publishing 1985

How the Racers Ski Warren, Witherell 1965

Soft Paths Hampton and Cole, Stockpole Books 1993

The Basic Essentials of Minimizing Impact on the Wilderness Hodgeson, ICS books 1994

How to Sh*t in the Woods Meyer, Ten Speed Press 1991

307

PUBLICATIONS:

Blunt Magazine
Dickhouse Publishing Group, Inc.
815 N. Nash
El Segundo, CA 90245
(310) 640-7082
Subscriptions: (800) 366-6670

Eastern Edge
4 River Road
Bondville, VT 05340
Phone: (802) 297-3432
Fax: (802) 297-3409

Fresh And Tasty Magazine
100 Spring St.
Cambridge, MA 02141
(617) 547-6520

Heckler
PO Box 507
Sacramento, CA 95812
Phone: (916) 443-0373
Fax: (916) 444-8972
e-mail:Hecklermag@aol.com

Medium Magazine
2635 east 3300 south
Salt Lake City, UT 84109
Phone/Fax: (801) 467-0772
mediummag@aol.com

Plow Magazine
PO Box 67
San Clemente, CA 92647
Phone: (714) 361-7716
Fax: (714) 361-7715
plowmag@aol.com

SnoBoard
2814 Fairfield Ave., Suite #137
Bridgeport, CT 06605
Phone: (203) 367-5124
Fax:(203) 331-1578
snomag@aol.com

Snowboarder
33046 Calle Aviador
San Juan Capistrano, CA 92675
714.496.5922

Transworld Snowboarding,
Blast & Warp
353 Airport Rd.
Oceanside, CA 92054
619.722.7777
www. twsnow.com

W.I.G. Magazine
PO Box 1082
Park City, UT 84060

•A•

Absorption - To use your body to accept rather than fight the forces placed upon it.

Active Air - To Jump up into the air. Compression and powerful extension to loft the rider.

Aft, Aftward - Toward the tail of the board

Air - To leave the ground. Can be the name of a trick — Big Air, Mute Air, Weak Air. To catch air. Air active — jumping, compression and powerful extension to loft the rider. Jump up into the air. Air passive — absorbing of the legs, knees toward the upper body. This can be demonstrated by standing upright and bringing your legs up off the ground so quickly that you are momentarily "suspended" in the air and then you fall. This skill is necessary for both effective bump riding and the "crossunder" turn.

Alpine - Riding in a carve heavy style. The design of a snowboard system that caters to the high speed carving aspects of snowboarding. This is usually composed of a stiff board with lots of sidecut, hard boots and a plate binding system.

Angulation - Using your body in a manner to maximize stability and conserve energy when you ride. It brings your body closer and lower to the board to maximize your cone of balance. Flexing at specific joints in the body.

Anxiety - A negative form of excitement associated with anticipation.

Asymmetry - A snowboard design theory that compensates for the fact that you shift and move differently over your toeside than your heelside.

Avalanche - A very large snow slide. These slides can bury you. You can learn how to read/ deal with the possibility of this dangerous snow condition by reading text and taking classes about this specific subject. (See Appendix)

Awareness - Your ability to sense what is going on within and around you.

•B•

Backcountry - Any terrain that is out of bounds of a resort. This means you have to hike for your runs and you are at Mother Nature's mercy.

Bail - The latch that clips your hard boot into your binding. To fall or mess up while riding a snowboard

Balance - A relative state to the position/movement of your body over the board. The ability to keep your body over the board on the snow and therefore be in a position to control the board. In this case I like to think of the snowboard as a moving tightrope. Good balance helps to keep you on top of the tightrope, all the way down the hill.

Bank - A large berm or physical object covered with snow. A leaning turn, it is easy to do. However it is not very powerful or stable at speed.

Banked Slalom - A crazy race that rides through highly raised walls. Imagine a race through a huge halfpipe. This is what a banked slalom race is like.

Base - Bases are the P-tex bottoms of snowboards. They are what makes the board go fast. Extruded bases are not very fast but they hold wax for a long time. Sintered bases are faster but they require more maintenance, and they are more expensive as well.

Base Shot - Damage to your snowboard that is

so sever that you can see the core of your board. This is a good indication that you need to take your board to the shop for major reconstructive surgery.

Base Structure - The little grooves in the base of your board that add to the surface area and speed of your board.

Bevel - An alteration of the 90 degree angle on your edges. A wedge underneath the feet to pronate or supinate the foot

Bindings - The plastic/metal mousetraps that "bind" your feet into the top of the snowboard.

Black List - An ever shorter list of resorts that for some obscure reason do not allow snowboarders to ride on their slopes.

Bladders - The soft inner portion of your snowboard boot. This liner supports, holds and keeps your feet warm when you ride.

Blind - A spinning trick/movement that starts rotating into a direction that you cannot see when you start to spin. This makes for a much scarier spinning trick.

Blunt - A sideways wheelie.

Boardercross - The unholy union of a downhill snowboarding race in a motocross elimination format. Insane courses are set, and whoever gets to the bottom first, wins. There is a minimal set of rules, and all racers must wear a helmet.

Body Separation - By using different parts of your body in a certain manner you can increase your ability to manipulate your board. The three parts are: your head, your body from the hips up, and your body from your hips down.

Bomb - To descend down a hill at very high speeds, best achieved by not turning at all.

Boning - A wonderful word that is used to describe (among other things) straightened out leg(s). Very stylish in the air. Not so stylish if you use your legs in this fashion when you make your turns on the snow.

Bonk - To ride by or over an object and slap it with your board.

Boots - The connection between your foot and the binding of the board. Hard boots are made of plastic and look like (or they are) ski boots. Soft boots are made of rubber fabric, and leather. Hybrid boots combine the plastic shoe of a hard boot, with the flexible upper of a soft boot.

Bumps - (See Moguls)

•C•

Camber - Boards are built to bend like a bow. When a board is pressured, energy builds inside the board. Just like drawing an arrow. The board then releases this energy and projects you into the next turn. This is called "re-cambering". Just like an arrow leaving the drawstring of a bow.

Camp - A place to get better at snowboarding and whatever else the camp has to offer. Expensive, but always worth it.

Carve - A turn that uses high edge angles. As a result, the sidecut of the snowboard defines the shape and the radius of the turn. A carved turn cuts through the snow, it does not skip, slip or skid.

Center of Gravity (COG) - The absolute center of your whole body. This is denoted in the illustrations of the book by the black and white crosshair in the circle, just like the crash test dummies wear.

Centripetal - A force that holds you in a turn. These forces are generated with your body and snowboard.

Centrifugal - A force that draws you away from a turn. These forces are generated by inertia and gravity.

Commitment - Your mental ability to stay with a planned course of action, even though it may not be easy to do.

Conditions - The current weather and or type of snow you are riding over.

Cone of Balance - An imaginary cone that represents where you can move and be balanced over your board.

Contact Length - The amount of edge in contact with the snow underneath the board.

Co-contraction - The flexion of muscles on both sides of a joint.

Core - The stuff in the center of your snowboard. It affects all of the characteristics of your ride. Some new cap designs use the outer cap of the board to work with/ as the core of the board.

Cornice - A large overhanging snow lip.

Counter Rotation - A forced turn movement. Getting the board to turn around by swinging (twisting) the upper body opposite to the direction of the board's desired travel.

Cross-Over Skier - A skier that tries snowboarding, likes it and end up "Crossing over" into the sport of snowboarding.

Cross-Over Turns - We call these cross-over turns because your body crosses and rises over the board from one turn to the next. During the turn you sink down to pressure your board. You extend out of this turn to release your edge and start to transfer your weight toward the other side of the board. You have to move over the board. In this sense the board dictates the movement of the body.

Cross-Under Turns - The board crosses under the body as the COG maintains a steady height over the snow and travels down the hill. Pressuring movements are very different than cross-over turns. The board is pressured almost as soon as it is placed on edge. As the turn ends, the board is accepted into the body. The board is then set on the new edge. Now the body dictates the direction of the board. Cross-under turns are a much more forceful kind of turn. You manipulate your board underneath you and your movements dictate the direction of the board. It takes a good sense of balance and a lot of practice to do it.

Crud -A snow condition made up of broken up snow.

Crust - A hard top layer of snow that covers the hill. This snow can collapse under your weight and break through to the softer snow underneath. This kind of snow condition can make for difficult riding.

•D•

Dehydration - The loss of water from inside your body. If you lose enough water, your body will have difficulty operating.

Design - The specifics of construction, materials, and shape of your snowboard equipment. Ideally the design of your snowboard makes riding as easy for you as possible.

Detuning - The dulling of a portion of the edges to prevent hooking in and out of your turns. This happens to the total edge of your board over time.

Down-Dominant Turns - This is a crossover turn that emphasizes a gradual sinking body motion into the turns. This is to set the rider over the board during the turn. High speed turns are best done with down dominant turns for maximum stability and consistency. This kind of turn makes longer turns, and plowing through the tough stuff. Down dominant turns require patience because they rely on the shape of the board to determine the shape of the turn.

Downhill - Something that is further down the hill than you are. A race format that requires that you get down the hill as fast as you possibly can. Lotsa fun!

Drag - Drag slows you down. This is caused by friction between the contacting surfaces of your board and the snow. Drag can be greatly reduced with wax. In reference to your feet on the board. Drag can be caused with your toes and heels being too far over the edge of your board and digging into the snow.

Drill - An exercise or an exaggeration of a movement(s) specifically designed to improve a part/ all of your riding. This can also mean to poke holes into your board, so you can attach your bindings to your ride.

Duck Stance - A stance that has both feet pointing outwards from 0 degrees across the board.

•E•

Edges - The metal strips on the sides of the base of your board. These strips "bite" into the snow. This allows you to control both your speed and direction. If your board does not have metal edges, you will not be able to control yourself on harder snow conditions.

Edge Angle - The angle that your board's metal edges contact and dig into the snow. The higher this angle the more your edges will bite in and hold onto the snow.

Edge Control - The ability to make adjustments to the angle of the boards' edges in relation to the snow.

Emergency Stop - An immediate stop (usually a heelside turn) used to help prevent a collision.

Epoxy - An extremely strong glue that holds golf clubs, jet airplanes and snowboards together. Great for minor repairs to the top and sides of your board.

Eurocarve - Another name for a very low leaning type of turn.

Exercise - (See Drill)

Extension - This kind of movement generally increases the angle of the body's joints. A movement that you can use to lengthen your body.

•F•

Fakie - Riding your snowboard backward from the way you usually ride. Switstance is another name for fakie.

Fall - The thing that every snowboarder has done, and will probably do so again. It is important to learn to fall as safely as possible, being that falls are when most injuries take place.

Fall Line - The most direct line down the mountain. Think of a stream running down the hill. It's route is dictated by the pull of gravity, the most direct way down the mountain possible.

Falling Leaf - A sideslip on the uphill edge that can be directionally controlled by shifting one's weight from side to side.

Fear - A negative form of excitement that can overtake your consciousness. Fear can add stress and tension to your state of being. Extreme fear can keep you from doing what you really want to do, and even freeze you in place.

Field of Vision - Area you can see with your eyes.

Flats - Terrain that has no grade of steepness to it. If you're bound with both feet on your board on this kind of terrain, you're not going anywhere.

Flat Light - A visibility condition that occurs when the light is partially blocked. Gray skies or snowy conditions can make visual definition difficult. When riding in weather like this, wear goggles and try to stay near the side of the trail, or near some other physical reference to guide yourself safely down the hill. Bump riding is good in conditions like this because the bumps are visible, where flat terrain can be deceiving.

Flex - A movement that you can use to compress your body. This kind of movement generally decreases the angle of the body's joints. The amount a board will bend in any different direction.

Flex Pattern - The manner in which a snowboard bends. It can usually be altered by the thickness of the board's core. Most boards have a stiffer flex pattern at the middle of the board, and are softer at the tip and tail.

Fluid - A series of movements that flow easily from one to another.

Focus - One's ability to focus your mental power on the task at hand effectively. Sometimes this is referred to as "the zone".

Force - A power in our world that has the ability to affect other things around it.

Forced - An abrupt movement that uses the body's strength more than its structure to make an immediate. This kind of turn uses much more strength than necessary to accomplish it's goal.

Fore - Toward the tip of the board.

Freeriding - Riding the whole mountain, any way you want to. A description of equipment that is designed for freeriding.

Freestyle - A type of riding that is full of tricks, spinning and other gravity defying feats. A description of equipment that is designed for freestyle riding.

Frostbite - The freezing of the body's tissues. This is usually a byproduct of your boy trying to centralize its heat resources and prevent hypothermia.

•G•

Garland - A long staggered turn in one direction.

Giant Slalom - A race format that uses medium to long radius turns through a set course.

Goofy - An old surfing term that refers to riding right foot forward.

Grab - To hold onto your board in the air.

Gravity - A constant force that pulls us toward the center of the earth.

Guiding - A gradual committed movement that uses the body's structure and a minimal amount of effort to accomplish a desired task.

•H•

Habit - An internalized process that has become something that you don't think about anymore. A pre-conscious thought.

Halfpipe - A manmade 12- 30 ft. wide trench in the snow that you can ride in. This kind of terrain is perfect for tricks, flying in the air and doing crazy things.

Handplant - To pull a trick in the air (usually in a half or a quarter pipe) and support yourself with one or both hands over the snow.

Hard Binding System - A boot/ binding system that accepts hard boots.

Heelside - The side of the board your heels are closest to.

Heel Strap - A collar that wraps around the back, bottom and front of the soft boot over the ankle. This will help your heel from "floating" in your soft boots.

Highback - A piece of a soft binding that allows the rider to place leverage upon the heelside turn in soft boots.

Heelstop - A stopping technique that is used when skating. This is accomplished by taken the trailing foot and planting it in the snow by the side of the board.

Horizon - As far as the eye can see. In this case I am referring to seeing down the hill, through the trees, to the lift, around the bend. If you can see it is within your horizon, and you can use your mind to anticipate it.

Hybrid Boots - A boot with hard soles and soft uppers. Some work in hard bindings, some are designed for soft bindings. If you like the control of a hard boot and the flex of a soft boot this might be a good choice for you.

Hypothermia - The reduction of the body's core temperature. If the body's core temperature drops below a certain point, you can die.

•I•

Ice - A very solid form of frozen water.

Ice Axe - A mountaineering tool that is specifically designed for use in the alpine environment. A must for super steep slopes where a self arrest is sometime the only way to stop.

Inverts - An aerial movement that places the rider upside down over the snow. Inverts are very dangerous. Falling on your head at speed can have serious and permanent implications.

Inserts - T-nuts that are built into the board during the manufacturing process. Arranged in a pre-determined pattern to match with your bindings. (See T-nuts)

•J•

Jump Turns - Up dominant turns that are powerful enough to totally rise off the snow. Basically it is a jumping 180 turn. Once the board is off the ground, it is very easy to turn. These kind of turns are necessary on very tight, very steep (or both) terrain. Jump turns also work well in very heavy snow or crusty conditions to free the board from the burden of the snow.

•K•

Kick (tip/tail) - The amount of lift that the end of the board rises over the snow.

Kicker - A deceptive little jump that will shoot you straight up into the air.

•L•

Leading Body Part - If you split your body vertically in two between your eyes, the leading half is the half of your body going down the hill first.

Learning - The assimilation, processing and realization of information about the world we live in.

Leash - A safety retention device that is designed to keep the board from leaving the rider in case of a binding release. Most resorts will not let you ride on their trails without one.

Length - The measurement of the board from one end to the other. Usually expressed in centimeters. However, not all manufacturers measure centimeters in the same way.

Lesson - A great way to start and improve upon your learning skills.

Leverage - The ability to pressure the board using your body and the forces of the turn.

Lifts - A more expensive, but less tiring way of getting up your favorite hill. There are many types of lifts, Some are easy to use, others take some practice to get used to.

Lip - The end of a jump, or terrain that will launch you into the air.

•M•

Maintenance - The daily and long term upkeep of your snowboard. This is to help your beloved board and make it last forever.

Mechanic - Someone who knows what they are doing as far as snowboard maintenance and repair is concerned.

Mental Anticipation - The ability to keep your mind further down the hill than your ability to act/ react to it. Generally speaking the further down the hill you can look, the better your ability to anticipate what's coming up.

Mental Visualization - Using your mind to see exactly what you want to do, before you actually ever do it. This technique can be used to make yourself a better rider off as well as on the snow.

Moguls - Man made snow bumps. Difficult at first, mogul riding emphasizes almost every skill inherent to snowboarding. Riding on steep uneven terrain like this will challenge you and make you into a much more effective rider.

Mondopoint - The European foot measurement scale. You think they'd use metric.

•N•

Natural Ready Stance - A body position that allows for powerful, quick reaction in just about any direction.

Night Riding - Done at a resort with trail lights, or in the backcountry under a full moon.

Nollie - An ollie that spring off the tip instead of the tail of the board.

Nose - (See Tip)

•O•

Offset - The measured deviation from a point, usually from the center of the board's sidecut to the midpoint of the board.

Ollie - A jumping technique that uses the snowboard as a springboard to increase the power of your jump.

Open - A spinning trick/movement that starts rotating into a direction you can see when you start to spin.

Out of Bounds - Past resort area boundary, if you go there you are on your own. The patrol cannot help you out of bounds.

•P•

Park - A manmade obstacle course full of things to ride, jump and fly over. This is usually the only area of the resort that the use of objects like wood, metal slides, and junked cars is allowed.

Passive Air - Absorption of the legs toward the upper body. This can be demonstrated by standing upright and bringing your legs up off the ground so quickly that you are momentarily "suspended" in the air and then you fall. This skill is necessary for both effective bump riding and the "cross-under" turn.

Pigeon-Toed - A stance on the board that has the toes pointing toward each other.

Poke - A quick airborne scootch.

Powder - Fresh, soft untouched snow that you can glide over like a ghost. The stuff snowboarding dreams are made of.

Pressure Control - The ability to increase or decrease pressure upon the board in contact with the snow. This can also be related to portions of the board (i.e. pressuring, loading up, the tip of the board).

•Q•

Quarter Pipe - A large lip that is like a half pipe, but only has one wall. Basically it is a big jump to vertical.

Quest for the Perfect Turn - The never-ending story of the snowboarder looking for the ultimate realization of the riding experience.

Quiet - Body or part of the body that is stable and free of extra movements.

•R•

Race - To ride with technique that is meant for competition. Snowboard design similar to alpine, but refined to go as fast as possible.

Regular - Someone who rides left foot forward.

Relax - Your ability to release tension from your mind and body.

Rental Equipment - Equipment that is contracted out on a short term basis for a fee. A good investment route to take when you are first learning to ride.

Repairs - Highly intensive maintenance.

Rest - A necessary amount of inactivity that your body needs to recuperate and replenish itself with.

Retention Plates - Metal or fiberglass plates that are placed inside the board. These plates are meant to hold the screws that your bindings attach to the board with.

Rotation - By twisting a part or the whole body around to get the snowboard to move in a specific direction. This kind of rotational motions is sometimes referred to as torque or twisting movements.

•S•

Safety - A prime concern for any snowboarder. This includes the environment, others around you and most importantly, yourself.

Scootch - Manipulating the board underneath your body using your leg muscles. This helps to stabilize the upper body and reinforces upper/lower body separation.

Self Arrest - To control yourself on extremely steep terrain. Best done with an ice axe.

Sensory Depravation - A teaching technique used to aid in the process of learning to snowboard. By blocking out the visual sense, other sensory pathways are focused upon to relay information to the mind. This information can be fully concentrated on without the sense of sight distracting the mind from this "secondary sensory information". This focused attention on this information can give you a new perspective your body, it's effect on your snowboard and the snow underneath you.

Shops - Place to rent, buy and maintain your snowboard equipment.

Shifties - A airborne scootch that is held for a long time before touchdown with the snow.

Shifting - The controlled movement that alters

315

your body's position over the board.

Shovel - A little device that is an absolute safety necessity in the backcountry. Shovels can also be used to build jumps and dig snowpits.

Sidecut - The shape of the side of the board. This in combination with the flex pattern of the board determines the size and quickness of the turns the board produces.

Sideslip - Traveling down the hill on the uphill edge. This uses your edge angle to reduce/ increase your rate of travel.

Sidewalls - The pieces that make up the sides of your boards.

Skating - A means to get about on the flats. Kind of like skateboarding on the snow.

Sketch - This is what happens when your edge starts to lose its grip on the snow. It sounds like a popping skid underneath you.

Skidded Turns - A type of turn guided with both feet. This turn makes a scraping sound across the snow.

Skills - The degree of your ability to do something in particular.

Slalom - A race format that emphasizes quick short turns through a set course.

Slides - Objects besides snow that you can ride over.

Snowpit - A pit dug into the side of the slope before descending. Reading the layers of snow in the pit can help you to determine if there is avalanche danger in the area.

Snurfer - Invented in 1963 by Sherman Poppen. This contraption is considered by many to be the predecessor of the modern snowboard.

Soft Binding System - A boot/ binding system that accepts soft boots.

Spotting - To watch or have someone watch you to make sure that you are safe.

Stance - The manner in which you stand over the board over your board. This relates to the distance be-

tween your feet. The angles of your feet, and the proximity of your feet to the tip and tail of your board.

Steepness (pitch, grade) - The angle of steepness of the terrain you are riding over.

Steering - A controlling movement that alters the position/direction of the snowboard as you travel down the hill. A good example are the movements required to skid your turns down the hill. To make a skidded turn you have to steer the board around and across the hill with both legs. As you are steering the board across the hill you can (with a little bit of edge bite as well) control both your speed and direction.

Stopping - A very important skill to have when you ride. The more your board points across the hill and you dig your edges in, the more quickly you will stop. Stopping speed is also affected by the speed that you are traveling at when you start to stop.

Straps - The bands that hold boots into bindings.

Stretching - A good way to warm up and prevent injury before and after your day of riding.

Super-G - A race format that is made for very long turns high speed through a course.

Swing Weight - The weight of the board in terms of spinning it around. The heavier the swing weight, the more difficult to rotate the board.

Switchstance - Switchstance is when you do a trick riding backward, just as you would do it forward.

Symmetry - Snowboard design that is identical comparing one side to the other. This can pertain to the shape, sidecut, flex pattern and stance. A twintip board is symmetrical in length, width, and construction.

•T•

Tail - The trailing end of your snowboard.

Tailward - Toward the tail end of the board (aftward).

Terrain - The mountain environment that you ride.

Tip - The leading end of a snowboard (fore, nose).

Tipward - A movement that is directed toward

the tip of the board.

T-nuts/Inserts - Small bolts that look like an inverted "T". These nuts are placed inside the board during production or drilled through the board later. These nuts spread out the forces placed upon them by the bindings. T-nutted snowboards are very strong and nearly impossible to rip out of.

Toeside - The side of the board your toes are closest to.

Torsional Flex - The boards ability to resist twisting along its length.

Transition - The change from one edge to the next between turns. The curved section of a jump, a quarter-pipe or a half-pipe. The change between the level part of the terrain and the lip of the jump, or vert of the pipe.

Trail - Designated (sometimes undesignated) routes down the hill at resorts.

Trailing Body Part - If you split your body vertically in two between your eyes, this is the half of your body going down the hill last.

Traverse - To ride across the hill in a continuous path that crosses the fall line.

Trees - Woodland mountain terrain that offer a great deal of riding possibilities. It can also be a very dangerous place to be. Never ride the trees alone.

Trick - A maneuver, grab , contortion or a combination of the above that is out of the ordinary. Any creative extension to your riding.

Tune-up - The regular checking/maintenance of your snowboard. Regular maintenance is the best way to invest in the safety, reliability and longevity of your snowboard.

Turns - A means of speed and direction control as you descend the hill.

•U•

Up-Dominant Turns - Turns that are emphasized with upwardly body motion from one turn to the other.

Slalom turns are like this, they are designed to be quick and explosive. These turns also work well to project yourself and the board up and out of difficult conditions. Up dominant turns rely heavily upon the athleticism of the rider to determine the shape of the turn.

UV Rays - Part of the spectrum of sunlight that can damage your body. Protect any exposed portions of your body with eyewear, sunscreen and clothing.

•V•

Vertical (vert) - The vertical portion of the wall of a halfpipe.

•W•

Waist - The thinnest part of a board along its length.

Warming Up - Body preparation for your day of riding. Often this can be achieved by stretching and taking an easy run or two to the bottom of the hill. Starting out "cold" can be inflexible and even possibly lead to injury.

Warranty - A guarantee of quality by a manufacturer. If the product falls apart due to bad construction or defect, the manufacturer agrees to replace the product. Often this guarantee is for a limited time only. Make sure to check the warranty of a product before purchase.

Wax - Paraffin or some crazy space age material that builds a barrier between your board and the snow. Different waxes are designed to work at different temperatures.

Wheelies - A scooch like movement that brings the board up on its end as you travel down the hill.

Wrist Guards - Little devices that you put on your wrists to prevent injuries to that joint.

•XYZ•

Zipper Line - An imaginary line that can be found between the bumps down the hill.

Kevin Ryan has been teaching people how to ride snowboards for the last ten years. He lives in Boulder Colorado with his partner Lisa and their son Maxwell. He has set up a 3D illustration/animation studio and is currently producing a video series and eventually a CD-ROM based upon the information inside this book.

If you have any questions pertaining to the information found in this book or about the story of snowboarding, Kevin can be contacted through Masters Press.